The Politically Incorrect Guide® to Christianity

The Politically Incorrect Guides® to...

American History
Thomas Woods
9780895260475

The American Revolution
Larry Schweikart
Dave Dougherty
9781621576259

The Bible
Robert J. Hutchinson
9781596985209

The British Empire
H. W. Crocker III
9781596986299

Capitalism
Robert P. Murphy
9781596985049

Catholicism
John Zmirak
9781621575863

Christianity
Michael P. Foley
9781621575207

The Civil War
H. W. Crocker III
9781596985490

Climate Change
Marc Morano
9781621576761

Communism
Paul Kengor
9781621575870

The Constitution
Kevin R. C. Gutzman
9781596985056

Darwinism and Intelligent Design
Jonathan Wells
9781596980136

English and American Literature
Elizabeth Kantor
9781596980112

The Founding Fathers
Brion McClanahan
9781596980921

Global Warming
Christopher C. Horner
9781596985018

The Great Depression and the New Deal
Robert Murphy
9781596980969

Hunting
Frank Miniter
9781596985216

Islam (And the Crusades)
Robert Spencer
9780895260130

Jihad
William Kilpatrick
9781621575771

The Middle East
Martin Sieff
9781596980518

The Presidents, Part 1
Larry Schweikart
9781621575245

The Presidents, Part 2
Steven F. Hayward
9781621575795

Real American Heroes
Brion McClanahan
9781596983205

Science
Tom Bethell
9780895260314

The Sixties
Jonathan Leaf
9781596985728

Socialism
Kevin D. Williamson
9781596986497

The South (And Why It Will Rise Again)
Clint Johnson
9781596985001

The Vietnam War
Phillip Jennings
9781596985674

Western Civilization
Anthony Esolen
9781596980594

Women, Sex, and Feminism
Carrie L. Lukas
9781596980037

The Politically Incorrect Guide® to Christianity

Michael P. Foley

Cataloging-in-Publication data on file with the Library of Congress

ISBN 978-1-62157-520-7
ebook ISBN 978-1-62157-539-9

Published in the United States by
Regnery Publishing
A Division of Salem Media Group
300 New Jersey Ave NW
Washington, DC 20001
www.Regnery.com

Manufactured in the United States of America

10 9 8 7 6 5 4 3 2

To the giants on whose shoulders I ride piggyback—G. K. Chesterton, C. S. Lewis, and Ronald Knox—this porcine exercise in apologetics is gratefully dedicated. And for all readers living in an age that gives great political power to people like Dianne Feinstein, I pray: May the Dogma live loudly within you!

Contents

A Note to the Politically *Correct* Reader

I congratulate you for picking up this volume; that act shows intellectual probity. I ask only one additional favor. Try to read this book with the benefit of the doubt. It may seem to you that Christianity is outrageously out of tune with the modern world and should therefore be confined to the ash heap of history. I meet you halfway: Christianity *is* out of tune with the modern world, but perhaps it is the modern world that needs the tune-up.

I appeal to your open-mindedness. Consider whether, to paraphrase John Stuart Mill, it is better to be a maladjusted Socrates than a well-adjusted sow—and if the sheep in Christ's flock may have more in common with Socrates than with swine.

I appeal to your tolerance and love of diversity. What could be more tolerant and diverse than a society in which some of its members march to the beat of a little drummer boy who played for a Jewish child in Palestine?

Lastly, I appeal to your sense of history. Both the Left and the Right in the United States are increasingly impoverished by an educational system that privileges STEM fields (science, technology, engineering, and math) and downplays the kind of critical and logical thinking that comes from a classical liberal arts education. As a result, our youth have far better job skills than life skills, skills that would enable them to think clearly about life's most important questions and a sense of their place in history. Worse, they *think* they know their place in history because of a few shoddy sound bites that they may have picked up along the way. The moment they are challenged on these half-digested nuggets they retreat to "safe spaces" where they can bewail all the "microaggressions" against them. One of the shoddy sound bites they have picked up is the idea that Christianity is the product of a dark and superstitious age and an enemy of genuine human progress. If you have any knowledge of the Bible or Church history, you know that this claim is tendentious at best. In the interest of accuracy—and to reclaim a deeper understanding of our human journey—is it not time to move beyond caricatures such as these?

Why should you give this book the benefit of the doubt? Well, you've come this far, haven't you? At the very least you'll learn how the other half thinks, the half that still embraces the history that paved the way for your own values today. Think of this book as the ultimate test of your toleration. If you read it cover to cover without casting it into the fireplace, you pass!

And if it seems that here or there I am guilty of a cheap shot against Christianity's detractors, I ask for your forgiveness. My aim has been to scratch rather than to wound. And to be honest with you, the principal audience I had in mind in writing this PIG was not so much you (even though I am thrilled that you are joining the conversation) but my brethren in Christ who, believe it or not, feel increasingly oppressed and worried about their future in the brave new world that perhaps you wish to see.

Sincerely,
Mike Foley
September 14, 2017
Triumph of the Holy Cross

Introduction

I have been asked by my friends at Regnery to write a politically incorrect guide to Christianity. Even though it is impossible to do justice to the greatness of the Christian faith, it is relatively easy to describe Christianity as politically incorrect for one simple reason: it is. In fact, Christianity has the distinction of being the world's most politically incorrect religion—for three reasons.

First, the term "political correctness" was coined by Marxists in the 1930s to signify whatever conformed to the Party line, and Christianity is the religion par excellence that does *not* conform to a Marxist worldview.

Second, in current usage, "politically incorrect" means anything of which the Left disapproves, and what it disapproves of with the greatest vehemence is orthodox Christianity. Indeed, it is not an exaggeration to say that for much of the Left, progress is measured by how far one is able to move away from traditional Christian beliefs and practices. In 2004, Professor Philip Jenkins called anti-Catholicism the "last acceptable prejudice" in America. While a statement perceived "as racist, misogynistic, anti-Semitic, or homophobic can haunt a speaker for years," wrote Jenkins, "...it is still possible to make hostile and vituperative public statements about

Roman Catholicism without fear of serious repercussions." (Jenkins quoted a statement by Peter Viereck in 1960: "Catholic-baiting is the anti-Semitism of the liberals.") Looking out over the horizon at America and the rest of the so-called First World today, one can only wonder if the "last acceptable prejudice" is broadening its franchise to include Christians of all stripes. In the new world at our doorstep, Muslims are accorded the protected status understandably reserved for Jews following the horrors of the Holocaust, while Christians are increasingly fair game for unfair denigration.

Third, if you take "politically incorrect" more broadly, to mean anything that does not perfectly align with the body politic or political life, Christianity is again your prime suspect. As we will explain in chapter four, Christianity is the world's only "transpolitical" religion. Christianity's transpolitical character, its looking beyond policies and laws, beyond the will of the people and the muscle of the State, beyond ethnic loyalty and nationalist identity, is *the* unpardonable sin to those for whom politics is everything. To such folks, Christianity is a dangerous distraction from the all-important work of building their utopias here and now.

Yes, Christianity is the world's most politically incorrect religion, and thanks be to God, it always will be.

CHAPTER ONE

About the Big Guy

In 1897, an eight-year-old girl named Virginia O'Hanlon wrote to the editor of the *New York Sun* asking if her friends were right when they claimed that there was no Santa Claus. The reply of veteran newsman Francis Pharcellus Church has become the most reprinted editorial in history:

> VIRGINIA, your little friends are wrong. They have been affected by the skepticism of a skeptical age. They do not believe except they see. They think that nothing can be which is not comprehensible by their little minds. All minds, Virginia, whether they be men's or children's, are little. In this great universe of ours man is a mere insect, an ant, in his intellect, as compared with the boundless world about him, as measured by the intelligence capable of grasping the whole of truth and knowledge.
>
> Yes, VIRGINIA, there is a Santa Claus. He exists as certainly as love and generosity and devotion exist, and you know that they abound and give to your life its highest beauty and joy. Alas! how dreary would be the world if there were no Santa Claus. It would be as dreary as if there were no VIRGINIAS. There would

Did you know?

★ Atheism, not belief in God, grows out of psychological needs left over from bad relationships with earthly fathers

★ The possibility that we might choose evil is a necessary condition of our capacity for love

★ God did not create us because He needed someone to love

★ If the Resurrection didn't really happen, Christianity is pointless

> be no childlike faith then, no poetry, no romance to make tolerable this existence. We should have no enjoyment, except in sense and sight. The eternal light with which childhood fills the world would be extinguished.... Nobody sees Santa Claus, but that is no sign that there is no Santa Claus. The most real things in the world are those that neither children nor men can see.

Now, beginning a chapter on the existence of God with a defense of Santa Claus may seem to be a foolish thing to do. But I suspect that behind Mr. Church's flawed affirmation of Santa Claus is an implicit yearning to affirm God. And while some of his reasoning is not solid, some of it is. Substitute "God" for "Santa Claus" in his editorial and you start to get the idea.

Yes, Virginia, There Is a God

So sorry, Virginia, Santa Claus isn't real (unless of course you mean Saint Nicholas of Myra), but that doesn't mean there is no grounding for love and generosity and devotion. It doesn't mean that there is nothing behind life's highest beauty and joy. And it doesn't mean that the most real things aren't those that you cannot see. Virginia, allow me to introduce you to God.

And to help you with this introduction, let me start by explaining to you what God is *not*. I know that this is an odd way to introduce somebody. If I introduced you to Bob I would not say, "Virginia, I'd like you to meet someone who isn't Sam, Cheryl, or Cindy." But God is unique, so please humor me.

God is not several gods. Much early religion was polytheistic, and it is easy to see why. Polytheism is a quick, non-scientific way of naming disparate forces in nature and explaining their apparent conflict with each other. If the wind is troubling the sea, one can say that the god of the wind has had a spat with the goddess of the sea. Polytheism is also a way of projecting the human heart's troubling unconscious desires onto the big screen, so to speak, thereby exorcizing them. Think of all the patricide, incest, and cannibalism in the stories of the Greek gods. No wait, Virginia, *don't* think about them. I forgot that you're only eight. Anyway, as we'll see momentarily, the recognition of one transcendent and supreme God is based on a much different foundation from a belief in many gods.

God is not a body. He is not a material entity, and He is certainly not a mighty humanoid in the sky with a long beard or a thunderbolt. God is spirit. What does that mean? Virginia, some of the brightest philosophers have gotten that one wrong, and I tremble to go further. But let me at least speak in "nots" a little more. Spirit is a kind of being that is *not* confined by space, time, or matter. Spirit has no shape or size, no smell or sound, no taste or feel. And yet spirit is real; in fact, there is a way in which spirit, a purely intelligible reality, is more real than the things that we can see, smell, hear, taste, and touch, but that are always undergoing a process of change that can lead to their destruction. Material things come and go, but spirit, as Frank Sheed puts it, "is the being which has a permanent hold upon what it is, so that it can never become anything else." This may be difficult to understand, but it is not religious mumbo jumbo. One of the keystones to the philosophy of the great philosopher Plato, who lived centuries before Christ, is precisely this distinction between the "sensible" and the "intelligible" worlds. Plato would be the first to tell you that a materialist—a believer in the material or empirical as the only form of reality—is living in a dark cave and missing the glorious reality that lies outside. (We'll talk a little more about materialism in chapter ten below.)

God is not the byproduct of psychological illusion or primal fear. This was one of the signature claims of Sigmund Freud, but recent and methodical psychologists such as Paul Vitz have convincingly argued the opposite: atheism, not theism, is the product of a dented psyche. Vitz discovered that famous Christian believers such as Blaise Pascal and Dietrich von Bonhoeffer had

A Book You're Not Supposed to Read

Faith of the Fatherless: The Psychology of Atheism by Paul C. Vitz, 2nd ed. (San Francisco: Ignatius Press, 2013).

strong and loving fathers while famous atheists such as Marx, Stalin, Freud, and Hitler had fathers who were weak, unloving, or absent. Hopefully, Virginia, you have a good dad; if you don't, you may have to work out some issues concerning your earthly father before you can readily love your Heavenly Father. But don't worry: you won't be the first, and it's not an insurmountable problem.

God is not a superstitious rejection or replacement of science. This one you hear a lot these days thanks to the so-called "New Atheists"—Christopher Hitchens, Richard Dawkins, and so forth. Three points on science and religion are in order here.

Three Books You're Not Supposed to Read

New Proofs for the Existence of God: Contributions of Contemporary Physics and Philosophy by Robert J. Spitzer (Grand Rapids: Eerdmans, 2010); *Is There a God?* by Richard Swinburne (Oxford University Press, 2010); and *Atheist Delusions: The Christian Revolution and Its Fashionable Enemies* (New Haven: Yale University Press, 2010) by David Bentley Hart all do a good job of refuting "New Atheist" arguments claiming that belief in God is anti-scientific.

First, modern empirical science can neither prove nor disprove God's existence for the simple reason that *empirical* science only studies *empirical* phenomena (duh!), and God, as we said earlier, is not empirical but spirit (if only Richard Dawkins had read this book!).

Second, it is folly to think that the more we learn from science about how nature works the less room there is for God in our understanding. Even if one day we achieve a perfect and complete scientific grasp of the entire universe and its laws, it would still not cast a single doubt on God's existence or His providential governance over everything. Why not? Because God is not one cause among other causes—one domino knocking down another after being Himself knocked down by a previous domino.

God is not a part of the vast intertwined nexus of causes and effects that science studies. He is not a cause *immanent within* this unfolding structure; rather, He is the *transcendent* cause *of* the structure. As we shall see in a moment, God is the First Cause, which means that He operates on a level of causation entirely different from all other causes, yet preserving the natural integrity of those secondary causes.

Completing, Not Competing

"Belief in God is a rational option, which completes the scientific quest for understanding the universe and does not compete with it."

—**Keith Ward,** *Pascal's Fire*

Let's put it this way, Virginia. It is tempting to think of things in this world as partly caused by nature and partly caused by God, so that when we can't explain something in nature or when something appears to be happening outside of nature, we then ascribe it to God. But this is quite wrong. It is not the case that things happen partly in a natural way and partly in a divine way; instead, they are *wholly* natural and *wholly* divine but on different planes. The metaphor that Thomas Aquinas gives is of an author and a pen. It is equally true to say that the author wrote this sentence and that his pen wrote this sentence. We rightly attribute the same effect (the sentence) to both causes (the author and the pen), only not in the same way. (We'll look at miracles, which are a special case, in chapter six.)

A Category Error

"If there was a controlling power outside the universe, it could not show itself to us as one of the facts inside the universe—no more than the architect of a house could actually be a wall or staircase or fireplace in that house."

—**C. S. Lewis,** *Mere Christianity*

Third, the job of science is to understand *how* things happen and *what* this or that thing is. But as C. S. Lewis observes in *Mere Christianity*, "*why* anything comes to be there at all, and *whether* there is anything behind the things science observes—something of a different kind—this is not a scientific question."

Both/And, Not Either/Or

"It is also apparent that the same effect is not attributed to a natural cause and to divine power in such a way that it is partly done by God and partly by the natural agent; rather, it is wholly done by both, each according to a different mode, just as the same effect is wholly attributed to the instrument and also wholly to the principal agent."

—**Thomas Aquinas,** *Summa contra Gentiles*

That is not to say that the why and whence questions about being cannot be answered, but it is to say that they cannot be answered by modern empirical science.

Positive Attributes

Fortunately, that marvelous spiritual entity known as the human mind, with its gifts of reason and judgment, is still capable of discovering that there is a God. How? I'm glad you asked, Virginia, for now we can move from what God is not to some of the things He is. I say "some of" because the following list is by no means exhaustive.

God is the First Cause. Every effect comes from a cause or series of causes, and these causes are themselves the effects of other causes: the wood of a house comes from trees (and lumbering), the trees come from nature, and nature comes from ____? We can trace any sequence of cause and effect on and on, but we can't trace it forever, for an infinite regression is logically impossible. There must be some first cause that got the entire chain of cause-and-effect going but is itself uncaused—for if it were caused by something else, it would not be the first cause. So there is a First Cause (an uncaused Causer, if you will), and this First Cause we call God.

God is the Mind whose expression we find in the pattern of creation. "The more we try to map out the pattern of nature," writes Ronald Knox, "the more are we driven to the conclusion that it exhibits the working of a Mind greater than any human mind." The great symphony of the universe, in which countless parts come together to form a harmonious whole, implies a great Conductor—especially considering that most of the parts to this symphony have no mind or reason of their own yet somehow act according to a rational pattern. Where does this rational pattern come from if not from a Reason or Mind greater than the entire array of patterns? This Reason or Mind we call God.

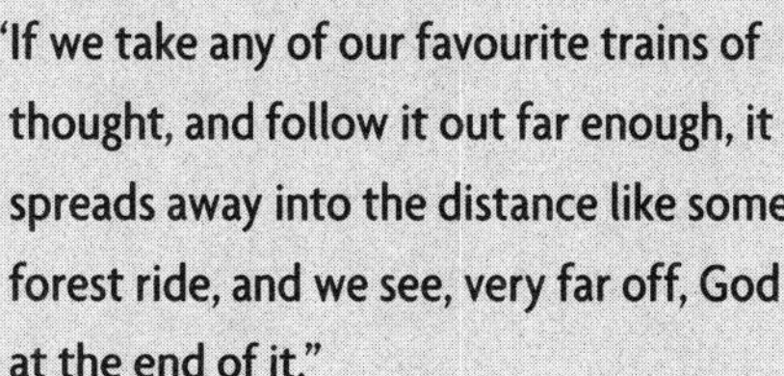

It Can't Be Turtles All the Way Down

"If we take any of our favourite trains of thought, and follow it out far enough, it spreads away into the distance like some forest ride, and we see, very far off, God at the end of it."

—**Ronald Knox,** *The Creed in Slow Motion*

God is the Goal for which everything else exists. Just as you cannot really understand something without understanding its origins, so too can you not really understand something without understanding its end or purpose. But what is the purpose of existence? Why is there a universe? Why I am here? Again keeping in mind the impossibility of an infinite regression of causes (in this case "final causes," which is an old name for goals or ends), there must be a Supreme Good to which everything that exists is ultimately ordered. And this Supreme Good we call God.

God is the Supreme Good behind morality. Despite all our talk today about an endless diversity of values in a multicultural world, a close study of history reveals a recurring moral code held more or less in common by all peoples—including prohibitions against theft and murder and admonitions to honor parents and care for children. At the very least, when we disagree over what is right and what is wrong, we presuppose that there is a right and wrong over which to disagree. Even moral relativists betray that fact (although they won't admit it) when they talk about moral progress or contrast liberal societies like Sweden's with Nazi Germany or denounce any leader they don't like as another Hitler. This tendency is so widespread that it has given rise to "Godwin's Law," the principle that "as an online debate increases in length, it becomes inevitable that someone will eventually compare someone or something to Adolf Hitler or the Nazis."

The Law Written on Our Hearts

"The moment you say that one set of moral ideas can be better than another, you are, in fact, measuring them both by a standard, saying that one of them conforms to that standard more nearly than the other."

—**C. S. Lewis,** *Mere Christianity*

But how *can* we contrast Sweden and the Third Reich or compare President Trump to Adolf Hitler? The comparison of two things presupposes a standard independent of both. And how is it that I have an awareness of this independent standard? Saying that it is a biological or evolutionary impulse is incorrect. As C. S. Lewis explains, the moral voice in my head often tells me to act *against* this or that urge or *against* mere self-preservation. Saying that morality is a social convention doesn't cut it either: true, you may have learned rules of decent behavior from your society, but that doesn't necessarily make the rules a mere societal construct (you learned the multiplication table in school too, but that doesn't make multiplication mere human artifice). No, it is more plausible to conclude that the independent moral standard to which we appeal in all discussions about morality is itself independent of human will. The standard, in other words, comes from God, who has implanted a sense of moral duty and moral discrimination into our hearts.

One final word, Virginia, and then I'll stop addressing you. We have framed our talk about the existence of God in intellectual terms, for indeed it is the mind and not the will that judges whether or not God exists. But a *moral* element can also interfere with these deliberations, warping our judgment and even making people—as we saw in the cases of Marx, Freud, Hitler, and Stalin—enemies of God. When we sin, the thought of God makes us feel uncomfortable, and so we try to forget about Him, even to the point of convincing ourselves that He does not exist. In the words of Fulton J. Sheen: "If you don't behave as you believe, you will end by believing as you behave."

A Note on Evil

One of the most common objections to theism in general and to Christianity in particular is how a God who is omniscient (all-knowing), omnipotent (all-powerful), and omnibenevolent (all-good) could permit so much evil in the world. It is indeed a vexing question, especially when one is personally suffering from some evil. But there are several considerations to keep in mind:

1. Despite our emotional reactions, in the dispassionate realm of logic, divine omniscience, divine omnipotence, divine omnibenevolence, and evil's existence are not mutually exclusive.
2. If you want love, you must have free will, and for our wills to be free they must have the capacity to choose evil. God, you might say, is a hopeless (or rather, hopeful) Romantic: He chose to create a world in which evil could ruin much of His creation's original goodness in order to have a creature that could love Him back—and He did so not out of any need to be loved (He already has, as we'll see in a moment, His own Triune Self) but simply out of the goodness of His heart, to share the thrill of existing, knowing, and loving with piddling creatures. Love and free will are as intrinsically connected as circles and roundness. The loyalty that a dog shows

More Books You're Not Supposed to Read

The Problem of Pain by C. S. Lewis (New York: HarperOne, 2015), originally published in 1940, is an accessible "theodicy"—the classic term for an argument explaining how evil in this world is not incompatible with an all-seeing, all-powerful, and perfectly good God. For a more detailed and academic argument, see Alvin Plantinga's *God, Freedom, and Evil* (Grand Rapids: Eerdman's, 1977). *The Doors of the Sea: Where Was God in the Tsunami*? by David Bentley Hart (Grand Rapids: Eerdman's, 2011); and *Why Me? When Bad Things Happen* by Mike Aquilina (Huntington: Our Sunday Visitor, 2009), also address questions raised by evil in a world created by a good God.

Accepting the Risk

"The happiness which God designs for His higher creatures is the happiness of being freely, voluntarily united to Him and to each other in an ecstasy of love and delight compared with which the most rapturous love between a man and a woman on this earth is mere milk and water. And for that they must be free. Of course God knew what would happen if they used their freedom the wrong way: apparently He thought it worth the risk."

—C. S. Lewis, *Mere Christianity*

to its adopted human pack is not, strictly speaking, love, for love is more than an instinct. It's a choice that comes only from free will, and free will comes only with a mind endowed with the capacity to truly know the difference between good and evil. You'll get no argument from me—a dog's devotion to his master is a wonderful thing. But we have to be honest. Dogs inevitably "love" us just because they're made that way; they can't choose not to. God wanted more than Pavlovian animal responses; He wanted a universe crowned with free lovers. And that meant making a universe filled with potential haters.

3. This fact alone makes God a greater Lover than we are. According to birth rates charted by the U.S. Department of Health and data from market research firm Euromonitor, Americans today are having fewer babies and owning more small dogs: the age group of women (15–29) that is foregoing motherhood is the same age group buying the most pooches. There are a number of reasons for this trend, but one of them is that people are replacing children with dogs, treating their pets more like members of the family by spoiling them with premium dog food (now 57 percent of the dog food market), expensive health-monitoring equipment, dog-friendly vacations, and even canine ice cream trucks. Why? Because a dog doesn't grow up to become a teenager who tells you that she hates you as she drops out of college to shack up with her

deadbeat boyfriend. People prefer Fido's safe but limited "love" over the risks and sacrifices of having children with a real capacity to love and hate them. Thank God that God did not follow this strategy. For all of our blather about "love wins," we hardly know the first thing about love.

4. Make no mistake: God abhors evil and did not create it, but once free creatures commit evil, God makes it His problem. The moment that Adam and Eve disqualified themselves from Paradise, God took pity on them and replaced their homemade fig-leaf aprons with animal skins that could withstand the rigors of a life east of Eden. All of sacred history follows the same pattern: God constantly bails out sinful mankind and saves him from himself by employing a variety of strategies that culminate with the ultimate solution of God making Himself a vulnerable human being and allowing Himself to be victimized by evil men. As C. S. Lewis observed, "It costs God nothing, so far as we know, to create nice things: but to convert rebellious wills cost Him crucifixion." As we'll see in our section on the Atonement, the Cross is a scandal to so many precisely because it means that an all-powerful God voluntarily became weak for our sake in order to enter into our suffering and share the burden of it.
5. What we experience as evil on a micro level is part of a greater order that is good. Evil is evil, and God abhors it; but God is so good that He can repurpose evils. An earthquake is an evil thing, especially to the people that it kills, but on a large scale this breakdown (the violent shifting of tectonic plates) actually restores an equilibrium to nature (releasing pent-up elastic energy under the earth's surface). Tragedy can strike a family, but out of it can come innumerable blessings that bring

them together and even heal old wounds. We can even go so far as to say, as does Thomas Aquinas, that it is not despite God's infinite goodness but because of it that He allows evil to exist and produces good out of it. After all, the God who produced something out of nothing in creation is the same God who produced the greatest good out of the greatest evil in the Crucifixion.

6. Of course, it is not always easy to see how God is bringing good out of the evil in our lives, for we lack the right perspective. Augustine of Hippo compared our situation to that of a man standing three inches in front of a wall mosaic. At such a close distance, all the man can see is an ugly disarray of imperfect little stones. It is only when he steps back and looks at the entire mosaic through God's eyes that he will see how all the chaos and the imperfections of the tesserae somehow come together to form a perfect, beautiful, and unified whole. Or think of a toddler who needs a painful medical procedure. As the little boy is being pricked with painful needles by scary masked strangers in a cold and windowless room, he looks plaintively at his father as if to ask, "Why are you letting this happen to me?" His loving and heartbroken father cannot explain in any way the boy could understand how this bad experience is ultimately a good thing. Something similar obtains for us in relation to our Heavenly Father and the evils we experience this side of the grave.

Seeing the Big Picture

"Corruption and defects in natural things are said to be contrary to some particular nature; yet they are in keeping with the plan of universal nature; inasmuch as the defect in one thing yields to the good of another, or even to the universal good... A lion would cease to live, if there were no slaying of animals; and there would be no patience of martyrs if there were no tyrannical persecution."

—**Thomas Aquinas,** *Summa Theologiae*

7. Finally, Christians can cooperate with God in this process of making good lemonade out of evil lemons so that suffering can even have a *redemptive* quality to it. We can do this by gladly accepting the suffering in our lives as God's will for us (a tall order, I know, but don't knock it till you try it). We can unite our sufferings with the sufferings of Jesus on the Cross. Paul mentions both of these things in an arresting line in the Epistle to the Colossians: "I now rejoice in my sufferings for you, and fill up that which is behind of the afflictions of Christ in my flesh for His body's sake, which is the Church" (1:24). Paul does not mean that Christ's sacrifice on the cross was somehow deficient: the Atonement was infinitely sufficient. Rather, Paul is talking about joining our Lord—taking up his own cross to follow Jesus—by offering up his own suffering for the sake of Christ's Church.

But God Meant It for Good

"Suffering is an evil thing in itself. But the suffering which comes to us in this way, suffering which we can't avoid because it is God's will for us, can be turned from an evil thing into a good thing, if we treat it in the right way."

—Ronald Knox, *The Creed in Slow Motion*

Now the point of all this is not to go around looking for suffering or to do absolutely nothing when suffering comes, as if instead of going to the dentist when we get a toothache, we are required to stay home and "offer it up." The point is simply to accept suffering that cannot be avoided as providential and to use that opportunity to offer up a sorrowing but devoted heart as a living sacrifice, holy and pleasing to God (see Romans 12:1). The point is to echo the patience of Job: "Shall we receive good at the hand of God, and shall we not receive evil?"(2:10) and "The Lord gave, and the Lord hath taken away: Blessed be the name of the Lord" (1:21).

To those who think that this theology of suffering leads to a kind of fatalistic attitude, let history set the record straight. The Christians who accepted suffering in their lives as their own cross to carry are the same people who built hospitals and orphanages, cleaned the wounds of lepers, and launched the largest philanthropic efforts the world has ever seen, to reduce the suffering of others.

The Trinity: God's a Party

In our initial explanation to Virginia, we looked at how far the human mind can go by itself in acknowledging the divine. The good news is that, when we are honest with ourselves and not deceived by immoral decisions or by claims spuriously made in the name of science, we can know by human reason alone that there is a God. The bad news is that this knowledge of God amounts to little more than acknowledging a "known unknown," like an X in mathematics. Now, we should not be ungrateful for even this little bit of knowledge; after all, the first step in solving an equation in math is identifying an unknown and then working out its properties. And indeed, in so-called natural theology, we can work out some of the properties of this Divine X, as we have seen above. But that is a far cry from genuine familiarity with God, let alone love and friendship with Him.

Fortunately, God has not left us orphans but has instead gone to a great deal of trouble of introducing Himself to us. In addition to leaving clues in our mind, in our conscience, and in the world around us, God has intervened in human history through divine revelation. His first major step was to pick one man to be the father of a special people whom He would call His own and whom He would teach, slowly but surely, that He is One and that He is Spirit and that He really, really loved them. It would not be an easy process, for the children of Abraham (the people of Israel), had polytheistic and carnal-minded neighbors whose habits and beliefs rubbed off on them, often making them forget their Divine Lessons. But eventually, when the basic reality of monotheism had sunk in, God dropped the real bombshell: that God is not only One but Three-in-One.

Which brings us to the doctrine of the Trinity, that there are three Persons in one God. The First Person in the Holy Trinity is the Father, who proceeds from nobody and nothing else. From the Father proceeds the Son, the Second Person. We call this procession a "begetting" or a "generating" rather than a "making" because the Son is not a creature who was made by the Father; rather, He is of the exact same stuff or substance as the Father (the technical term is "consubstantial") roughly in the same way that a child is the same kind of stuff as his parents. The Son is also the perfect reflection of His Father, which is why He is referred to as Image or Word (Colossians 1:15; 2 Corinthians 4:4; John 1:1ff). Finally, when the Father beholds His Son and vice versa, the result is a procession of Love, but this Love is not just a movement or emotion; it is a third distinct Person called the Holy Spirit. As Ronald Knox explains,

> From all eternity there has been a multiplicity of life within the unity of the Godhead. God the Father, from all eternity, has spoken a Word; or if you prefer to put it in a rather more luminous way, from all eternity He has thought a thought of Himself. When you or I think, the thought has no existence outside our own minds; but when the eternal Mind thinks of itself, it produces a Thought as eternal as itself, and that Thought is, like the eternal Mind, a Person. And so you get two Persons within the Blessed

Lord of the Dance

"And that, by the way, is perhaps the most important difference between Christianity and all other religions: that in Christianity God is not a static thing—not even a person—but a dynamic, pulsating activity, a life, almost a kind of drama. Almost, if you will not think me irreverent, a kind of dance."

—**C. S. Lewis,** *Mere Christianity*

Trinity, the eternal Mind and its eternal Thought. And now, you can't imagine two Divine Persons as existing side by side, can you, without their having some relation to each other, some attitude towards each other; and what that attitude will be it is not difficult to guess; They will love one another. And this Love, which springs at once from the eternal Mind and its eternal Thought, binding them to one another, is the Holy Spirit. That is why we say that the Holy Spirit proceeds from the Father and the Son. He is the conscious response of Love which springs up between them; He goes out from each of them to the other.

Love Overflowing

"Why did God want to create the world? From all eternity to all eternity he lives in heaven, utterly self-sufficient; nothing outside himself could possibly contribute to the happiness and to the glory that is his. Why did he want there to be anything else? It's no good telling me that he must have been lonely with nobody to know, nobody to know him, with nobody to love, nobody to love him. Because, you see, the doctrine of the Holy Trinity knocks all that argument on the head... There is no loneliness, then, imaginable in God's existence; the Divine Life would have full scope for its activities, even if there were nothing else."

—**Ronald Knox,** *The Creed in Slow Motion*

The key phrase here is "from all eternity." One of the things that makes the Trinity difficult to understand is that it is in eternity, and eternity does not play by the rules of time. For us to picture the processions of the Divine Persons, we have to picture first the Father, then the Son, and then both of them "spirating" the Holy Spirit (that's the technical name for the procession of the Third Person, if you must know). This temporal image gives the impression that there is a "before" and "after" in the Trinity. But there isn't. "Before" and "after" are temporal categories, and the divine processions do not take place in time. Indeed—and please forgive me for speaking this way—the processions take place before there was a before or after to speak of. At no time, then, was there only the Father or only the Father and the Son. Father, Son, and Holy Spirit are co-eternal.

Now if you are an atheist (new or old), you will be tempted to dismiss this as religious mumbo jumbo. But note that your problem is not with religion but with metaphysics, the kind you get in good Greek philosophy. A good metaphysician never imposes the categories of time onto eternity. Another mark of sound metaphysics is to know that spiritual substances such as the divine nature do not have parts and cannot be separated, and so you should have no problem with the Christian teaching that the three Persons in the Trinity are distinct but not separate and that they do not share a divine nature the way three friends share a pizza but rather each possesses divinity in its entirety—that is, each is God whole and entire.

It's a Mystery

"The heart of humanity... is... satisfied by the strange hints and symbols that gather round the Trinitarian idea... Suffice it to say here that this triple enigma is as comforting as wine and open as an English fireside; that this thing that bewilders the intellect utterly quiets the heart."

—G. K. Chesterton, *Orthodoxy*

The Trinity is not easy to understand, but that does not mean it is incoherent or absurd. If Christians taught that there were three gods in one God or three persons in one Person, *that* would be irrational. But the Church is careful with its language, and if you understand what the Church means by "Person" and what it means by "God," you will see that there is nothing preventing more than one Person in the Godhead. We are confronted here not with a contradiction but with a mystery in the older sense of the word, a reality that is so great that it outstrips our ability to fathom it. A man contemplating the Trinity is like an owl staring at the noonday sun.

Of course, that doesn't stop us from trying to understand, nor should it. Christians have come up with dozens of comparisons for the Trinity, from the triangle to the fleur-de-lis to the "triquetra" to St. Patrick's shamrock. No analogy for God is perfect, but the one that comes closest to mirroring the inner life of the Trinity is not outside but within us: in fact, you're using

★ ★ ★

Just for Fun

Check out "St. Patrick's Bad Analogies" by Lutheran Satire on YouTube. It's really hard not to be a heretic where the Trinity is concerned.

it right now to read these words (and no, I don't mean your eyes). The human mind in the act of knowing is trinitarian. For knowing is a unity, but it also consists of three things. First there is an insight or discovery, that "aha!" moment when the light goes on. From this insight proceeds the "word," a definition or conceptualization of the insight you just had. And from the insight and its conceptualization there follows delight, the love of the discovery. One of the neat things about this "psychological analogy" of the Trinity (as it is traditionally known) is that it deepens our understanding of what it means to say we are made in the image of God. Apparently, man is made not simply in the image of the one God but in the image of the entire Trinity. Very cool.

Feminist Objections

Feminists don't like the Trinity. Some would like to see "Father" replaced by "Mother." Others try to sneak the feminine into the Trinity by confusing the categories of grammatical gender and biological sex and arguing that because the word for Spirit in Hebrew has a feminine gender, the Holy Spirit is of the female sex. God is not opposed to using the occasional feminine category to describe Himself or His actions (see Isaiah 66:13 and Matthew 23:37), and it is true that strictly speaking, there is no sexual differentiation in either the divine nature or in the divine persons. But the male nouns and pronouns are nevertheless important for three reasons.

First, even though the Trinity is not male, it *is* masculine in relation to us. That is, the proper relation between the Triune God and our soul is the same as the proper relation between Christ and His Church—namely, the relation between husband and wife (Ephesians 5:24–25). In these pairings,

God is the husband while human beings, whether they happen to be men or women, are the bride. Even though I am a man, my soul is feminine vis-à-vis God, insofar as it should be receptive of and responsive to the initiative of its Heavenly Spouse. And note that I said "receptive" and not "passive." There is a huge difference between being a passive blob that is merely worked on whether it likes it or not and being a receptive agent who is freely and actively cooperating with the initiator. The image to keep in mind is not a sculptor molding a lump of clay but Fred Astaire leading Ginger Rogers in a graceful (in both senses of the word) dance. To put it in biblical terms, the ideal model of Christian discipleship in relation to the Trinity is the humble handmaid of the Lord who is willing to do whatever He says. The Virgin Mary's utterly receptive and free "Yes" to the marriage proposal of God the Father resulted in her espousal to the Holy Spirit, which resulted in the Son of God's being conceived in her womb and in her heart (Luke 1:26–38; 2:19, 51; 11:28). Feminists hate all this, but they shouldn't. It actually puts men in their place, forcing them to be subordinate in the same way that they expect their wives to be subordinate (what's sauce for the goose . . .).

Second, the male relation between father and son is the best way to describe the relation between the First and Second Persons of the Trinity. It is fatherhood and not motherhood that gives us both resemblance and transcendence: a son not only resembles his father in both blood and sex, but the father is also more "transcendent" in relation to his son than is his mother, whose intimate ties to her children through conception, gestation, and nursing are more suggestive of "immanence." Not surprisingly, many pantheists—who hold that God is immanent in or basically the same as nature—think of the divine as maternal (Mother Earth, Mother Nature, and so forth).

Third, while feminists charge that the masculinity of the Christian God provides cover for the oppression of women, they are overlooking the role that goddess-worship has played in *degrading* women. In most of the ancient cosmogonic myths where the primordial goddess is maternal, men end up slaughtering the goddess (Tiamat, for example, in the Babylonian *Enûma Elish*) to create the world as we know it. The point of these stories is not to expose male violence but to justify it, to portray it as necessary for erecting mighty empires. Violence against the feminine, these myths teach, is the egg you must crack to make a good cosmic or imperial omelet. Scripture, on the other hand, rejects this justification of violence in the first two chapters of Genesis by portraying creation as the peaceful product of God's nonviolent Word and by portraying violence, even in the animal kingdom, as a deviation from God's original plan that only enters into the equation as a consequence of human sin. Feminists claim that the fatherhood of God justifies the oppression of women, but while it is certainly true that bad men can abuse good theology, the opposite is true: rather than justify oppression, the Trinitarian masculinity of the Creator constitutes a rejection of violence against the feminine. By trying to abolish God's masculinity feminists are unwittingly removing a bulwark protecting women from male violence.

Glory Be to the Father and to the Son and to the Holy Spirit

Knowing about the Trinity has other advantages too. For starters, it highlights the sheer gratuity of creation. God did not have to create Heaven and Earth because He was lonely; He already had his own Triune Self to keep Him company. God created a vast universe of creatures simply out of the goodness of His heart, to share the thrill of existing, knowing, and loving with myriads of little beings who don't have to be here.

Further, the Trinity teaches us the meaning of selfless charity. The Father and the Son love each other so selflessly and perfectly that their love is not a thing but a distinct Person (try wrapping your head around that mystery for a while). The selfless love of the Divine Persons for each other and for us reminds us how we should be in our relation to God and each other.

One more beautiful thing about the Trinity is how we are swept up into it. The Christian life is the life of fellowship with Father, Son, and Holy Spirit, with the Spirit leading us to the Son and the Son to the Father and all three Persons dwelling in us. The Christian disciple, as we noted a moment ago, is like the Virgin Mary, Jesus' first disciple: responding to the Father, overshadowed by the Spirit, and conceiving and "begetting" Christ in his heart. The bliss of Heaven is nothing less than joining the immense communion of saints in participating fully in the very life of the Trinity. The Good News is that God is a party—and you're invited.

The Incarnation: What If God Were One of Us?

The reason we know that God is a party to which we are invited is that the Father sent the Son to extend the invitation, and the Son sent the Holy Spirit to convince us to accept it. When did the Son extend this invitation? When He became one of us.

The doctrine of the Incarnation is that the Second Person of the Holy Trinity, who is co-eternal with the Father and the Holy Spirit, entered into human history and took flesh ("became incarnate") by taking on our human nature. In this way the eternal Son of God became Jesus of Nazareth, born in a manger in Bethlehem in 4 B.C. or thereabouts (it should be A.D. 1, but some scribe miscounted). Jesus—a.k.a. the Christ or "Anointed One"—is therefore

The God-Man

"Orthodox theology has specially insisted that Christ was not a being apart from God and man, like an elf, nor yet a being half human and half not, like a centaur, but both things at once and both things thoroughly, very man and very God."

—**G. K. Chesterton,** *Orthodoxy*

★ ★ ★

The Perfect Man

Jesus Christ was "was in all points tempted like as we are, yet without sin" (Hebrews 4:15). But if Jesus never sinned, how can He be like one of us? It's easy to assume that sinning is a part of human nature, but it's not. Rather, sin is a *corruption* of human nature even when it is inherited, as in the case of the spiritual birth defect known as original sin. Adam was made without sin and was fully human (indeed, he was the prototype of humanity), and his decision to sin reduced his humanity rather than augmented it. Likewise, Jesus Christ the "New Adam" was conceived and born without sin, but unlike Adam He perfectly followed the will of God.

one Divine Person with a fully divine nature and a fully human nature.

And when Christian teaching says "fully," it means it. The history of the early Church is filled with heresies trying to split the difference one way or another, arguing either that Jesus wasn't fully divine (Arianism and Adoptionism) or that Jesus wasn't fully human because, they erroneously claimed, He lacked a human nature (Monophysitism) or a human soul (Apollinarianism) or a human will (Monothelitism). Some heretics even tried splitting Christ's personality or personhood, maintaining that there are two persons in Jesus Christ (Nestorianism). But the Church held firm to the teaching it received from the Apostles. Jesus Christ is "of the same stuff as" or consubstantial with God the Father and God the Holy Spirit in His divinity, and consubstantial with us in His humanity. In fact, Jesus is like us in all things except sin.

The Incarnation is indeed Good News for us, for it means that we have a God-Man who can act as a mediator between God and man, and Lord knows we need one. There is already quite a gulf between man and God on a natural level. As mere mortal creatures, we are hardly on par with our transcendent Creator. But when you put sin into the equation, that gulf grows even wider. How good it is, then, to have someone with a leg on both sides of the chasm to bridge the gap.

And the fact that Father, Son, and Holy Spirit all wanted this mediation to take place rather than to let man continue to abuse his own dignity and waste away into nothingness shows the immense and disproportionate love that God has for us. As St. Augustine points out, "Christ came that man might learn how much God loves him." God saw that man was bent over by sin and ignorance, his gaze bent downwards toward the lowly and ephemeral things of life. And so God humbly became man in order to meet us where we are, condescending to our level in order to meet our gaze and redirect it back up to the true, the good, and the beautiful. And when I say "condescend," I really mean it. C. S. Lewis captured the shock of the Incarnation when he wrote, "The Eternal Being, who knows everything and who created the whole universe, became not only a man but (before that) a baby, and before that a foetus inside a Woman's body. If you want to get the hang of it, think how you would like to become a slug or a crab."

★ ★ ★

Participation in the Divine Life

"O God, who in creating human nature wonderfully dignified it and still more wonderfully restored it, grant that... we may be made partakers of the divinity of Him who deigned to be made partaker of our humanity, Jesus Christ our Lord, Thy Son. Amen."

—Prayer from the Extraordinary Form of the Roman Rite

But the Incarnation is more than mediation; it is also an elevation of our nature. When God shares in our humanity, we get to share in His divinity: in St. Athanasius' arresting words, God became man so that man might become God. It is not that we are absorbed into God's nature, losing our individuality in a vast divine ocean, but that our individual natures become shot through with God's love and light, making us His "adopted sons." The Incarnation is not only the beachhead on which God begins to reconquer the territory stolen by the Devil; it is also the beginning of the transformation of that territory into a whole new kingdom.

Just in Time

And the Incarnation came in the nick of time. Ever since Adam's Fall, humans have gladly cooperated in our own dehumanization, debasing our own dignity and distorting the divine image in which we were made. God became man in order to restore this image before it was wiped out entirely through human folly and malice, but He did so only after a long preparation. One reason for this delay was to *persuade* us rather than suddenly *force* us to get our act together and return to Him. "It belongs to despotic power," writes St. Gregory Nazianzus, "to use force; it is a mark of God's reasonableness that the choice should be ours."

Another way to look at God's timing is that like any good author, He wanted to build up a sense of suspense and help His audience see, by exhausting virtually every other option, how fitting His surprising "ultimate solution" to the problem of sin would be. The Old Testament sometimes gives the impression that God is a hapless manager trying a variety of stopgap solutions in response to the problem of human sin—the Flood, the division of languages after Babel, the Covenant with Abraham, the Mosaic Law, the Israelite kingdoms, the prophets' dire warnings, and so forth—all of which invariably fail. But the deeper reality behind the mystery of the Old Testament is that the all-knowing God is not learning from His mistakes but teaching mankind about ours; He is patiently showing *us* that no other solution to the problem of sin is quite right except the scandalous idea that the Word of God should Himself become part of the race making all the trouble.

So God did not kiss the earth with His Son too soon, but neither did He wait too long. He did not wait until the Jewish people as a whole had lost all hope for a Messiah or until the Gentile world had lost all moral decency and reverence for the divine. God chose the perfect moment in history, right after the imperial ambitions of Alexander the Great and then the Romans had created a remarkably unified world that could receive a remarkably universal Gospel, and right before the ancient priestly religion of Israel was destroyed along with its Holy Temple. Perfectly timed, the Incarnation was a sea change that would alter the course of history and begin a chain reaction that would forever improve the world.

Only Another Myth?

Detractors charge that Christianity is just another ancient "myth" about a demigod or hero who is either a savior figure (like Hercules) or who dies and is born again (like Dionysus). We will tackle the question of whether the Bible as a whole is mythological in chapter six. In the meantime, let us note the enormous differences between pagan myths and the life of Christ. The Gospels, for instance, do not have the hazy "Once upon a time" fairy tale quality of mythology but a crisp concern for historical accuracy, as is evident in statements such as "Now in the fifteenth year of the reign of Tiberius Caesar, Pontius Pilate being governor of Judaea, and Herod being tetrarch of Galilee, and his brother Philip tetrarch of Ituraea and of the region of Trachonitis, and Lysanias the tetrarch of Abilene, Annas and Caiaphas being the high priests, the word of God came unto John the son of Zacharias in the wilderness." (Luke 3:1–2). Moreover, there is a world of difference between saying that a person is half-man and half-god (like Hercules or Theseus or Aeneas) and saying that He is fully man and fully God. The half-and-half version reduces the divine to the level of the mortal by yielding to the rather lazy human desire for compromise. The Christian version soars above all comfortable categories by insisting on the astonishing claim that two completely different natures, one thoroughly human and the other thoroughly divine, exist in one and the same Person. Mixing things dilutes them, but the

All the World Being at Peace

"For all intents and purposes, when our Lord came, there was a single world-empire, the Roman Empire, there was a single world-language, the Greek language. That had never happened before; it has never happened since. Our Lord came just at the right time; or rather, if you look at it from a more sensible point of view, Providence had arranged the right time for our Lord to come in. Up till 30 B.C., he would have found the world distracted by a long series of civil wars. After A.D. 70 he would have found Jerusalem a heap of ruins. Just in those hundred years, everything was favourable, you see, to the spread of a world-wide Gospel."

—**Ronald Knox,** *The Creed in Slow Motion*

doctrine of the Incarnation keeps Christ's natures bold and unmixed, in your face and beyond your understanding. The half-and-half solution is fine for coffee but not theology.

But even if the differences outweigh the similarities (and they really do), how do you explain the similarities? Atheists claim that the overlapping elements "prove" the falsity of Christianity since they are derivative, even plagiarized. C. S. Lewis, on the other hand, sees these early myths as "good dreams" sent by God to the heathen to prepare them in some small way for the Christ event, just as He sent Moses and the prophets to the Israelites to prepare them. Perhaps Lewis is right, but we can also take his concept of a dream in a different direction. In dreams, the details of an underlying truth are usually distorted. Perhaps then, the "dreams" of ancient myths are best seen as a bizarre and often deviant longing for Christ, whether or not they were ever intended to prepare or succeeded in preparing anybody for Him.

For what the aforementioned atheists overlook is that in addition to a priority of time there is a priority of being. In the order of time an acorn may come before a tree, but in the order of being the tree comes before the acorn. Similarly, savior and resurrection myths may dot the landscapes of literature and folklore centuries before Christ, but the coming of Christ perfected and completed those myths. And this is true not just of myths; many aspects of Christianity can be understood in this light. Washing rituals, for instance, are common in different cultures and religions, with the implicit goal of spiritual cleansing or purification; yet the only religious washing that does what it promises is baptism. Acknowledging the feminine in the spiritual life has taken all kinds of wrong turns, some of them quite sinister or disparaging to women. The solution was not worshipping a female deity but honoring a handmaid who humbly said yes to God: not a mother goddess but the Mother of God.

Of course, some religious and cultural acorns fail to grow into oaks because they are warped by sin. In some respects, offering up a bloody sacrifice is a healthy acknowledgment of one's own sinfulness and creatureliness before God (think Abel or Noah in the Old Testament). But this impulse took a satanic turn in pagan sacrifices that scapegoated innocent human victims. It took the Crucifixion to reveal the true meaning of sacrifice. Or take the Eucharist and its relationship to cannibalism. The Romans accused the early Church of cannibalism because of the Christian belief that the bread and wine consecrated in divine worship is really the Body and Blood of Christ. But is the Eucharist an instance of cannibalism or is cannibalism, especially as a religious practice, a perverse and demonic mimicry of Holy Communion? Just as all pagan blood-sacrifices are distorted knock-offs of the one true Sacrifice of Calvary (even if they took place *before* the Crucifixion), so too are all ritual acts of cannibalism a twisted attempt to replace the Bread of Life with the mammon of one's own iniquity. The Eucharist is not another form of cannibalism; rather, cannibalism is an ungodly deformity of the Eucharist, a blind way of seeking but never obtaining a union with life and divine power. Holy Communion may even be called the supreme instance of anti-cannibalism, insofar as it exposes the bankruptcy of all its evil impostors.

Atonement: The Passion, Death, Resurrection, and Ascension of the God-Man

The Son did more than extend an invitation to the party that the Trinity was throwing; He paid for our ticket with His own blood. The Atonement is the reconciliation of God and man that makes them "at one" with each other (see 2 Corinthians 5:19). This reconciliation, which was needed because sin has alienated man from God, was made through the suffering, death, Resurrection, and Ascension of Jesus Christ. The Bible uses a number of images to help us fathom the great and inexhaustible mystery of the Atonement: that Christ came to "conquer" death, sin, and Satan (1 John 3:8);

that Christ gave His life as a "ransom for many" (Mark 10:45, Matthew 20:28); that Christ "redeemed" or bought us back from bondage or servitude by paying the ultimate price (1 Corinthians 6:20); that Christ took on our punishment instead of us (2 Corinthians 5:21; 1 Thessalonians 5:9); that Christ's suffering heals us (Isaiah 53:5; 1 Peter 2:24); that Christ's suffering is a model for us to imitate (1 Corinthians 11:1, 1 Peter 2:21); and so on.

Perhaps we can sum up the Atonement by rubbing two principles together. The first is that "the greatness of an offense is measured by the dignity of the person against whom the offense is committed." By itself, sticking out your tongue is a neutral act. When you stick it out at your coworker it becomes a minor offense. When you stick it out at the Queen of England it becomes a more serious offense. And when you stick it out at God, it is an infinitely greater offense, for God is infinitely greater than the Queen of England (and, as we'll see in a moment, the Fall was more than just sticking out one's tongue).

The second principle is that when it comes to making reparation for an offense, "the greatness of the reparation is measured by the dignity of the person who is making it." If sheep belonging to Downton Abbey hopped the fence and ate old Mr. Molesley's award-winning roses, reparation would have to be made. Let's say that Mr. Molesley would only be satisfied by a member of the estate's dressing up like a sheep and making braying noises in the village square. Perhaps old Molesley was picturing how funny Thomas the footman would look in a big fluffy costume, or better yet, Carson the grave-faced butler. But imagine Molesley's astonishment if Lord Grantham himself deigned to be humbled in this fashion. It would more than make up for the nibbled roses.

When we apply these two principles to sin and reparation, we come across an awful truth: when man sins against God, there is no way he can make it up on his own. He has committed an infinite offense but he lacks the infinite dignity to rectify it; he has fallen but he can't get up. Hence the God-Man

Jesus Christ. As fully human, Jesus became one of us and made reparation on our behalf. As fully divine, Jesus' infinite dignity gives His human act of reparation an infinite efficaciousness. Both Jesus' divinity and His humanity are essential to the equation. Atonement always involves some kind of loss or suffering, but God as God cannot suffer: God needs to become man in order to take on man's suffering and to suffer like a man. But if Jesus were a mere man and nothing more, His every action would not have infinite merit. His humanity had to be yoked to His divinity in order to give His human deeds that kind of reverberating power.

And so the Divine Person Jesus Christ suffered through His human nature and suffered terribly, allowing His Blood to be shed through scourging, through a crowning of thorns, through falling while carrying a heavy cross, through the torment of Crucifixion. The slain blood of Abel once cried out for vengeance (Genesis 4:10), but the Precious Blood of Jesus Christ "speaketh better things" than Abel's (Hebrews 12:24). It cries out not for vengeance but for peace and forgiveness. For reconciliation. For atonement. And its cry is heard.

And One Mediator Also between God and Men

"Now clearly a mediator between God and men should have something in common with God, something in common with men . . . the Mediator between God and men, the man Christ Jesus, appeared between sinful mortals and the immortal Just One: for like men He was mortal, like God He was just. . . ."

—Augustine, *Confessions*

Not Attuned to the Atonement

The Atonement is great news for mankind, yet from the start it has been scandal to the Jew and folly to the Greek (see 1 Corinthians 1:23). It was a scandal to the Jews not only because they expected "signs" or displays of superhuman power (1 Corinthians 1:22) but because they (rightly) thought of God as a transcendent spirit utterly distinct from man. Even though there are hints in the Hebrew Bible that God would eventually take flesh, it would never have occurred to the average Jew that the long-expected Messiah would be not only a Son of David but also the Son of God—much less that God's Chosen People would collaborate in His murder (talk about a blow to the collective ego). Islam takes this even further. Muslims deny that Jesus, whom they revere as a prophet, died at all (Qu'ran 4:157–158). They say either that the Crucifixion never took place or that God substituted someone else, like Judas Iscariot, on the cross for Jesus. Underlying this fanciful rejection of Jesus' death is the idea that God would never allow one of His latter-day prophets to be so mistreated. The God of Islam triumphs by crushing His enemies through raw power, not by sharing in our weakness and suffering.

As for the Greeks, they probably sniffed at anything they had to take on faith. They wanted "wisdom" (1 Corinthians 1:22), which meant to them what it means for many of us today, an intelligible account of the whole, every part of which is rationally verifiable. The Christian account of the whole is certainly intelligible (it makes sense), but not all of it is rationally verifiable, for even the high and mighty must believe the word of some Galilean fishermen about what they heard and saw. To do that seems sheer folly to the intellectually proud.

The accusations of scandal and foolishness did not die with the ancient Greeks or Hebrews, but they changed over time. Today some feminists charge that the Father's "demanding" His Son's death is the supreme act of child abuse, providing patriarchal heterosexual men with an excuse to beat their wives and children. Atheists denounce the idea of an angry, sadistic God who can only be satisfied by His Son's blood: they sometimes try to back up their claims by twisting or exaggerating the teachings of great theologians like Anselm of Canterbury. Some call Jesus' self-offering on the cross a form of human sacrifice.

But God has made clear in the Bible that, unlike the deities worshipped by Israel's neighbors, He does not much care for sacrificial bloodshed (see Psalm 51:17, Hosea 6:6, and Hebrews 10:8). So why did God require bloody sacrifices in the Old Testament, and why was He pleased with His Son's bloody sacrifice in the New?

The answer says more about us than about Him. The sin of Adam was not an innocent misdemeanor; it was a conscious effort to become God without God. And becoming God without God means making oneself God's enemy, an aspiring deicidal maniac. Man was already "god-like," having been created in His image and likeness (Genesis 1:26); his listening to the serpent and eating the forbidden fruit in order "to be as gods" (Genesis 3:5) sprang from a desire to become *his own god* who could make up his own version of "good and evil." And this goal of becoming one's own god sooner or later entails wanting to get the real God out of the way. Ever since the Fall, then, man has had a dark and bloody heart (see Genesis 8:21), and not just towards his fellow man. Of course, the smart thing for man to do would be to realize what a spiritual cancer this dark heart is and to seek forgiveness from God. Instead, however, we humans make it worse by turning to self-denial and deceit; rather than bringing our sin out in the open and getting it cured we cover up our interior wickedness like Adam and Eve trying to hide their shame with aprons made out of fig leaves. (Genesis 2:7–8). Hence the prophet Jeremiah declares that the human heart is not only "desperately wicked" but "deceitful above all things" (17:9). Sad but true.

One way to understand all the blood sacrifices in the Bible, then, is as a divine response to help mankind acknowledge the bloodiness of his own heart—for, as any psychologist will tell you, the first step to a cure is admitting that

A Book You're Not Supposed to Read

Desperately Wicked: Philosophy, Christianity, and the Human Heart by Patrick Downey (Westmont, IL: IVP Academic, 2009).

you have a problem. God Himself deplores violence, which is why in the book of Genesis violence is not a part of His original creation: before the Fall, even the animals were vegetarian (Genesis 1:29–30), and in contrast to other creation stories from the ancient world, the Hebrew God creates peacefully through His word rather than violently through His might. But once human sin violated this divine order and introduced violence into the world, God was willing to use violence in order to help man help himself. He commanded bloody sacrifices in the Old Testament as a way of teaching Israel to acknowledge its own sinfulness and dependence on God: the shedding of animal blood was a ritual reminder of our own hidden desire to shed each other's blood and of the fact that all gifts come from God. God was "pleased" with the sacrifices made in the Old Testament not because He loves the smell of burning flesh in the morning but because when they were done in the right spirit and not merely as some kind of attempted bribe, they bespoke a contrite heart. And that was their intention all along.

And God is even willing to use violence Himself. We see this very early on, when God makes clothes out of animal skins for Adam and Eve because their dorky fig-leaf aprons are not going to cut it outside Eden (Genesis 3:21)—even though His original plan was not even for animals to kill animals. In other words, God shed blood in order to bail out sinful mankind, and this pattern, which repeats itself throughout the Bible (think of God's protection of Israel), culminates in the ultimate act of God's allowing His own blood to be shed in order to redeem us.

And thus we come full circle. As we noted, it has been man's secret desire to kill God ever since the Fall. And what was God's ultimate solution to this iniquity? It was to let man do exactly what he wanted. God let man kill God, so out of the greatest evil that man could commit the greatest good might come. God was not pleased that His Son should be treated thus by man; He was pleased that His Son would so valiantly offer Himself for worms like us, in the same way that a father is proud of his soldier son who offers his life for his country while deploring his son's violent demise. And paradoxically, although this death is a sacrifice and although it involves a human being, it is not a "human sacrifice" but rather the supreme answer to human sacrifice, exposing all such sacrifices as demonic mimicries of the God-Man's willing sacrifice of Himself. Jesus Christ voluntarily offered His life when He could have just as easily kept it, making Him not only the Victim but the High Priest and thereby transforming His murderous execution into a holy offering. Jesus the High Priest then took this offering of His own Precious Blood into Heaven at His Ascension and presented it to the Father. The Father was not pleased with the sight of blood per se but He was moved by the sight of His Son's still open wounds, everlasting witnesses of His sacrifice and of His love for His flock. Just as we are moved to give more money to a homeless person the more disfigured and wretched he looks, so too is the Father more moved to grant whatever the Son asks at the sight of His crucified and risen body. It is a circle of love: the Father sent the Son to redeem us out of love, and He grants the Son's petitions for us out of love.

The Resurrection and Ascension

Unlike Muslims, most secular nonbelievers do not doubt that Jesus of Nazareth was crucified under Pontius Pilate around the year A.D. 33; what they doubt is that He rose again on the third day. According to Augustine of Hippo, the Devil above all tries to seduce unbelievers into mocking faith in the Resurrection. The Devil apparently has been pretty successful in modern times. Every Easter in mainstream publications like *Time* or *Newsweek* or their online heirs, you can count on an "exposé" on "what *really* happened" to Jesus, where the "historical Jesus" (a reconstructed picture of Jesus by biblical scholars who either lost their faith or never had it) is "discovered" to be some nice moral teacher who never really came back to life and whose overzealous disciples blew things out of proportion. Even liberal

Two Books You're Not Supposed to Read

Both *Jesus on Trial: A Lawyer Affirms the Truth of the Gospel* by David Limbaugh (Washington, D.C.: Regnery, 2014) and *Cold-Case Christianity: A Homicide Detective Investigates the Claims of the Gospels* by J. Warner Wallace (Colorado Springs: David C. Cook, 2013) look at the case for the Resurrection—one from the perspective of a lawyer used to sifting testimony and evidentiary documents, the other from the point of view of a police investigator—and conclude that the evidence is solid.

Christians have been hopping on this bandwagon since the nineteenth century, treating belief in the bodily resurrection of Jesus Christ as a major impediment to the acceptance of Christianity by the sophisticated.

But the atheists who deny the Resurrection are right about one thing. If the Resurrection is just a metaphor—if Jesus Christ did not rise body and soul from the dead that first Easter Sunday morning—then the entire Christian faith is in vain. That's exactly what Paul says in 1 Corinthians 15:14. The Gospel hinges on the Resurrection. It is the ultimate confirmation of Christ's divinity, which is essential to the Atonement; it is the ultimate proof that God's mercy is greater than man's sin; it is the ultimate victory over death, which ever since the Fall has had power over mankind; and it is the ultimate promise of the resurrection of our own bodies at the end of time. The Resurrection is not the problem; it is the solution.

And if I may put it this way, it is oddly plausible. Modern empirical science cannot prove that the Resurrection is impossible, only that it is highly unlikely. And they are right: a man rising from the dead *is* highly unlikely unless that man happens to be God (which is also highly unlikely but likewise not impossible). On the other hand, the testimony of the disciples is strangely compelling. Most men will not die for what they know is a lie, but they will die for what they believe to be true. And every one of the Apostles except John died for his faith without retracting a single word. According to tradition, Peter even went so far as to ask to be crucified upside down since he was not worthy to die like his Savior. Finally, when the Bible is read in light of the Crucifixion and Resurrection, not only do all of the promises that Jesus makes about dying and returning make sense, but an entire world of clues in the Old Testament opens up, revealing a pattern of foreshadowing that begins on the very first page of Genesis.

★ ★ ★

Archaeological Evidence

There is forensic evidence that Peter was crucified upside down. In the 1950s, bones were discovered in a catacomb directly beneath the high altar of St. Peter's Basilica in Rome. When the skeleton was reconstructed, it was discovered that the foot bones were missing, which suggests that Peter's feet were severed after his death in order to remove the body from its cross.

Finally, when Jesus went up to Heaven body and soul in his Ascension, forty days after He rose from the dead (see Acts 1:2–11), He was not so much ending His earthly ministry as beginning a new level of heavenly intercession. For when Jesus ascended into Heaven, there was not a welcome home party with a "Mission Accomplished" banner spread across the clouds. Jesus' work was not yet done. He entered into the "Holy of Holies" as both High Priest and sacrificial Victim, bringing His own blood as the price for our redemption (see Hebrews 9:11–13). Taking His seat at the right hand of the Father, He could then send the Holy Spirit to sanctify His Church below and keep it from the jaws of death, and He could prepare a place in Heaven for His elect.

CHAPTER TWO

High-Proof Spirits

God has spent a lot of time and effort trying to help mankind, but the human race was not His first or even His highest creation. Both of those distinctions belong to the angelic orders.

The first chapter of Genesis fails to say exactly when angels were created. Some ancient exegetes interpreted God's creation of the light on the first day as His creation of angels and His separation of the light from the darkness as His separation of the good angels from the bad after the fall of the latter (Genesis 1:3–4). Some modern Christians hold that angels were created along with the celestial light-bearing bodies on the fourth day (Genesis 1:14–18). The problem with both of these views is that they assume that angels were created at some point in time, and although angels are not co-eternal with God, neither are they temporal beings—they may have a beginning like all of God's creatures, but it is not a beginning *in time* (that's a mind-blowing thought, I know, but nobody said that understanding the sacred mysteries of Christianity would be easy). The more likely view is that they were created when God created the heavens in Genesis 1:1, assuming that the "heavens" here refer to the spiritual realm of bliss where saint and angel abide and not simply the sky. But regardless of when they

Did you know?

★ Angels don't learn things; they already know everything they will ever know

★ The correct pronoun for angels is "he"

★ There are nine different angelic orders

came into being, angels are a recurring feature in the Bible. By the time we get to Paul's Epistles, we even know the names of the nine angelic "choirs" or "orders."

What are angels? They are pure spiritual beings. Like humans, they are creatures with an intellect and will, but unlike us they do not have bodies (nor do they have wings and harps—those are just symbols). To understand the implications of an angel's lack of corporeality, one needs a good dose of sound metaphysics. Here is a sampling:

- Angels are pure intellect. Because angelic knowing does not occur through the mediation of a brain, angels do not reason their way gradually from data to conclusion or learn one thing at a time. Rather, they know things immediately according to their essence, and they know them all at once.
- Angelic knowledge is not limited by the physical senses; therefore, they can know whatever they want about what is happening in the physical world. Angels are not, however, omniscient (see Matthew 24:36). They cannot know the future unless God reveals it to them as He did to the prophets, and they cannot read our thoughts. On the other hand, because angels are extremely astute, with a wider view of events than human beings have, they are very good at predicting the future and guessing what is on our minds.
- Angels know about time and the succession of events, but they do not experience time. To an angel it does not feel like a long time since he has been created by God because "long time" and "short time" mean nothing to him. Keeping a star in motion for a billion years or talking to a human being for a couple of minutes are the same to him.

- Angels do not have emotions; they do not move from one passion to another, for that requires a succession of different moments in time.
- Because they are spirits, angels are not "in" a particular place the way that a material object is in a physical location, like a chair in a room. When it comes to being in a particular place, angels fall somewhere along the spectrum between man and God. Whereas human beings, by virtue of our bodies, can be in only one place at one time, God is perfectly and entirely present everywhere. Angels, on the other hand, are neither physically confined to one place nor omnipresent. Rather, they are present in a place insofar as they exert their power there. They are where they act, whether that be on a single person or an entire galaxy.
- Angels can manipulate air and solid matter to take on any appearance they want (hence their various apparitions as men in the Bible), but this is more like a hologram; it is not a genuine incarnation, as when the Second Person in the Trinity became Jesus Christ.
- Angels can use their intellect and will to affect the material world in other ways as well. An angel struck the Apostle Peter while he was asleep, lifted him up, unlocked the chains on his wrists, and opened the city's formidable iron gate (Acts 12:7–10). The apocryphal or deuterocanonical books of the Old Testament afford additional examples of angelic power over the material (see Daniel 3:49–50).
- Angels constantly behold the face of our Heavenly Father and give glory to Him, even when employed in various ministries. We can say that they glorify God through their ministries: their entire being and activity are a single act of worship.

And why are they called angels? "Angel" is from a Greek word meaning "messenger," which itself is a translation of a Hebrew word for "one sent." The word applies specifically to the lowest rank of celestial spirits (who indeed serve as messengers between God and men), but the Bible also uses the term generically for all nine ranks of heavenly spirits, since all of them in some way have been sent by God. Basically, while "spirit" describes their nature or essence, "angel" describes their office or job.

Ye Watchers and Ye Holy Ones

What kind of job can an angel have, you ask? Here's where the speculation on angels gets really interesting. We know on the authority of the Bible that there are nine choirs or orders of angels: Seraphim, Cherubim, Thrones, Dominations, Virtues, Powers, Principalities, Archangels, and Angels (though the order of these ranks is disputed—see Ephesians 1:21 and Colossians 1:16). We also know that angels have power over the material world, which in the Scriptures is principally manifested in special interventions to save God's people. In the Old Testament, angels protected Lot and Isaac, assisted prophets, led Israel, and even killed Israel's enemies (2 Kings 19:35). In the New Testament, the angel Gabriel announced the births of John the Baptist and Jesus. Angels will also help Christ round up the wicked at the end of time and cast them into the everlasting fires (Matthew 13:41–42).

But in addition to these miraculous interventions, angels may have more "ordinary" jobs, keeping creation running smoothly. The fifth-century Christian mystic Pseudo-Dionysius organized the nine orders of angels into three "spheres" and speculated about their roles:

First Sphere: Heavenly servants of God the Son incarnated.

1. *Seraphim.* Known for their ardor, the seraphs or "burning ones" serve at the heavenly court and continuously sing, "Holy,

holy, holy, is the Lord of hosts: the whole earth is full of his glory!" (Isaiah 6:3).

2. *Cherubim.* Guardians of the way to the Tree of Life (Genesis 3:24) and the throne of God (Ezekiel 28:14–16), cherubs are characterized by a fullness of knowledge.
3. *Thrones.* Living symbols of God's justice and authority (like a king's throne), these spirits are known for their immediate knowledge of the types of divine works.

Second Sphere: Heavenly governors of creation, both spiritual and material.

1. *Dominations.* As their name would suggest, Dominations or Dominions have dominion over the lower angels, ruling and guiding them.
2. *Virtues.* According to Thomas Aquinas, "virtue" in Greek and Latin signifies a "certain virile and immovable strength," and so the Virtues are those spirits who have a certain strength with respect to their divine operations in receiving divine gifts. They fearlessly undertake the divine things appointed to them with great strength of mind.
3. *Powers.* Powers have the capacity to receive divine things from above and to lead inferiors to those things. According to some, they supervise the heavenly bodies, maintaining the order of the cosmos, and opposing the evil spirits that manipulate matter in the universe.

Third Sphere: Heavenly guides, protectors, and messengers to mankind.

1. *Principalities.* Princes on earth are those who lead others, and Principalities are those spirits who are leaders in a sacred order. They preside over the archangels and angels and charge them with fulfilling their roles.

2. *Archangels.* Archangel means "chief angel." They guard over nations or peoples. Michael the Archangel, for instance, was the patron of ancient Israel and is currently the protector of the Church.
3. *Angels.* Angels are the spirits most involved in human affairs, including our guardian angels. Along with archangels, they also "announce to men either great things above reason or small things within the purview of reason" (Thomas Aquinas).

Skeptics say that this kind of angelology detracts from the laws of nature that are discovered by science—as if we were forced to choose between a scientific or a spiritual account of nature. But why not have it both ways? Appreciating the role of angels in the cosmos does not lead to a loss of faith in the scientific method: it simply underscores the fact that God uses a vast number of intermediary causes and agents to execute His will. The recognition of this vast hierarchy of causes and agents increases our awe of His majesty and power. Angels are a part of the *natural* order. Today we misuse the term "supernatural" to refer to anything paranormal or out of the ordinary, but in Christian theology "nature" refers to the order of creation and "supernature" to the order of grace wrought by Christ, for grace is a special gift from God that heals nature if it has been wounded by sin and elevates it to new heights. Even though angels are endowed with grace and may be supernaturally commissioned carriers of grace to others (just as we can be), they are natural beings like us.

Finally, the existence of the nine angelic orders is a testimony to the fact that we are not alone but protected by throngs of great spiritual patrons who mediate the will of God. I suspect that one of the reasons modern man has become obsessed with the possibility of extraterrestrial life is to fill the void left in his heart by his dismissal of angels. We cannot stand the thought that we are alone in the universe, and so having rejected beautiful luminous spirits, we scour the skies searching for creepy-looking aliens in UFOs.

Your Guardian Angel—and Your Local Feminist

One of the best known kinds of angel is the guardian angel. The Bible does not explicitly state that each person is assigned an angel to help him through life, but there are several biblical hints to that effect (Genesis 16:6–32 and 24:7; Judith 13:20; 1 Kings 19:5; Psalm 33:8, 34:5, and 90:11; Hosea 12:4; Acts 12:7; and Matthew 18:10). In the Christian tradition, guardian angels have been accepted as a normal part of existence: the only debate was whether each guardian angel is assigned to one human being from the beginning to the end of that person's earthly life and then assigned another, or if each angel is assigned to only one person for all eternity. Thomas Aquinas believed that the latter opinion was the more probable—so it is well to be on good terms with your guardian angel, since he'll be sitting next to you in Heaven. And if Aquinas is right, there are a *lot* of angels, something that is to mankind's benefit.

Angels can also be guardians of families, parishes, occupations, and guilds, while archangels are usually guardians of larger entities such as nations. One of the reasons that "Michael" was the most popular boy's name in the United States in every year but one from 1954 to 1998 was that St. Michael, the warrior archangel who defeated Satan, had been invoked to protect our armed forces against the wicked legions of Hitler and Tojo. The returning GIs remembered Michael's patronage and gratefully named their sons after him.

And speaking of naming, feminists don't like it when people call angels "he"—or when they call women "angels." The latter complaint is understandable: calling a woman "angel" comes across as a bit patronizing despite the fact that, in reality, angels are superior to and more powerful than

★ ★ ★

Spirited Spoof

On November 15, 2016, the Christian satire site *The Babylon Bee* published a news story entitled, "God Apologizes for Gendered Language In Bible," reporting that the Almighty had "issued an apology Tuesday for the gendered language found throughout His Word, the Holy Bible." The Lord had explained, "The fact that gendered language has been non-offensive for millennia is no excuse, since through my omniscience I knew that by the time the 21st Century rolled around it would no longer be considered acceptable." God added "that it was never His intention to advance the agenda of the patriarchy" and said, "My choices were unfortunate and regrettable, and I have no intention of trying to mansplain them away. I will do better."

human beings. But as for the first objection, we beg to differ. Angels have the power to assume any appearance they want, but whenever they appear as human beings in the Bible they always appear as male. This fact alone makes the use of the masculine pronoun for angels appropriate. Besides, even though angels are by nature sexless (see Matthew 22:30), they are typically masculine vis-à-vis human beings, inseminating the receptive human soul, so to speak, with messages from God.

Of course, one thing we have never heard a feminist complain about is the exclusive use of the masculine gender for Satan and his demonic minions.

The Devil Is in the Details

Demons or devils are fallen angels, celestial spirits who have rejected God and been cast out of Heaven by Michael the Archangel to suffer everlasting torment. To understand these nasty creatures, we need to put our metaphysical thinking caps back on:

- God created all of the angels at once. And, of course, like everything else He made, God created them good.
- Immediately upon his creation, each angel already knew everything that he would ever know, including the difference between good and evil (remember, angels don't learn gradually, like humans slogging through time). Using this

knowledge, a number of angels chose to rebel from God. Why did they do so, knowing that it meant eternal damnation? Well, why did Adam eat the fruit knowing that he would die and lose Paradise? Like all too many human beings, some angels simply choose to be stupid. Evil is the enduring mystery wrought by the stupid.

- What was their incentive in rebelling? It is speculated that the devils were guilty of pride and envy: pride in desiring to be like God (the serpent used the same temptation to ensnare Adam and Eve) and envy about *us*. They knew that it was the Son of God's plan from all eternity to become a lowly human being and not a cool angel like themselves, and they grew green—or rather red—with envy. And so, instead of rejoicing in God's mercy over vile bodies like ours, they declared *Non serviam*—"I will not serve." Their rejection was a rejection of God in general and of Christ in particular, for all heavenly spirits were created to serve the Son of God (see Colossians 1:16).
- Damnation in return for a single decision may sound harsh, but angels are pure spiritual beings living outside of time. One of the advantages of living in time, as we human beings do, is that we have many occasions to change our minds. Not so with angels. Angels truly live in the moment: all past, present, and future is to them like a single Now. And it is either an eternal Now of love and obedience or an eternal Now of hatred and mutiny.
- The damnation of demons is due not to a lack of God's mercy but to their rejection of mercy. God respects the choices of His creatures. He will not drag anyone, angel or human, kicking and screaming into Heaven against his will.

- The bad angels impudently declared that they would not serve God, but that does not mean that they are exempt from God's service. As we have already seen, God's goodness is so good that it makes good use even of evil. God uses the malice of these heavenly draft-dodgers to His own advantage, allowing some of them to vent their hatred of mankind by torturing souls in Hell and thus executing His divine justice and others to prowl about the world seeking the ruin of souls by tempting men to sin (more below on how this fulfills God's will).
- We don't know how many angels turned away from God. According to some of the Church Fathers, the wise saints from about A.D. 100 to the early Middle Ages, the Bible verse about the dragon's tail sweeping a third of the stars from the sky and casting them to the earth (Revelation 12:9) refers to the proportion of good versus bad angels. Moreover, it is speculated that the world will end only when God has filled the empty seats, so to speak, left by the bad angels with the elect, those human souls that are saved. Let us hope, then, that God created trillions upon trillions of angels! (Theologians such as Thomas Aquinas have speculated that God created incomparably more angels than human beings, since purely spiritual beings are more perfect than beings that are both spiritual and material.)
- Because of their powerful nature as celestial spirits, demons are terrifying and not to be taken lightly. It is important to remember, though, that they have been weakened rather than strengthened as a result of their sin. Our culture likes to think of the rebel as powerful because he has found his inner strength rather than wimpily following authority. Demons, however, are rebelling against the very Source of

their strength and in so doing are corrupting (and hence compromising) their original excellence and capacities. They may "work like the Devil" and do a significant amount of damage, but their work does not hold a candle to that of the angels, let alone to that of God.

The Devil and All His Friends

The demon who garners the most attention is the Devil. The words "devil" and "demon" refer interchangeably to a fallen heavenly spirit, but "the Devil" refers to the chief of the fallen angels. Jesus Christ calls him a murderer from the beginning, a liar, the father of lies (John 8:44), and the prince of this world (John 12:31). The Bible also calls the Devil Beelzebub (from the Hebrew for "lord of the flies"), Satan (from the Hebrew for "accuser"), "the god of this world" (2 Corinthians 4:4), and the morning star or Lucifer (from a traditional application of a passage about the king of Babylon in Isaiah 14:12 to the Devil). According to a similar interpretation of Ezekiel 28:14, originally directed against the king of Tyre, it has been speculated that Satan was from the order of cherubim before he fell. If this is true, it must be another sore spot for Satan that he was defeated by Michael, a lowly archangel—that's like a colonel getting bested by a staff sergeant. Satan is also identified with the serpent in the Garden of Eden and the dragon mentioned in the Book of Revelation: "And there was war in heaven: Michael and his angels fought against the dragon; and the dragon fought and his angels, and prevailed not; neither was their place found any more in heaven. And the great dragon was cast out, that old serpent, called the Devil, and Satan, which deceiveth the whole world: he was cast out into the earth, and his angels were cast out with him" (12:7–9).

The Devil is bad news: as the prince of the power of this air, he now works on "the children of disobedience" (Ephesians 2:1–2). But he is no

A Book You're Not Supposed to Read

The Screwtape Letters by C. S. Lewis (New York: HarperOne, 2015) is a tour de force of Christian apologetics, written in the form of letters of advice to a devil on the front lines in the business of human temptation, from a superior in the diabolical hierarchy.

match for Christ, who won the decisive victory against him and gives the spoils to us. Even when we are under his sway, the Devil does not own us: we are *God's* creatures. Satan has no rights over his captives; Christ's atonement was paid to God alone and not to a fallen creature.

St. Michael drove the demons out of Heaven, but as we have already seen, angels don't occupy a physical location like we do. It is therefore not a contradiction to say that, on the one hand, *all* devils are in Hell and that, on the other hand, some are in Hell torturing damned souls while others are on earth tempting human beings. Just as angels carry Heaven within them by constantly beholding the face of God no matter what they do (Matthew 18:10), all demons carry Hell within them insofar as they are smart enough to see that their rebellion causes them nothing but misery and despair and that they have lost eternal happiness. And a portion of these demons, while they go about harboring their inner Hell, have the task of marauding the earth and tempting man.

Why tempt us? In their pride and envy, demons hate every single man, woman, and child, looking down on us as inferiors and deeply resenting Christ's special love for us. Demons carry the principle "Misery loves company" to a whole new level. They will do anything in their power to make the dramatic farewell curse "See you in Hell" come true. They are utterly treacherous creatures: even if you cooperate with them on a grand scale, like Hitler or Stalin, they will still take glee in punishing you for all eternity for the cooperation into which they duped you.

Why does God allow these infernal pests to plague our world? We don't know the full answer to that question any more than Job knew why God allowed Satan to wreak such havoc on his life. But we can hazard a partial answer: God allows demons to tempt us for the same reason that He allowed the serpent to tempt Adam and Eve, namely, to build up virtue. Moral and spiritual excellence are strengthened by confronting and overcoming temptations. Our souls are like our muscles: they need to be exercised, and the more they exercise, the stronger they become.

And take heart: Christ and His angels are our spotters in this spiritual gym: more than that, they are doing most of the heavy lifting.

There Are Limits

Since it is important to know thine enemy, let us take a look at what demons can and cannot do to us.

Demons can't:

- Read your mind. As we saw above, angels aren't omniscient. They are, however, pretty good guessers, and this is true of fallen angels as well. If a devil sees you watching Internet porn, he doesn't need to be a genius to know what strategy to employ against you. He can also take advantage of life's pitfalls, such as the loss of a loved one, to send false signs that lead you astray.
- Make you sin. Even in the case of diabolical possession (which we'll get to in a minute), a demon cannot turn you away from God. He can take over your body but not your soul. "The devil made me do it" is always a false statement when made in reference to moral decisions.
- Buy your soul, even if you want to sell it. "Selling your soul to the devil" is an old yarn, but in reality the sale is never binding.

As long as you are alive, you can repent of your sins and return to God.

Demons can:

- Appear to perform miracles, because as angelic substances they have the power to manipulate matter. Pharaoh's sorcerers, for example, appeared to turn their staffs into serpents and water into blood (Exodus 7:8–13).
- Cause death and disease, again because as angels they have the power to manipulate matter. In the Book of Job, the Devil stirred up a violent wind that collapsed a house and killed Job's children; he also caused severe boils to break out all over Job's body.
- Give ideas to human beings and make them believe that they can read minds and see into the future (demons can't do those things either, as we have seen above, but they are good at faking it). In the Acts of the Apostles, a slave girl was a successful fortune-teller until Paul exorcized the demon that had been possessing her, much to the disappointment of her owners. In the same way, demons can influence today's psychics and soothsayers.
- Tempt you. They are extremely skilled at taking advantage of your desires for wealth, pleasure, honor, and so forth, and heightening the allure of those objects.
- Oppress you. "Oppression" is the technical name for an *external* attack from the devil—for example, an assault on your finances, relationships, employment, or health. The woman whom Jesus cured of a "spirit of infirmity" is a probable example of demonic oppression (Luke 13:10–16). Instances of oppression do occur, but they are very difficult to diagnose

because similar misfortunes are also part of the ordinary course of life. When truly weird things happen, however, they can be traced to demonic oppression.

- Obsess you. "Obsession" is the term for an *internal* attack by a demon. The Apostle Paul may have been plagued by demonic obsession when he spoke of being attacked by "a messenger of Satan" (2 Corinthians 12:7–9). Examples of obsession include evil thoughts that you cannot shake, emotional wounds that refuse to heal, and recurring evil dreams. These symptoms, however, can also be purely psychological, so extreme care should be taken (in consultation with a qualified spiritual director) before concluding that demons are directly responsible.
- Possess you. A demon cannot be "in" someone physically because they are not physical beings that occupy space. But demons can possess a person, taking control of his body, moving his limbs and his tongue at will. The Bible attests to demonic possession as a real phenomenon, but psychological disorders sometimes have similar symptoms. Otherwise inexplicable phenomena such as speaking in languages the possessed person does not know, knowledge of hidden events (see above), and exhibitions of preternatural strength (above and beyond the kind of strength that people get when they're high on PCP) are signs of diabolical possession and not mental illness. Possessions are rare, but when they do occur, they are usually the result of somebody toying with the occult—anything from playing with a Ouija board to New Age crystals to more serious practices such as voodoo or Satanism. Dabbling in the occult does not guarantee diabolic possession, but it opens a portal to the demonic—and if a demon happens to be

in the neighborhood when you open the door, you could be in for trouble. Think of it as going into shark-infested waters with a bleeding wound.

- Infest a certain place or thing. Even though demons can't be "in" a place or thing spatially, they can have a certain power over it. Just as certain places on earth are centers of holiness (churches, or the miraculous healing spring at Lourdes, France), certain places can be centers of iniquity. Often these places were the location of evil doings such as Satanic practices or extreme moral perversity. A portal had been opened, and the demons came in and claimed squatters' rights.

An Exorcist Tells His Story by Gabriele Amorth (San Francisco: Ignatius Press, 1999).

The First Radical

Has Satan infiltrated the Left more than the Right? Two of the most powerful liberal politicians in the last generation, Hillary Rodham Clinton and Barack Obama, were deeply influenced by a man who praised the Devil. In 1971, a Chicago-based community organizer named Saul Alinsky wrote a book called *Rules for Radicals: A Practical Primer for Realistic Radicals*. The book has three opening epigraphs: one from Rabbi Hillel, one from Thomas Paine, and one from Alinsky himself. The paragraph from Alinsky praises Lucifer as "the first radical known to man who rebelled against the establishment and did it so effectively that he at least won his own kingdom."

But Alinsky does not discuss Lucifer in his book, and his opening paragraph expresses uncertainty as to whether our knowledge of the Devil is myth or history, and so it would be a stretch to call him a devil-worshipper—an attention-grabbing polemicist would be a more accurate characterization.

And although Alinsky's praise for the Devil is certainly objectionable, his methods for effecting political change have also been used on the Right. So calling Barack and Hillary the spawn of Beelzebub simply because of their affinity for Alinsky is a stretch.

★ ★ ★

It's Working on a Lot of People

"The devil's finest trick is to persuade you that he does not exist." —the famous line from Charles Baudelaire's "The Generous Gambler" that was popularized by the 1995 movie *The Usual Suspects*

If the Left is more saturated with Satan than the Right, it could be due to two causes. First, the Left is more apt to deny the Devil's existence; leftists are less likely than conservatives to believe in God, and even less likely to believe in evil. The Left in general has difficulty in coming to terms with the mystery of iniquity. Moral relativism means that nothing can be called objectively evil, and the fixation on a person's upbringing rather than his own moral choices minimizes the role of evil in human affairs. If your ideology cannot come to terms with evil and is more comfortable talking about syndromes rather than sins, you certainly will have difficulty recognizing a Prince of Darkness. The Devil, of course, is quite pleased with having his existence denied, for it makes it easier for him to do his work.

Second, insofar as leftists value autonomy and self-expression over duty, service, and conformity to the moral law, they echo the Devil's rebellious cry of *Non serviam*—I will not serve. It was for "rebell[ing] against the establishment" that Alinsky praised Satan. Perpetual rebellion is endemic in leftist thought even, ironically, when the Left becomes the establishment. Hence the Orwellian name for the socialist party that ruled Mexico for most of the twentieth century, the PRI or Institutional Revolutionary Party. Huh?

On the other hand, some members of the Alt-Right see themselves as Overmen who are "beyond good and evil," which is Nietzsche's formula for becoming a god and attempting to replace the Christian God—in other words, for acting like Satan.

The key point, whether we're talking about the Right or the Left, is whether the person or group conceives of rebellion as an end unto itself—whether they think it is better to rule in Hell than to serve in Heaven.

Finally, it is important to remember that sound political theory or even sound theology is not enough to be rendered immune from Satan's wiles. If the Devil can quote Scripture for his own use, he can also take advantage of good political and moral convictions and make them an occasion for the pride that goes before a fall.

A Note on Dualism

Pop Quiz: Based on this chapter and on your knowledge of Christianity, who is the opposite of the Devil? Think before you answer.

Are you ready? If you answered God or Jesus Christ, you are *in*correct. Strictly speaking, God has no opposite. As we learn from the meaning of the holy name YHWH, God is "He who is": that is, He is pure and transcendent Being. And since the opposite of pure Being is nothing, nothing is the opposite of God. Or think of it this way: How could a measly creature—who, despite his unique role in rebelling and his distinctive pitchfork and pointy tail, is nevertheless one among a countless number of other creatures—be the opposite of his Creator?

Neither is the correct answer to this question Jesus Christ, even though Jesus battled and defeated Satan. As true God, Jesus has no opposite; and Jesus' humanity would not find its diametric opposite in an angelic substance (that distinction goes to the first Adam, which is why Paul calls Jesus the New Adam).

So let's try again. Satan is the head of the fallen angels; his counterpart, then, would be the leader of the angels who remained true to God. And so the opposite of Satan is St. Michael the Archangel (see Jude 1:9; Revelation 12:7).

We conducted this quiz to highlight the danger of dualism, the mindset that sees good and evil as equal and opposing forces forever locked in conflict. It is true that good and evil aren't exactly friends, but are they equal? Dualist religions have two gods—typically a good god who creates spirit, and an evil god who creates matter (hence the material world is vilified). But Christianity is not a form of dualism. Christians believe that God created everything, and that all His creation is good. Evil, by contrast, is not a separate "thing"—paradoxically, it is the *privation* of the goodness of God's things. Evil is a parasite that relies upon the good for its existence. Even Satan must depend on the original goodness given to him as an angel in order for him to corrupt it. If Satan were so thoroughly corrupted that he became 100 percent evil, he would cease to exist. Don't get me wrong: the Devil is as evil as evil can be, but total evil = total privation of goodness = nothing left of the good = nothing.

So the next time you see a cartoon or commercial with a little angel on one shoulder and a little demon on the other, repeat to yourself over and over: "I accept that angels are trying to help me and devils are trying to hurt me, but I reject the dualistic implications of this image."

CHAPTER THREE

About Us

One of the advantages of knowing the truth about God is that it also reveals the truth about ourselves. The quest for self-knowledge goes back at least as far as Socrates, and it features prominently in Christian thought as well. (Just ask Pierre Courcelle, who filled two entire volumes of his *Connais-toi toi-meme; de Socrate a Saint Bernard* [*Know Thyself: From Socrates to St. Bernard*] with excerpts from Church Fathers and medieval sages on the subject.) Christianity is a mirror that reveals who we truly are. Let's look at four of the things we see in that mirror.

Did you know?

★ There are seven basic ways to deal with human desire, and only one of them works

★ Both the Old and New Testaments demonstrate that God likes "organized religion"

★ An elaborate vocabulary has been invented to portray proponents of Christian morality as backwards and oppressive

The Restless Animal: Seven Options

Man is a rational animal, in the old formulation, a being endowed not only with five bodily senses but also with the faculty of understanding. This alone makes him rather freakish. Unlike angels (which are pure spirits) and unlike animals (which are material beings with perishable souls) human beings are intellects connected to intestines, minds attached to matter. But it gets even weirder. This intelligent mortal creature with finite capacities has infinite dreams. This limited agent has

Owner of a Lonely Heart

"For Thou hast made us for Thyself, and our hearts are restless till they rest in Thee."

— **Augustine,** *Confessions*

limitless desires. For unlike every other creature in the animal kingdom, whose desires are commensurate to its nature and hence circumscribed, man is the restless animal that is not content until he has satisfied a seemingly insatiable appetite.

The Christian explanation of this condition is that man's infinite desire is a desire for the Infinite, and the Christian solution is that man will only be happy when he sees God face-to-face in Heaven. For the human intellect does not merely desire this or that truth but all truth, and the human will does not merely desire this or that good thing but the universal good. Until we attain complete and total truth and goodness, we will remain unhappy. No amount of pleasure, wealth, health, power, or success will fill that hole; we may be temporarily satisfied by the delight of a new discovery or the possession of a new toy, but after a while the high wears off and we are restless again. The only real solution to our remarkable wanderlust is permanent union with universal Truth and Goodness.

And that is quite a tall order. It's difficult, to say the least, to see how we could achieve it on our own. And since we can't make it to God through our own efforts, we need God to condescend to us and intervene in our lives if we are ever to attain the happiness we seek. After all, God *is* Truth and Goodness. He is the cause of all that is good and true, and all other things are only true or good by participation in Him. He alone is true and good by virtue of what He is. All of which is to say that we have a natural desire for a supernatural end, so that desire can only be fulfilled supernaturally.

The Beatific Vision

"Final and perfect happiness can consist in nothing else than the vision of the essence of God."

—**St. Thomas Aquinas,** *Summa Theologiae*

The problem of human happiness requires a superhuman solution.

Put another way, all of our desires, even the most carnal ones, are a faint expression of our yearning for God. Freud got it exactly wrong: the love of God is not suppressed sexual libido; sexual libido is a whisper of the love of God. To paraphrase the novelist Bruce Marshall, the man who knocks on the door of a brothel is looking for God (while Freud would have us believe that a man who shows up at church is looking for a brothel).

Now if you don't buy the Christian solution to the problem of man's infinite restlessness, you have only a few basic alternatives. Let's look at six of the more historically popular options.

Stoics on Suicide Watch

"The keener eye will not fail to observe behind all the brave banners and heroic symbols the profound inhumanity, the submerged anxiety, the senile rigidity, the tension of such an attitude. And our admiration becomes tinged with consternation and horror as it becomes apparent to us how closely such self-sufficiency verges on despair."

—**Josef Pieper,** *Happiness and Contemplation*

Stoic Resignation

You can live an upright life like the Stoics of old. You'll be off the emotional roller coaster, protected from the crazy highs and miserable lows that the thrill-seekers around you go through; but you'll live without hope of fulfilling your ultimate desire for happiness. Your life will be, to paraphrase Thoreau, one of quiet desperation.

This description fits yesteryear's non-believers better than their counterparts today—think old New England Yankees or Southern aristocrats, versus kvetching bloggers both Left and Right. The Old Left, which was largely Marxist, tended to be Stoic about personal suffering while engaging in very un-Stoic complaining about political grievances. With the rise of the New Left in the 1960s, however, came an increase in whining across the board.

A Book You're Not Supposed to Read

Makers and Takers: Why Conservatives Work Harder, Feel Happier, Have Closer Families, Take Fewer Drugs, Give More Generously, Value Honesty More, Are Less Materialistic and Envious, Whine Less... and Even Hug Their Children More Than Liberals by Peter Schweizer (New York: Doubleday, 2008).

According to Paul Schweizer's *Makers and Takers*, today's liberals are statistically much more likely than conservatives to be angry about everyday matters and to complain about their families and jobs (note that we are not talking about weightier political matters such racial segregation). This un-Stoic behavior has reached its apogee with the so-called snowflake millennials who, whatever their virtues, have never been accused of suffering with a surfeit of quiet dignity. Perhaps the only thing that today's Left and the ancient Stoics have left in common is higher suicide rates.

Sisyphean Illusion

If you can't accept the bleakness of life with Stoic resignation, you can try to convince yourself that the ache in your heart is actually a good thing. Sisyphus was a trickster condemned by the gods to roll a boulder up a mountain and then watch it roll back down again for all eternity. The French author Albert Camus (1913–1960) latched on to this Greek myth as a symbol for the absurdity of our existence, an image of how we desperately want there to be meaning and purpose in the universe but all we find instead is meaninglessness. Rather than become suicidal over this fact, Camus taught, we must try to live life to the fullest, embracing and celebrating our Sisyphean condition through 1) constant revolt; 2) freely thinking and behaving as we choose; and 3) a passion for pursuing different experiences. Not even a bright fellow like Camus could avoid certain contradictions in this position—such as the fact that he was using his rational mind to argue that there is no reason or coherence in the universe. When Sigmund Freud defined an illusion as a wish-fulfillment not grounded in reality, he was trying to discredit religion, but that description arguably fits Camus' thought better.

Most of us do not have the leisure to sit in a sidewalk café all day, stroking our beatnik goatees and worrying about nonbeing and nothingness. Even the Old Left didn't like Camus: they loathed his rejection of communism, and they believed that they *had* found meaning in the historical process that would bring about their classless utopia. But today you see Camus' Sisyphean illusion alive and well, in practice if not in name, in the New Left, which denies any cogent purpose to the universe—New Left founder Ernst Bloch said we need to *create* God—and instead lives by:

1. constant revolt, expressed in a range of ways, from angry bumper stickers to "awareness-raising" to frequent protest marches;
2. asserting the freedom to define reality as they please—usually in order to wiggle out of universally binding moral obligations; and
3. a zeal for experimentation, from trying new ethnic foods and Eastern meditation techniques to engaging in previously taboo sexual activity and drugs. This zeal has been significantly refined and domesticated over the decades (the 1960s hippies have become "bourgeois bohemians" in David Brooks's phrase), but it is still present today. Don't get us wrong. We're all for drinking life to the lees and trying new things, but not as a means of providing meaning and purpose to life or filling an existential void.

Buddhist Self-Annihilation

If you cannot satisfy your desires or even pretend that you are fulfilling them, abolish them. The Second Noble Truth of Buddhism is that the root of all suffering is desire; the Third Noble Truth is to extinguish desire

Making It Up as You Go Along

"At the heart of liberty is the right to define one's own concept of existence, of meaning, of the universe, and of the mystery of human life."

—Justice Anthony Kennedy, explaining in the 1992 Supreme Court decision *Planned Parenthood v. Casey* why a wife has no obligation to tell her husband that she is going to have their unborn child aborted

through detachment. Christianity also speaks of detachment from temporal goods, but for the purpose of attaching to the Supreme Being in a blissful and loving union; Christians seek not so much the abolition of desire as its fulfillment. Buddhism, on the other hand, recognizes no Supreme Being that fulfills man's restless heart and therefore teaches desire's annihilation as the key to Nirvana (which literally means "extinguished"). But is man—by definition the restless and desiring animal—still human after he has been stripped of his desires? Which is the happier ending: abolishing my humanity in order to become god (or nonbeing), or sharing in the divinity of a God who humbled Himself to share in my humanity out of love?

While in its native Asia Buddhism has historically supported the conservative status quo, American converts to Buddhism are mostly leftists (think Richard Gere). For many, Eastern religion has become a shallow way to signal that you are "deep." In fact, if you are dilettantish enough, you can ensure that Buddhist practices and beliefs will not interfere with your feel-good egocentrism. Eastern religious practices (think yoga) will even help you stay in shape so you can continue to secretly worship bodily health rather than extinguish your desire to live forever in Berkeley, California, or Burlington, Vermont.

Consumerism

Or you can also simply concentrate on fulfilling your passing worldly desires, ignoring the deep transcendental desire behind them all. This is the solution proposed by Thomas Hobbes (1588–1670), and it is in some respects the very foundation of modernity. Hobbes denied that there is a transcendent end or Supreme Good that will complete man and make him happy. Instead, he claimed, happiness is nothing more than "a continual progress of the desire from one object to another, the attaining of the former being still but the way to the latter." (Actually, Hobbes was smart enough to know that this was not genuine happiness, and so he named his new version "felicity.") The consumerism that we have with us today and the endless promises from Madison Avenue that this or that product will make us happy are the fruits of Hobbes's thought.

Consumerism is usually associated with the capitalist Right, though ironically many of the old capitalists were strict adherents of the Protestant Work Ethic who did not buy into it (maybe they were just pushers, not users). But one of the more fascinating sociological shifts in recent American history is how the Left has become consumerist. White upper middle class leftists proudly own Priuses, Apple products, REI gear, and Ikea furniture. And they gladly spend money at local coffee shops, farmers' markets, gourmet bakeries, microbreweries, and any another business that combines virtue signaling with inflated prices. They are able to practice this form of consumerism with a clear conscience because of two distinctions

The Difference between Buddhism and Christianity

"The opposition exists at every point; but perhaps the shortest statement of it is that the Buddhist saint always has his eyes shut, while the Christian saint always has them very wide open. The Buddhist saint has a sleek and harmonious body, but his eyes are heavy and sealed with sleep. The mediaeval saint's body is wasted to its crazy bones, but his eyes are frightfully alive. There cannot be any real community of spirit between forces that produced symbols so different as that. Granted that both images are extravagances, are perversions of the pure creed, it must be a real divergence which could produce such opposite extravagances. The Buddhist is looking with a peculiar intentness inwards. The Christian is staring with a frantic intentness outwards."

—**G. K. Chesterton,** *Orthodoxy*

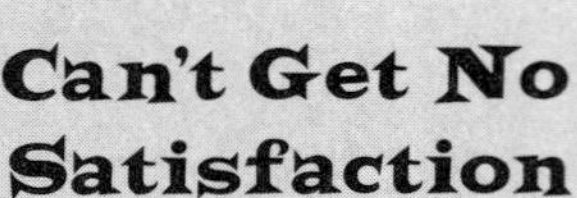

Can't Get No Satisfaction

"To which end we are to consider that the Felicity of this life consisteth not in the repose of a mind satisfied. For there is no such *Finis ultimus* (utmost aim) nor *Summum Bonum* (greatest good) as is spoken of in the books of the old Moral Philosophers."

—**Thomas Hobbes,** *Leviathan*

they make: 1) If you have a mere "want" like a speedboat or sports car, it would be vulgar to buy it; but if you have a genuine "need" to reduce carbon emissions on your way to a Whole Foods Market, then you can and probably should buy a top-of-the-line bicycle, and 2) If your spending is tied to some activist cause such as fair trade or the environment, then it is permissible and perhaps even meritorious.

Diversion

If the never-ending treadmill of consumerism is not working for you, a similar way to stop thinking about your God deficit is to dive into diversions. Blaise Pascal (1623–1662) is the master analyst who first explored this psychological dodge in detail. Man's condition, Pascal argues, is one of inconstancy, boredom, and anxiety. We cannot help wanting to be happy, but we are profoundly unhappy. We cannot live in the present, but either dwell nostalgically on the past or gleefully anticipate the future. It's always like the high school prom: there is a long and exquisite buildup as the day approaches, but during the actual event there really is no single moment that lives up to your expectations: indeed, it is something of a letdown, even if you later rave enthusiastically about it. "Since we are always preparing to be happy," Pascal observes, "it is inevitable that we should never be so."

To forget that he is unhappy, man turns with gusto to various diversions such as sports, entertainment, and hobbies. While these activities are pleasant, they do not provide true happiness: for one thing, they "are liable to be disturbed by a thousand and one accidents"; for another, it is not really the hobby's aim that we crave but the process of achieving it. What hunters really want, Pascal opines, is the hunt itself. If you threw a free dead deer at a hunter's feet as he was slipping on his Realtree scent-blocking camouflage, he would be mightily disappointed. "All our life passes this way," Pascal concludes. "We seek rest by struggling against certain obstacles," but once these obstacles are overcome, we can't stand it and soon latch on to some new thing to obsess over or worry about. That's right: worry about. We would rather take on new burdens in our personal and professional lives and worry ourselves to death than risk boredom.

Ah, to Be Young!

"Anyone who does not see the vanity of the world is very vain himself. So who does not see it, apart from young people whose lives are all noise, diversions, and thoughts for the future? But take away their diversion and you will see them bored to extinction."

—Blaise Pascal, ***Pensées***

Diversion is as old as humanity itself, but it has reached new levels in the digital age, when constant distractions from our electronic devices keep us thoroughly diverted from the quiet if unsettling task of self-knowledge. Technology was developed to save time so that we could have genuine leisure and introspection, but we have instead used technology to fill up our days and make life more complicated. Why? Because we can't stand being in a room alone with ourselves—without our iPods or smart phones, that is.

Both Left and Right indulge in diversion with respect to entertainment and hobbies, although their pastimes often differ: liberals like communing with nature while conservatives like stalking it down and shooting it. As for more serious activities, we suspect that the Right's go-to diversion is business while the Left's is political activism. A man whose personal life is a train wreck can bury himself in his work or in various *causes célèbres*—and with corporate America's elite now listing to the Left, he can make the former an extension of the latter. There is a generational element operative here as well: with their addiction to social media and electronic technology, millennials are particularly vulnerable to the self-delusion

The Power of Silence: Against the Dictatorship of Noise by Robert Sarah (San Francisco: Ignatius Press, 2017).

of diversions, although it is difficult at this time in history to know whether their addiction is a passing byproduct of youth or whether they will remain thus stunted for the rest of their lives. One sign of hope is that according to a survey conducted by the Barna Group and Cornerstone Knowledge Network, 77 percent of millennials prefer "Sanctuary" over "Auditorium" and 67 percent prefer "Quiet" over "Loud," in contrast to the phrenetic diverting worship services of many Gen-X-dominated churches.

Sedation

Finally, if your burning desire for bliss still can't be quenched, turn down the heat. One popular way of being less hot for happiness is to become more "cool," cultivating an unflappable persona complete with aloof reactions, wry irony, inhuman or bug-like eyes (I think they're called sunglasses), and dark clothes. But if you can't pull off the simmering nonchalance of a young Marlon Brando or Ryan Gosling, you may need to reach into the medicine cabinet for something stronger. Numb or deaden your existential desire for God by turning to legal or illegal drugs. Become a pothead or join the Prozac Nation in order to suspend consciousness of your misery.

The Left is not as free and easy with recreational drugs as it was in the 1960s and '70s, but it still pushes (with increasing success) for legalized marijuana. Several studies have linked liberal political views with greater drug use: one reported in Peter Schweizer's *Makers and Takers* found that among heavy drug users the ratio of Democrats to Republicans was more than eight to one. Even the artistic tastes of the Left lean toward works that look like they were made under the influence of powerful hallucinogens.

And both sides turn to the bottle, though not necessarily the same one. According to a 2014 report from research firm National Media, Democrats prefer clear liquors such as vodka and gin while Republicans prefer dark liquors like scotch and bourbon. The good news is that people who take shots of Jägermeister are less likely to vote; the bad news is that wine snobs are more likely.

The Religious Animal

The more that man finds the truth (especially as he comes to recognize that Truth is a Person), the more he wants to worship it. The desire to adore God is an inherent part of being human, just like reverence before the wonder of nature. A glimmer of humanity's native religiosity may be seen in the fact that all human beings have a natural inclination to latch onto a cause greater than themselves and that when they try to reject everything above them and live only for themselves, they become a little less human. All people instinctively despise a selfish person, though those on the Left may despise those who don't care about the earth or the proletariat while those on the Right despise those who don't care about their country or freedom.

What We Really Want

"Most people, if they had really learned to look into their own hearts, would know that they do want, and want acutely, something that cannot be had in this world. There are all sorts of things in this world that offer to give it to you, but they never quite keep their promise.... Creatures are not born with desires unless satisfaction for those desires exists. A baby feels hunger well, there is such a thing as food... A car is made to run on gasoline, and it would not run properly on anything else. Now God designed the human machine to run on Himself. He Himself is the fuel our spirits were designed to burn, or the food our spirits were designed to feed on. There is no other."

—**C.S. Lewis,** *Mere Christianity*

> **Giving the Game Away**
>
> "All this entails a monstrous double standard: *because secularism pretends to be neutral, it gets away with murder.* In other words: one belief system—secularism—is privileged in our society simply because it denies being a belief-system! If secularism ever owned-up to what it actually is—a belief-system with its own metaphysic, its own ethics, its own disciples, and its own heretics—the game would be over. Secularism would just be another creed among others without any special privileges attached to it."
>
> —**Roger Buck,** *The Gentle Traditionalist: A Catholic Fairy-Tale from Ireland*

And both sides loathe a traitor, even the side that benefits from his treachery. Man is at his best when he is on a mission from above.

On the other hand, man is at his worst when he is on a mission that he thinks is from above but isn't (think Nazism and communism) or when he is on a mission from above but gets his directions really, really wrong (think militant Islam and the historic abuses of Christianity, which we'll get to in Part Two). Man is an undeniably religious animal that either finds his cause in his religion or turns his cause into a religion. Even atheism is a religion of sorts with clear dogmas on divinity, the afterlife, and humanity's ultimate concerns. We can even say that there is a new secular religion that has its own metaphysics (only the material world counts); its own ethics (including the right to suicide, abortion, marijuana, and transgendering); its own evangelization (its adherents disseminate their beliefs with the help of public shaming and government enforcement); and its own witch hunts.

So the question for the human race is not really between religion and non-religion but between the right religion and the wrong ones.

Spiritual but Not Religious

Yet you've heard it many times: "I'm spiritual but not religious." It has become such a cliché that it has its own abbreviation (SBNR) and an entry on Wikipedia including endorsements from feminists, Wiccans, and other neo-pagans. I once had a coworker who had fathered several children, each with a different women, and was going to the hospital to see his latest son. When I asked him why he wasn't married to the mother of this child, he smiled sheepishly and replied that what they had as a couple was "very spiritual" and that marriage was too "religious."

Picking the Wrong Side

"On a semi-light/semi-serious note, there is a being in this universe who is spiritual but not religious. Satan, being a fallen angel, is a pure spirit. There are no creatures more spiritual than Satan. So being spiritual doesn't necessarily put us on the team we want to be on."

—Mike Schmidt

He got one thing right. The word "religion" means a "binding" of man to God, which also entails a binding of man to man—or, in my coworker's case, what should have been a binding of man to woman. We have it on good authority that if you do not love your neighbor, honor the brotherhood of fellow Christians, and help the poor, there is something loose and sloppy about your binding to God.

But does it have to be "organized religion"? Well, when people care about something, they make sure that it is organized in such a way that it flourishes. The new secular religion, for instance, has highly organized organs for preaching its gospel and enforcing its doctrine: the media, entertainment industry, government, and so forth.

Both Old and New Testaments are proof that God likes organized religion. Despite what you may have heard from your skateboarding youth minister, Jesus was not a hippie who flaunted rules in the name of hanging loose: He was a Lord who laid down a hierarchical structure for His Church.

So do you have to go to church to be a Christian? That was the very question a sophisticated member of society faced long ago when he contemplated converting to Christianity. Marius Victorinus was an educated and well-respected intellectual in the Roman Empire who found himself persuaded by the claims of Christianity. One day he told a Christian friend that he had

★ ★ ★

A Hierarchical Church

Consider the following: Jesus distinguished between his generic disciples or followers and "the seventy-two" who were given a special mission (Luke 10:10). Further, he distinguished between the seventy-two disciples and His twelve Apostles, to whom He told things that He did not tell others and whom alone he invited to the Last Supper. And even within the organization of the Twelve He made distinctions. Only Peter, James, and John were allowed to see His transfiguration on Mount Tabor (Matthew 17:1–8), and accompany Him to the Garden of Gethsemane (Matthew 26:36–46). Finally, of these three, Jesus singled out Peter as the head of His new Church (Matthew 16:18), even though Jesus loved John as the "beloved disciple." The early Christian community after the Ascension reflects their Lord's plan. In Acts, the Apostles are clearly the leaders of the Church, calling councils and making decisions on behalf of the entire community; and Peter is clearly the leader of the Apostles.

converted. Victorinus's friend answered, "I shall not believe it unless I see you in the Church of Christ." Victorinus asked with faint mockery, "Then is it the walls that make Christians?" In truth, Victorinus was afraid of looking silly in the eyes of his important friends. It was only when he realized that Christ might deny him before His angels (see Luke 12:8–9) if he were ashamed to confess Christ before men that he changed his mind and was baptized.

What is the point of this story, which St. Augustine relays in his *Confessions*? Although Christianity is primarily concerned about the heart or the inner man, the walls of a church *are* important. Christianity is an incarnational religion that makes the spiritual present with the aid of the tangible—sacred spaces, sacred times, sacred images, and sacred acts. Christians have always practiced their beliefs in a structured community. The Church is the *Body* of Christ.

The fact is, man is a religious animal, and if he doesn't bind himself to the true religion, he will bind himself to a false substitute of some kind.

The Sinful but Redeemed Animal

Man is a restless and brilliant animal who has a taste not only for the material but for the eternal transcendentals of truth, goodness, and beauty. Yet he fails to achieve the happiness and wisdom for which he so desperately yearns and instead, like the old country Western song puts it, keeps looking for love in all the wrong places. Shakespeare gets at this paradox of human existence: Hamlet is right when he praises man as "the beauty of the world" and "the paragon of animals" who is "in action… like an angel, in apprehension…like a god!" Yet Puck is also right: "Lord, what fools these mortals be!"

How does one account for these astonishingly contradictory aspects of our humanity? Only Christianity provides a satisfactory answer: God created us good, but our first parents disobeyed Him, and we have inherited their original sin.

As we have seen, not only was man created good; he was made in the image and likeness of God Himself. And this tremendous dignity does not concern any physical resemblance to God—who is spirit, not a biped with opposable thumbs—but the great gifts of reason and free will, which enable us to know eternal truth and choose good.

Given these tremendous assets, one would expect humanity to be in a very good place, not in the mess in which it currently finds itself. Enter original sin. Although he was created good, man has a sort of spiritual birth defect that gives him a tendency to do evil. Original sin damages but does not destroy our original goodness: it screws us up just enough that even though we maintain the power to resist evil, we freely give in to it. We know that there is a

Organized Religion

"Any idiot can find God alone in the sunset. It takes a certain maturity to find God in the person sitting next to you who not only voted for the wrong political party but has a baby who is crying while you're trying to listen to the sermon. Community is where the religious rubber meets the road."

—Lillian Daniel

Fallen

"There are in faith two equally constant truths. One is that man in the state of his creation, or in the state of grace, is exalted above the whole of nature, made like unto God and sharing in His divinity. The other is that in the state of corruption and sin he has fallen from that first state and has become like the beasts. These two propositions are equally firm and certain."

—**Blaise Pascal,** *Pensées*

universal Moral Law—or *Tao*, or Rule of Decent Behavior, as C. S. Lewis calls it—but we fail to practice it. For Lewis, these two facts "offer an explanation of how we got into our present state of both hating goodness and loving it."

Another effect of these "two equally constant truths," to quote Blaise Pascal, is that we can know what our true happiness consists of, but we have no hope of attaining it on our own. Ironically, Pascal concludes, "man's greatness comes from knowing he is wretched: a tree does not know it is wretched. Thus it is wretched to know one is wretched, but there is a greatness in knowing one is wretched.... It is the wretchedness of a great lord, the wretchedness of a dispossessed king" who cannot shake the knowledge of his former greatness.

This knowledge of our own wretchedness would be unbearable were there no solution to this grave situation. Happily, there is. The Christian doctrine of original sin is made easier to bear by the Christian doctrine of grace, that supernatural aid won for us by the life, death, and Resurrection of Jesus Christ, who both heals our wounds and elevates us to an intimacy with God hitherto unimaginable. The good news is that, as C. S. Lewis puts it, "God Himself becomes a man to save man from the disapproval of God"—with the result that man becomes an adopted son of God and even shares in the bliss of His divinity.

Now if you are inclined to reject Christianity, chances are you also reject this account of our greatness and wretchedness. Instead of seeing yourself as a "fallen angel," you may prefer to see yourself as a "rising ape" and put your faith in a secular doctrine of progress that portrays you and your fellow apes as rising to ever higher states of perfection. But does progressivism (which we'll talk about more in chapter ten) really capture either the grandeur of our existence or the enigma of our evil deeds? Ours is an age that likes to reduce lofty human achievements to chemical processes in the brain and prefers to talk about syndromes rather than sins.

It Gets Us

"That a religion may be true, it must have knowledge of our nature. It ought to know its greatness and littleness, and the reason of both. What religion but the Christian has known this?"

—Blaise Pascal, ***Pensées***

Nor is the Progressive Myth consistent. Evolutionary biology, which leftists use to "disprove" Creation, interprets our selfish and wicked behavior as a normal and natural consequence of our struggle to survive—in other words, there is no such thing as evil. And yet the Progressive Left also insists that human beings are born perfectly innocent and good; their environment makes them bad—in other words, evil exists, but it is somebody else's fault.

These beliefs simply don't do justice to the complexity of the human condition. When you think of man as a nasty animal, you deny his comprehension of the transcendent—in particular, his capacity to recognize the eternal Law of Decent Behavior. When you think of man as a helpless pawn of his environment, you fail to acknowledge his ability to make choices that shape his destiny. Either way, you're giving short shrift to what is quintessentially human, blinding yourself to man's greatness and downplaying his wretchedness.

Christianity offers the most accurate mirror to our true condition, yet it also offers us a remedy for the disfigurement that we see looking back at us. For the Christian, it is a glorious thing—an occasion for gratitude—to declare himself a sinful but redeemed animal.

The Nuptial Animal

The truth that God created human beings "male and female" (Genesis 1:27) is reflected in our biology, but it goes far beyond our generative organs and even our chromosomes. To be a man or a woman is to be called to a life of self-giving in one of two complementary ways. This complementary self-giving is especially realized in the "great mystery" of marriage, in which husband and wife give themselves to each other, with the ordinary result of the creation of new life. The supreme model for this "nuptial" character of humanity is Jesus Himself, who in an act of total sacrifice gave His body to His bride and bestowed eternal life on her (see Luke 22:19). The one-flesh communion of husband and wife is a sign of the one-flesh communion of Christ and His Church (Ephesians 5:25–33).

To say that human beings are nuptial animals does not mean that everyone can or should get married. There is a long Christian tradition of some believers following the example of Paul and choosing a life of celibacy (see I Corinthians 7:8). It does mean, however, that manhood and womanhood are good things in and of themselves that are designed to work together. Even when they are not married and literally parents, adult men should act virtuously like good, responsible fathers and adult women should act virtuously like good, responsible mothers.

The Christian view of the sexes is at odds with what we might call the neo-Nietzschean belief, in which manhood and womanhood are seen as competing quests for power, as if the goal in life were to gain domination over others. (Read the Wife of Bath's Tale and the Merchant's Tale in Chaucer's *Canterbury Tales* for hilarious spoofs of male and female chauvinism). Christianity rejects this lust for power and affirms the astonishing paradox that you will only gain your life once you give it away in a sacrificial offering of love (see Matthew 10:39). Manhood or womanhood reaches its fullest expression when it becomes a form of (sometimes) humiliating service, rather than a form of self-exaltation or an expression of the will to power.

Christianity has an integrated anthropology, a view of the human person that sees both body and soul as part of a harmonious union. The Christian faith does not reduce manhood or womanhood to mere sexual activity: Jesus

Christ and the Apostle Paul were real men even though they were celibate. Nor does Christianity endorse only one cultural expression of manhood or womanhood. It can even be playful with sexuality: Christian literature is filled with imagery of men's souls acting feminine like a bride vis-à-vis Christ the Bridegroom and women's souls acting masculine like a warrior vis-à-vis pagan persecutors. The bottom line is that Christianity sees both maleness and femaleness as marvelous gifts that are a cherished part of our embodied existence.

The Meaning of Man

"The more one forgets himself—by giving himself to a cause to serve or another person to love—the more human he is and the more he actualizes himself."

—**Viktor E. Frankl,** *Man's Search for Meaning*

The recognition of mankind as a nuptial animal whose very body has meaning and purpose is one of Christianity's most beautiful and ennobling contributions, yet it has become the most reviled aspect of the Faith among the West's cultured elite. Why? Because it runs afoul of two idols dear to the modern age: the autonomous self, which seeks meaning in what it invents for itself rather than in what it discovers about itself, and sexual license, whose promoters have done their best to make people ashamed of being sexually ashamed. Both of these principles have been operative in feminism for decades, and they have taken on new life in the LGBT movement.

Chesterton remarked that the Christian creed can sometimes be unattractive on the outside and attractive on the inside, whereas modern philosophy is the opposite. The controversy over humanity's nuptial nature is a good example of this phenomenon. What could be more repressive than limiting sexual union to one man and one woman in a lifelong covenant—and for the sake of having children? And what could be more liberating than to "love the one you're with" and not worry about whether the other person is the same sex as you, identifies as transgender, or is married to

What Is Marriage?: Man and Woman: A Defense by Sherif Girgis, Ryan T. Anderson, and Robert P. George (New York: Encounter Books, 2012).

someone else? But at the core of this seemingly emancipating philosophy is despair, as Chesterton explains in *Orthodoxy*: "And its despair is this, that it does not really believe that there is any meaning in the universe; therefore it cannot hope to find any romance; its romances will have no plots. A man cannot expect any adventures in the land of anarchy. But a man can expect any number of adventures if he goes travelling in the land of authority. One can find no meanings in a jungle of scepticism; but the man will find more and more meanings who walks through a forest of doctrine and design."

As we will see more clearly in chapter ten, the world has gone from rejecting Christian sexual morality to rejecting human nature as normative. For Christians, human nature is good because it was created by a good and loving God; even the Fall, which corrupted human nature through original sin, did not obliterate that original goodness (even Christians who hold the most extreme view of mankind's total depravity after the Fall do not deny that human nature is *essentially* good; while an egg may be rotten, "eggness" is still good)—though it does, as we will see in a moment, sometimes make it difficult to discern between what is natural and what is unnatural. And one of our natural endowments is our sexual identity, which finds its fulfillment in either a lifelong monogamous union with a person of the opposite sex ordered towards the procreation and care of offspring or in a vocation of spiritual fatherhood or motherhood.

LGBT

Homosexual and transgender ideologies diverge sharply from this classical and Christian worldview in three respects.

First, the dichotomy between sex and gender is seen as so great that one's so-called birth sex is considered either a myth ("assigned by a doctor") or a mere biological fact that is irrelevant to one's true identity—unless, of course, *I* the autonomous self, want it to be relevant. Granted, there is a difference between sex, being born male or female, and gender, an artificial societal construct that determines how men and women are expected to behave in a given culture. If there were no difference, ladylike behavior would be the same in Portlandia as in Victorian England. And granted, there will always be a danger of mistaking cultural norms for what is natural—as Americans once did in prohibiting miscegenation—which is why great prudence and care are needed before drawing any conclusions. But to say that there is no normative purpose or meaning to our embodied sexuality simply because gender roles have varied in history would be a massive leap in logic.

Second, whereas the Christian sees human nature as an integrated combination of body and soul (both of which are good and meaningful), transgenderism is based on a schizophrenic dualism that divorces "self" from "body." In an Orwellian twist, my "nature" is now my "true self" while my body is merely a conglomerate of biological operations that offers no guidance or has no bearing on the meaning of life. The body, in other words, is no longer seen as a gift endowed with sacred purpose but a mere possession that the autonomous self can reconstruct or deconstruct according to its druthers. Milder forms of reconstruction include cross-dressing; more extreme forms include hormonal treatments and "sex changes" or sex-reassignment surgeries—which are, of course, a misnomer, since sex is determined by having XX or XY chromosomes and physicians cannot alter this substructure no matter how much they alter the plumbing. In any case, human nature (integrated body and soul) no longer provides norms for living the good life, and perfecting one's nature thus defined is no longer seen as the key to happiness. At best, my bodily nature is now raw

A Book You're Not Supposed to Read

Making Gay Okay: How Rationalizing Homosexual Behavior Is Changing Everything by Robert R. Reilly (San Francisco: Ignatius Press, 2014).

material for my self-expression; at worst, it is the enemy. (If you think we're exaggerating, do an Internet search of "transhumanism" or see chapter ten on the abolition of man). Ironically, the people who care so deeply for the environment, for conserving the world of nature, are often the same people who care so little for human nature and its proper flourishing.

The one interesting partial exception to this rule is the "born this way" argument—that because my sexual orientation is genetic, I ought to be able to live according to my impulses. This argument is popular in defending homosexuality (especially male) and to a lesser extent transgender identity, even though in the case of male homosexuality it contains a whiff of biological determinism that contradicts the idea of the autonomous self. Yet despite its appeal to something fixed and innate in the human person, this argument is not, strictly speaking, an argument from *nature*. Not all things that happen in nature are natural: a cow may give birth to a two-tailed calf, but that does not mean that it is natural for a cow to have two tails. As it turns out, there is no scientific evidence that same-sex attraction and cross-gender identification have a neurobiological basis or are genetically predetermined, but let's say for the sake of argument that they are indeed a product of biology. Does this mean that homosexuality is natural, or does it only indicate that someone can have a genetic predisposition towards a particular sexual activity in the same way that others have a genetic predisposition to obesity or alcoholism? And, of course, just because I have one of these predispositions does not mean that I should act on them. The nature of nature, so to speak, is more complicated than that.

Third, LGBT activists seek to overcome the "gender binary" of male and female, but all of their definitions rely on the fundamental distinction between men and women. To be a lesbian is to be a woman attracted to a woman, to be gay is to be a man attracted to a man, and to be bisexual is to be attracted to both men and women. The still-growing list of transgender identities involves some variation of male to female or female to male, or both, or neither (and note that saying "neither" forces you to finish the thought: neither *male nor female*). Rebelling against the binary only testifies to its inescapable normativity. Humanity remains what God made it: a nuptial animal.

Can We Talk?

It would be nice if we could hold discussions on sexuality in a sensitive, charitable, and dispassionate manner, but unfortunately we live in a world where that is increasingly difficult. On the Christian side there are a few breathtaking morons waving "God hates fags" signs, and on the other side there is a powerful combination of rhetoric, tactics, financing, and influence that stifles free speech and stacks the deck against fair and intellectually honest debate. Consider the following facts:

- There is now an elaborate vocabulary designed to portray proponents of Christian morality as backwards and oppressive. Besides the generic term "haters," critics of homosexual behavior and transgender identities are labeled "homophobes" and "transphobes," as if all opposition, no matter how principled or intellectually cogent, was nothing more than an irrational phobia. Allegiance to Christian sexual ethics is denounced as "heteronormativity," "heteropatriarchy," "intolerance," "hate speech," "trigger words," and so on. Control the language and you control the conversation.
- The new vocabulary and the doctrine behind it have been widely adopted and enforced by traditional and social media as

A Book You're Not Supposed to Read

The Health Hazards of Homosexuality: What the Medical and Psychological Research Reveals by MassResistance (CreateSpace Independent Publishing Platform, 2017).

well as by publishers, who often stipulate "inclusive language" and similar constraints in their contracts with authors. Liberal outlets such as *BuzzFeed* put out only heart-warming stories of transgender veterans and auntly septuagenarian lesbian couples while failing to report the negative aspects of the gay and transgender experience. When I used Google to search for "transgender," my screen was instantly festooned with a rainbow banner from top to bottom and what looked like little bits of colored confetti. One would never have guessed from this sunny and celebratory presentation that the LGBT community has higher rates of mental health problems, partner abuse, suicide, alcoholism, and drug addiction.

- LGBT groups and their allies disseminate propaganda with the explicit goal of confusing Christians about Christian doctrine. *BuzzFeed* put out a cringe-worthy, self-congratulatory video with the unintentionally apt name "I'm Christian, But I'm Not," which received a great deal of attention. The Human Rights Campaign recently finished a three-year, $8.5 million campaign called "All God's Children" that targeted Christians in Mississippi, Arkansas, and Alabama with blitzes of sentimental ads. During this time the HRC was accused of planting moles in conservative Baptist churches—sending transgender youth or gay couples into churches to ingratiate themselves with the community and then intimidate the congregation into accepting the new dogma.
- LGBT groups and their allies, such as the Southern Poverty Law Center, People for the American Way, and even the search

tool Guidestar, use smear tactics and black lists to silence dissent. For example, Guidestar now lists as a "hate group" the Alliance Defending Freedom, a network of 3,100 attorneys from around the country that defends religious freedom, the sanctity of life, and bakers who dare to decline making cakes for gay weddings. "Putting the Alliance Defending Freedom on a list with skinheads and the… Ku Klux Klan," notes Karl Zinsmeister of the Philanthropy Roundtable, "is like confusing Joe Lieberman with Joseph Stalin."

- At every level of education in the United States, there is pressure to conform to the LGBT agenda. Teachers are told not to refer to students as boys and girls *in pre-K*, while books such as *Jacob's New Dress* are designed to indoctrinate five-year-olds into the new androgyny. Upon entering middle school, students in some parts of the country are encouraged to read homosexual romance novels. Teacher training is tendentious. One woman spent $20,000 taking courses to get her principal's certificate at Texas State University but was not allowed to complete the internship necessary for certification because she disagreed with the premises of the LGBT movement. When she protested, the administration told her, "No one said life was fair." Because she does not have her certificate, she cannot be hired as a principal. And in school counseling, confused youth are often exhorted to "come out" as gay or identify themselves as transgender even though, in the words of American College of Pediatricians president Michelle Cretella, "the American Psychological Association's *Handbook of Sexuality and Psychology* admits that prior to the widespread promotion of transition affirmation, 75 to 95% of pre-pubertal children who were distressed by their biological sex eventually outgrew that distress."

- In order to comply with Title IX requirements, faculty at even private Christian universities must undergo annual sensitivity training in which they are warned about their "unconscious biases" and instructed to use "trans-inclusive language" in the classroom. The same training explains that one of the characteristics identifying male rapists is that they may "believe in gender stereotypes about women and men" (gasp!). The pressure does not stop there but extends to all areas of academia—research, teaching, service, administration, and credentialing. Researches are suborned to produce research supporting LGBT claims under threat of funding withdrawal or tenure denial. And should scholars produce solid research that is not favorable to the LGBT agenda, they are vilified and ostracized: just ask the authors and editors of the *New Atlantis* report on "Sexuality and Gender Findings." Of course, the LGBT cause has little difficulty finding in the halls of academia what Lenin called "useful idiots," willing Christian and non-Christian accomplices to do their bidding for them. The *Queer Bible Commentary* and the astonishing presence of Queer and Transgender Studies departments and centers on American campuses are a case in point.

A Study You're Not Supposed to Read

"Sexuality and Gender Findings from the Biological, Psychological, and Social Sciences" by Lawrence S. Mayer and Paul R. McHugh, in *The New Atlantis* 50 (Fall 2016).

- Sometimes eagerly and sometimes out of fear, America's major corporations now support, fund, and promote the LGBT agenda. Hundreds of corporations strive to keep their top rating on the Human Rights Campaign's "equality index." To achieve a top score, corporations must provide full medical benefits for "gender transition" such as sex reassignment surgery, mandate extensive "inclusive diversity training" for their employees, and donate no money whatsoever to any group with a policy unacceptable to the HRC. Corporations do, however, receive favorable points for donating to groups like the HRC!

According to Harvard professor Dr. Harvey Mansfield, "You can always tell who's in charge in a society by who is allowed to get angry." Indeed.

Leaving Jesus Out of the Equation

"The revisionist exegesis of Scripture is . . . that biblical injunctions against homosexuality refer to temple prostitution, pederasty, forced sex, and the like, not what goes on between 'committed' same-sex partners. It is a fashionable reading based on a contrived contextualization that goes against the plain meaning of the text, 2000 years of church teaching, and millennia of moral norms and social tradition. What's more, it fails to consider what Jesus had to say about sexual morality."

—Regis Nicoll

CHAPTER FOUR

The Rest of Creation

Man is a glorious freak, a creature of the world who does not quite fit into it. For Christians like G. K. Chesterton, this is a cause for rejoicing: "I had tried to be happy by telling myself that man is an animal like any other which sought its meat from God. But now I really was happy, for I had learnt that man is a monstrosity... The modern philosopher had told me again and again that I was in the right place, and I had still felt depressed even in acquiescence. But I had heard that I was in the *wrong* place, and my soul sang for joy, like a bird in spring. I knew now why grass had always seemed to me as queer as the green beard of a giant, and why I could feel homesick at home."

But doesn't this view alienate Christians from our environment, leading to ecological depredation, political disease, cultural wars, and misanthropy? Let's find out.

Did you know?

★ The scientific exploitation of nature is a function of the modern worldview that rejected the Christian attitude toward creation

★ Christians neither totalize nor totally reject politics

★ Nuns created much of the educational, health care, and philanthropic infrastructure in America

Nature: Mother or Kid Sister?

It is common nowadays to be told that Christianity is responsible for the West's lousy environmental track record. According to this accusation, the

An Essay You're Not Supposed to Read

"The Bible Made Me Do It: Christianity, Science, and the Environment" by Ernest L. Fortin in *Ernest L. Fortin: Collected Essays*, vol. 1, edited by J. Brian Benestad (New York: Rowman & Littlefield, 1996), 111–33.

biblical mandate to subdue and have dominion over the earth (Genesis 1:28) has led to the rapacious Western attitude towards the earth's natural resources. While the non-Christian non-Western man is supposed to be like the American Indian who, living in harmony with nature, uses every part of the buffalo and thanks the buffalo spirit to boot, the Christian Western man is supposed to be like the American cowboy who, disregarding nature, shoots buffalo just for the fun of it and thanks only his Winchester rifle.

It is a fetching argument, but folks who blame Christianity for the earth's manmade ills are forgetting three things:

First, the same book of the Bible that speaks of dominion over the earth also speaks of God's commanding Adam to "dress and keep" the Garden of Eden (Genesis 2:15). From this early instance of divinely-mandated human responsibility comes the notion of Christian environmental stewardship, the idea that God is the true owner of the earth and that we are stewards in charge of taking good care of it until we answer to Him on the Last Day. In the Bible, "dominion" and "rule" do *not* necessarily mean a violent or selfish despotism. In Genesis 1:16–18, for instance, the sun is said to "rule" the day and the moon is said to "rule" the night. Hardly a blank check for ecological tyranny, that.

Second, Christians have always seen the world of nature as bearing the fingerprints of its Creator. "The heavens declare the glory of God," declares the psalmist (19:1), and so too do the earth and all its marvelous furnishings and inhabitants. Academics and wags sometimes refer to the Christian "sacramental imagination," the idea that all creation is a *sacramentum* or divine sign of God's goodness and generosity. More than that, God's creatures even remind us of His saving deeds. The pelican, for example, was thought to have brought its dead chicks back to life by pouring out its own blood for them; hence it recalled Jesus Christ shedding His blood for His flock. Medieval bestiaries are full of lovely pious meditations, where all of nature is "haunted" or "enchanted" with deep theological meaning and as a result of which we approach nature with respect and gratitude, not greed or indifference. The sentiments of Duke Senior in Shakespeare's *As You Like It* are the sentiments of traditional Christianity: "Tongues in trees, books in the running brooks / Sermons in stones, and good in everything."

Third and perhaps most important, the ecological attitude that gave rise to deforestation, pollution, and the extermination of many species of plant and animal wildlife took hold sixteen centuries *after* the birth of Christianity and was not a fruit of the Christian worldview but a rejection of it. Modern science and modern economics are two of the principal culprits behind this development. Francis Bacon, the father of modern science, understood the new form of knowledge he was forging to have as its goal not wisdom but power, specifically, power over nature. Bacon argued for a new kind of science that "vexes and tortures" nature to force her to reveal her secrets so that man can use them against her through his inventions. Unlike biblical faith and classical philosophy, which viewed nature as a good thing to be cultivated and perfected, Bacon's new science viewed nature as an enemy to be exploited through

A Reflection on Stones

"God is a living stone, as St. Paul the apostle says in his writing, and St. John confirms it truly and without guile; God was a stone, and He was alive and covered all Paradise; from this stone all the stones have brightness and colour; from this stone all the stones have goodness and clearness; from this stone truly all stones have their foundation. And know, the apostle St. Peter calls the believers living stones; the saints are stones truly, the foundation of Holy Church, that is, they make it firm and stable and durable in Paradise; they are called living stones, they live for ever with God."

—*The Bestiary of Philippe de Thaon*, **translated by Thomas Wright** technological domination. Hence the conclusion of Ernest Fortin: "The Moderns, not the Ancients, are the ones who put nature on the rack and thereby set up an adversarial relationship between the investigator and the object of his investigation."

> ### Our Cute Baby Sister
>
> "Only the supernatural has taken a sane view of Nature. The essence of all pantheism, evolutionism, and modern cosmic religion is really in this proposition: that Nature is our mother. Unfortunately, if you regard Nature as a mother, you discover that she is a stepmother. The main point of Christianity was this: that Nature is not our mother: Nature is our sister. We can be proud of her beauty, since we have the same father; but she has no authority over us; we have to admire, but not to imitate. This gives to the typically Christian pleasure in this earth a strange touch of lightness that is almost frivolity. Nature was a solemn mother to the worshippers of Isis and Cybele. Nature was a solemn mother to Wordsworth or to Emerson. But Nature is not solemn to Francis of Assisi or to George Herbert. To St. Francis, Nature is a sister, and even a younger sister: a little, dancing sister, to be laughed at as well as loved."
>
> **—G. K. Chesterton,** *Orthodoxy*

As for modern economics, both capitalism and Marxism view natural objects not as divine signs of God's incomparable beauty or goodness but raw matter to be turned into something else through labor. When modern man sees a stone, he no longer sees a symbol for God or St. Peter or the Church; he sees dollar signs in a quarry or fodder for history's dialectical transformation of human society into a classless utopia. Stripping nature of its enchantment decreases respect for it, and the commodification of creation easily leads to exploitation. Pollution is obviously linked to the rise of industrialization in the capitalist West, but lest we forget, communist countries have an even worse environmental record, topping the list of the world's most egregious polluters.

Capitalism and Marxism are not moral equivalents; Marxism is far worse, and capitalism is not irredeemable. But like modern science, capitalism needs to be infused by a higher view of things in order not to be destructive—hence the need for a Christian society that provides a moral framework in which scientific and economic activity can be carried out responsibly and nature properly appreciated.

Christianity and Global Warming

The ecological issue dominating the news today is global warming, the idea that the greenhouse gases produced by the use of fossil fuels are causing a rise in the Earth's temperature that will result in environmental catastrophe and famine. Yet many Christians are suspicious about such claims, a fact that calls their commitment to environmental stewardship into question. Why are such Christians lukewarm about global warming?

First, some are skeptical not so much of rising temperatures but of the conclusions drawn from these findings. It boils down to an issue of causality. The earth's temperatures may have risen in the past century, and the output of carbon dioxide emissions may have also risen in the past century. But does that mean that the latter caused the former, or is the correlation simply a coincidence? Skeptics point to a paucity of evidence that definitively proves causality and worry that environmental alarmists are guilty of a *post hoc ergo propter hoc* logical fallacy.

Second, some Christians are skeptical of the politics of the global warming campaign, seeing the call to "save the earth" as a Trojan horse for an increase in centralized government control and a decrease in individual freedom and national sovereignty (France's Jacques Chirac, for example, called for "global governance" in response to climate change). Hence the tag line on the cover of Christopher Horner's *Politically Incorrect Guide® to Global Warming (and Environmentalism)*: "Global warming: the Left's last best chance to gain a stranglehold on our political system and economy." At the very least, the Left's strategic priorities would appear to be misplaced. Professor Lakshman Guruswamy is an internationally recognized expert in International Environmental and Global Energy Law. His position is simple. It is wiser to direct our political energies to providing solutions that we *know* will work to solve environmental crises rather than solutions that may or may not work. We *know* that polluted drinking water causes 3.5 million deaths every year, largely among children, and we know how to solve this problem. But we do not know with the same degree of certainty whether this or that policy will reverse global warming.

Third, some Christians are suspicious of contemporary environmentalism because of its lack of respect for human life and human nature. To its credit, the environmental movement that began in the 1960s has helped bring to light the costs of ruthlessly exploiting nature and renewed our appreciation for the virtues of responsible stewardship and for the marvels of God's green but fragile earth. Yet this same movement, which has served in many ways as a healthy reawakening, is peppered with absurdities. Often the same activists who defend endangered tadpoles and fruit flies blithely support killing millions of unborn babies and selling their body parts (if you're Planned Parenthood) to the highest bidder. In 2008, after liberalizing its abortion laws, Spain's socialist government introduced legislation to grant chimpanzees *legal rights* in order "to preserve the species from extinction"—this in a land with no native ape population. Huh?

Fourth, Christians are especially suspicious of environmentalism when it takes on the character of a religion. The new environmental religion comes complete with its own priests (climatologists), its own gospels (sacrosanct data about rising temperatures and shrinking glaciers), its own prophets (Al Gore, who unfortunately remains welcome in his own country), and perhaps most of all, its own apocalypticism, with the four horsemen of deforestation, global warming, ozone depletion, and fossil fuels all leading us to an ecological Doomsday more terrifying to the secular mind than the Four Last Things. If you think we're exaggerating, read David Wallace-Wells's "The Uninhabitable Earth" in the July 9, 2017, issue of *New York*

Magazine; with journalism as paranoid as this, it is not surprising that the American Psychological Association has identified a new disorder called "ecoanxiety." Concerns about the environment are valid, but when they are placed in a pantheistic or atheistic framework and when ecoanxiety replaces fear of the Lord as the beginning of wisdom, it is understandable that Christians would have reservations.

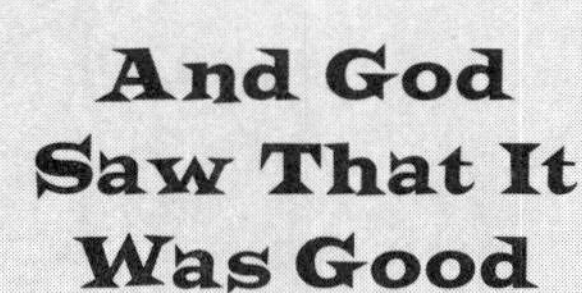

"God likes matter. He invented it."

—**C. S. Lewis,** *Mere Christianity*

Both the early modern antipathy to nature and the late modern idolatry of it stand in need of correction. Nature is not our enemy, but she is not our mother in the sense that she is the ultimate author of our life. Christians are right to seek a virtuous mean between these two extremes.

Three more observations and then we'll move on. First, the fact that not all Christians agree on the significance of global warming is proof that Christianity is a big tent. The Christian religion does not subscribe to a particular scientifically influenced account of reality, nor should it, for its primary goal is not to save the earth but something even more precious: your soul. Christianity does, on the other hand, provide an open forum in which these concerns can be debated, and bully for that. Second, the Christian duty to dress and keep the garden should be honored whether there is a danger of global warming or not. It strikes us as foolish to yoke the ancient Christian notion of environmental stewardship to the modern concern about global warming as if the only motive to avoid polluting were not wishing to soil our own nests: we should respect the earth whether or not rising temperatures are our fault. Christian care for the environment is based not on a fear of ecological consequences but on a respect for God's gifts.

Third, one reason for the skepticism about Christianity's environmental stewardship is a confusion over words. There is an old Christian concept called *contemptus mundi* or "contempt for the world," a phrase inspired by John 15:18–19, John 18:36, and I John 2:15–17. But in those verses "the world" does not refer to the earth or mankind or creation but to disordered human desire reeling away from God. As the great homilist Jacques-Bénigne Bossuet wrote, "the world" is not the sum total of visible and transient things but the *people* "who prefer visible and transient things to those invisible and everlasting." Oddly enough, "world" references an *artificial* environment or "set of values" created by the wicked rather than the *natural* environment created by God. It is not Yosemite National Park on a good day but Las Vegas on a bad day. That is why the French theologian Etienne Gilson could assert that "Christianity is a radical condemnation of the world, but it is at the same time an unreserved approbation of nature."

Indeed, contempt for the world leads not to a contempt for nature but to an appreciation of it, for it helps us to stop seeing nature through the eyes of greed and to start seeing it through the eyes of the God who lovingly made it and saw that it was good.

Politics: Composting the Dung of Romulus

Cicero was one of ancient Rome's greatest patriots—he lost his life for denouncing tyranny—but he was no political naïf. Writing to a friend about the more idealistic Cato the Younger (and alluding to Rome's mythical founder), he commented wryly, "Cato means excellently well, but he sometimes does harm to the commonwealth; for he talks as if we were living in Plato's republic and not the dung of Romulus."

Balancing civic-mindedness and sanity has never been easy. Patriotism can turn into nationalism, an ideology that has been used to justify injustices great and small. On the other hand, despising one's country can pave the way for dangerous delusions ranging from anarchism to communism to "new world order" utopianism, not to mention the basic indecency of not pulling one's own weight as a good citizen (there is something just plain vile about a person who does not feel the tug of love towards his or her country).

How does Christianity fare in navigating these tricky waters? Quite well, actually. Its secret weapon is its character as the world's only major "transpolitical religion." By that we mean:

Christianity is not a political religion: it is not a religion conceived or designed to support a particular regime, race, or form of government. Unlike Hinduism, Christianity did not emerge to justify a particular caste system. Unlike Shinto, it does not make an ideal state religion even when it is officially declared one. Unlike Buddhism, it can never be entirely subordinated to the political status quo, to the extent that its impact on social reform is negligible. And unlike Judaism and Islam, it does not have a body of law tied to a particular earthly homeland, for unlike these other two monotheistic religions, Christianity understands God's ultimate revelation or self-disclosure to be a *Person* (His Son Jesus Christ) and not a set of laws regulating an earthly territory or a chosen people.

Why Christians Are Reformers

"That external vigilance which has always been the mark of Christianity (the command that we should *watch* and pray) has expressed itself both in typical western orthodoxy and in typical western politics: but both depend on the idea of a divinity transcendent, different from ourselves, a deity that disappears… By insisting specially on the immanence of God we get introspection, self-isolation, quietism, social indifference—Tibet. By insisting specially on the transcendence of God we get wonder, curiosity, moral and political adventure, righteous indignation—Christendom."

—**G. K. Chesterton,** *Orthodoxy*

On the other hand, *Christianity is not an anti-political religion.* It denounces anti-Christian and unjust regimes, of course: in the Book of Revelation, St. John calls the pagan Roman Empire the Whore of Babylon who is "seated upon the seven hills" and "drunk with the blood of the saints and the martyrs of Jesus" (17:9 and 18:24). Nevertheless, the Christian faith

Ernest L. Fortin: Collected Essays: Classical Christianity and the Political Order: Reflections on the Theologico-Political Problem, vol. 2, edited by J. Brian Benestad (New York: Rowman & Littlefield, 1996).

does not denounce political life *tout court* but instead enjoins believers to pay their taxes (Mark 12:17), honor and obey civil authorities as divinely appointed (Romans 13:1–7), and be "subject for the Lord's sake to every human institution" (1 Peter 2:13).

And most important, *Christianity finds the ultimate meaning to life in something that lies beyond* ("*trans*") *political life and political community*, for Christians' ultimate allegiance is to God rather than men (Acts 5:29). While Christians are to "maintain good conduct among the Gentiles" (1 Peter 2:12), they are not to be "conformed to this world" (Romans 12:2). In the classic formulation, they are called to be in the world but not of it (see John 17:16). This tension is summed up nicely in the incident where the Pharisees try to trap Jesus by asking Him if it is lawful to pay taxes to the Romans. If He answers yes, He is a collaborationist and traitor to His people, the Jews; if He answers no, He is an insurrectionist and susceptible to Roman punishment. Jesus instead orders the Pharisees to show Him a coin and asks them whose image and inscription is on it. Caesar's, they reply. Our Lord's famous retort: "Then render unto Caesar what is Caesar's, and render unto God what is God's" (Mark 12:17). Note the implications: If something has someone's image and inscription on it, it belongs to that person. Roman coins are imprinted with Caesar's name and image and therefore belong to Caesar. But what bears God's image and inscription? *We do*, for man is made in the image and likeness of God (Genesis 1:27), and baptized Christians are inscribed with the name of Jesus (Revelation 22:4). Give your piddling lucre to the emperor, Christ is saying, but give *yourselves* to God.

Now this may not sound very patriotic, but it has the paradoxical effect of purifying patriotism and giving it a more solid grounding. Rather than have patriotic fervor stem from a blind and uncritical loyalty to one's own country simply because it *is* one's own country, patriotism now becomes a form of charity overflowing from the selfless love of neighbor. Thus it is more open to justice's demands for impartiality and self-sacrifice.

And this purified patriotism comes with an important reality check: no degree of Christian participation in politics, not even the establishment of Christendom itself, will overcome the limitations and inherent injustices of political life. Despite the believer's solemn duty to participate in the earthly city, the earthly city will remain the imperfect thing that it is until its elimination after the Second Coming. Not even a perfect Christian ruler or an ideal Christian society will be able to bring about the kingdom of God on earth. We enter the public forum for the sake of exercising virtue and bearing witness to the truth, but without expectations of victory. In the words of Mother Teresa, we are called to be faithful, not successful. This may sound rather obvious, but without this reality check one ends up in abject despair every time one's political hopes are dashed—see the histrionics displayed after Donald Trump's 2016 election to the presidency.

Unholy Alliances

At this point a skeptical reader might ask: Are you crazy? Doesn't Christianity have a long and tortured history with politics? Wasn't there an unholy alliance between altar and throne in the Middle Ages? Didn't the Byzantine Empire think of itself as the kingdom of God on earth? Didn't Elizabethan England force its subjects under threat of severe penalty to attend Sunday Anglican services? Weren't the Puritans trying to found their own theocracy in the New World?

Later we will look at some of the historic abuses of Christianity in detail. In the meantime, we offer three general points:

Transpolitical

"The second thing to get clear is that Christianity has not, and does not profess to have, a detailed political programme for applying 'Do as you would be done by' to a particular society at a particular moment. It could not have. It is meant for all men at all times and the particular programme which suited one place or time would not suit another. And, anyhow, that is not how Christianity works. When it tells you to feed the hungry it does not give you lessons in cookery."

—C. S. Lewis, *Mere Christianity*

First, it is precisely because Christianity is a transpolitical religion that it can be interpreted so diversely; its lack of a political program makes it like vodka in a cocktail—colorless, odorless, and without a strong flavor of its own, it mixes well with just about anything and still packs a punch. Popes crowning emperors and kings; conquistadors conquering the New World for Spain and God; Puritans enforcing blue laws; Maryland Catholics and Pennsylvania Quakers practicing toleration; Americans separating Church and State; Amish checking out of the whole system—every form of government from monarchy and empire to liberal democracy and communitarian rule has sought and received support from Christians, and all to some extent have abused that support.

Second, and this point is key: Christianity itself contains inherent limits to this abuse. It is not surprising that Christianity can be coopted for unholy use; most good things are like that, such as science (think of Nazi experiments on camp inmates), art, love, money, and so forth. We may even go so far as to say that most of the things in this world are potential allies of oppression. But as Chesterton points out, "There is only one thing that can never go past a certain point in its alliance with oppression—and that is orthodoxy. I may, it is true, twist orthodoxy so as partly to justify a tyrant. But I can easily make up a German philosophy to justify him entirely."

To give one small but symbolically important example. In the days of the Sun King, Louis XIV, Mass was celebrated in the Royal Chapel at Versailles with the king in a seat that was more prominent than the altar and the nobles circling around him, their backs to the sanctuary as they gazed attentively at their monarch. Yet despite this perverted arrangement, even here orthodox Christianity held its own. The nobles acted as if they were there to worship their earthly king, but the king they were reverencing was worshipping the true God. They were there to fulfill a worldly end, but the king's orientation testified to a power greater than himself that even he, an "absolute monarch," was forced to acknowledge.

Third, it may be said that Christianity's alleged political weakness is also its strength. By not being tied to any one regime or race, it is adaptable, and by being adaptable it maintains its capacity to transform the world. Consider this remarkable testimony from *The Epistle to Diognetus*, written by an anonymous second-century Christian author:

> For the Christians are distinguished from other men neither by country, nor language, nor the customs which they observe. For they neither inhabit cities of their own, nor employ a peculiar form of speech, nor lead a life which is marked out by any singularity... But, inhabiting Greek as well as barbarian cities, according as the lot of each of them has determined, and following the customs of the natives with respect to clothing, food, and the rest of their ordinary conduct, they display to us their wonderful and confessedly striking method of life. They dwell in their own countries, but simply as sojourners. As citizens, they share in all things with others, and yet endure all things as if foreigners. Every foreign land is to them as their native country, and every land of their birth as a land of strangers. They marry, as do all [others]; they beget children, but they do not kill their offspring. They have a common table but not a common bed. They are in the flesh, but they do not live after the flesh. They pass their days on earth, but they are citizens of heaven. They obey the prescribed laws, and at the same time

Compare and Contrast

"Mohammad had not only religious doctrines descend from Heaven and placed in the Koran, but political maxims, civil and criminal laws, and scientific theories. The Gospels, by contrast, speak only of the general relations of men to God and among themselves. Outside of that they teach nothing and oblige nothing to be believed. That alone, among a thousand other reasons, is enough to show that the first of these two religions cannot dominate for long in enlightened and democratic times, whereas the second is destined to reign in these centuries as in all the others."

—Alexis de Tocqueville, *Democracy in America*

surpass the laws by their lives. [They are persecuted], yet those who hate them are unable to assign any reason for their hatred. To sum up all in one word—what the soul is in the body, that are Christians in the world... Christians are confined in the world as in a prison, and yet they are the preservers of the world.

And it is precisely as the "soul" of this world that Christianity has, despite being a part-time ally of oppression, been a full-time ally of genuine progress and what Chesterton calls the "self-renewing energies of the West," from the *Magna Carta* to the Civil Rights Movement. It is no coincidence that the Christian West is the cradle of social reform, for even though the Christian knows that *sub specie aeternitatis* all great politics is but dung, he knows how to compost.

Christianity and Other Cultures: Honey Badger or Honey Bee?

Modern-day atheists such as Richard Dawkins lambast Christianity for being intolerant of other religions and cultures, but does the historical record support their claims? We will look at the Christian rapport with other religions later in chapter eight, but right now let us say three things about Christianity and culture.

First, because Christianity is made up of fallible people, Christians have sometimes confused the essential truths of their faith with their own cultural prejudices. Consequently they have rejected relatively innocent aspects of cultures different from their own. Think of dour Victorian missionaries frowning at the scanty clothing of tropical natives and you get the idea. (Yes, modesty is a universal virtue, but that does not mean that women in the South Pacific need to dress like women in Jane Austen's novels.) On the other hand, Christianity does affirm universal moral truths that must be obeyed at all places and all times, no matter what the local custom is—for example, its condemnation of infanticide.

Second, there have been unfortunate instances of cultural annihilation in Church history, but more often there have been examples of fruitful cross-pollination and development. The Hispanic New World is a good case in point. Christopher Columbus, who was a better mariner on sea than administrator on land, began a colonization of the Americas that led to the death and enslavement of countless Native Americans. Spanish settlement of the New World has been criticized for its destruction of pre-Columbian Native American cultures and peoples, and much of this criticism is valid. On the other hand, the Spanish did not launch a scorched-earth policy against the land's original occupants but fused their own culture and religion with native elements, thereby creating a unique and vibrant Hispanic culture—or rather, hundreds of unique and vibrant Hispanic cultures stretching from California to Argentina. Much was lost in that process, but not everything pre-Columbian was worth preserving (good riddance, we say, to the cannibalism of the Caribs and the human sacrifice of the Aztecs). And much was gained, especially the main prize, a civilization of Christian joy. In the words of Hilaire Belloc: "Wherever the Catholic sun doth shine, / There's always laughter and good red wine. / At least I've always found it so. / Benedicamus Domino!"

As Belloc's little ditty indicates, Latin America is not an isolated success. Ever since the Apostle Paul preached to the Athenians (see Acts 17:22–30), Christians have drawn from local cultures to explain the Gospel and ultimately transform them into something better. Nor is the resultant Christian culture monolithic. The different nations of Europe only became what they are today thanks to their Christian evangelization. When the Roman Empire expanded, it created more Romans, but at the expense of local identities. When Christianity expanded, it created more Christians *and* more nations, different peoples and cultures all worshipping the same God but in their own distinctive ways. This unity-in-plurality is what we mean by Christendom.

Third, Christianity does not so much destroy culture as preserve it. We would not have many of the glories of ancient Greece and Rome had Christianity not saved them from extinction. The valuables that Christianity has preserved run the gamut from priceless manuscripts dutifully copied out by monastic scribes to the concept of the rule of law to great architecture and engineering. Magnificent buildings like the Pantheon in Rome and the Porta Nigra in Triers, Germany, would have been pilfered to rubble by scavengers had they not been converted into churches (you're welcome, World Heritage Site lovers). Indeed, we can go so far as to join Chesterton in saying that Christianity is the only frame which has preserved the pleasures and the freedom of paganism. By introducing mortification of the flesh and the practice of "eating and drinking to the glory of God" (1 Corinthians 10:13), Christianity even preserved the Mediterranean love of food—converting the imperial Roman food orgy into the delicately balanced and moderate six-course French dinner (you're welcome, Foodies).

Christianity's enemies want to have it both ways. Out of one side of their mouths they accuse Christians of pursing a ruthless Carthaginian peace that salts the earth of different world cultures; out of the other side they yell "Gotcha!" when it is revealed that Christmas customs draw liberally from pagan yuletide traditions and the Roman Saturnalia. What they are missing is that Christians are called to embrace whatever is true, modest, just, holy, lovely, or virtuous wherever it is found (see Philippians 4:8).

In sum, although Christians have sometimes lamentably acted like a rampaging honey badger, not giving a hoot (this is a family-friendly PIG!), they have more often acted like the honey bee, gently taking the nectar from different cultures and transforming it into the sweetness of honey and the light-bearing qualities of candle wax. Christianity baptizes the best of what is human.

No Greater Commandment

"And there came one of the scribes that had heard them reasoning together, and seeing that he had answered them well, asked Him which was the first commandment of all. And Jesus answered him: 'The first commandment of all is, "Hear, O Israel: the Lord thy God is one God. And thou shalt love the Lord thy God, with thy whole heart, and with thy whole soul, and with thy whole mind, and with thy whole strength." This is the first commandment. And the second is like to it: "Thou shalt love thy neighbour as thyself." There is no other commandment greater than these.'"

—Mark 12:28–32

Love of Neighbor: Nobody Does It Better

Christians are animated by charity, which is *not* first and foremost philanthropy but what Paul calls *agape*, a divine love that the Holy Spirit pours forth into our hearts, enabling us to be superhuman lovers (see Romans 5:5). Charity is the love that prompted Christ to forgive the men who crucified Him (Luke 23:34), that enabled St. Stephen to ask forgiveness for the men who were stoning him (Acts 7:59), and that led Sir Thomas More to tell his condemners how he hoped they would all meet "merrily together" one day in Heaven. It is the love that enables Christians to distinguish between the sinner and the sin and to love the former and hate the latter at the same time and without confusion—a balancing act that baffles many political and social activists who "totalize" their animosities and vilify anyone who disagrees with them. Charity is an over-pouring of our love of God onto our fellow man. St. Augustine said it best: "Blessed, O Lord, is the man who loves You, his friend in You, his enemy because of You."

Of course, not every Christian exudes charity, but the overall record of Christian churches in aiding the less fortunate is unparalleled in world history. Consider three very brief examples: American Catholic nuns, the Salvation Army, and Compassion International.

Catholic nuns have been responsible for much of the educational, health care, and philanthropic infrastructure in this country. According to Elizabeth Kuhns, female Catholic religious built "the vast majority of Catholic institutions in the United States, founding 800 hospitals and more than 10,000 private schools." The Oblate Sisters of Providence, an African-American Catholic order, founded "the oldest continuously operating educational facility for black children in the U.S.," while St. Katharine Drexel, who founded the Sisters of the Blessed Sacrament and labored tirelessly for marginalized blacks and Native Americans, started more than sixty-five schools and missions, including Xavier University in New Orleans, the only African-American Catholic university in the world. Nuns helped found Alcoholics Anonymous and the Mayo Clinic, and they designed the first sewer system in Joplin, Missouri. Nine religious orders of Catholic women served so heroically as nurses on the front lines of the Civil War that they earned the unmitigated praise of Abraham Lincoln and a monument near the Lincoln Memorial in Washington, D.C. (One Sister of Charity was so admired by both Union and Confederate combatants in Kentucky that when she died of typhoid fever in 1861, both sides agreed to a truce so that they could hold a full military funeral for her.) Mother Joseph of the Sacred Heart, a missionary sister to the Native American populations on the Western frontier, was named the "First Architect of the Pacific Northwest" by the American Institute of Architects. American nuns have also ministered to cancer victims and the poorest of the poor, especially immigrant communities.

The Salvation Army lists as its objects "the advancement of the Christian religion... of education, the relief of poverty, and other charitable objects beneficial to society or the community of mankind as a whole." Since their founding in 1865, the Salvationists have sought to bring salvation and physical assistance to the poor, destitute, and hungry. Today they operate in 127 countries, running charity shops and homeless shelters as well as providing disaster relief and humanitarian aid around the world. In addition to their ubiquitous red kettles and bell ringers outside of stores around Christmas, the Salvation Army began (God bless 'em) National Doughnut Day in 1938 as a fundraising effort for victims of the Great Depression. In 2014, approximately thirty million people received their help.

Compassion International was founded in 1952 by the Reverend Everett Swanson, who went to South Korea to minister to American soldiers during the Korean War and saw hundreds of abandoned war orphans living and dying in the streets of Seoul. Vowing to help them, he started with a single orphanage and a program that provided food, clothing, medical care, shelter, and a Bible-based education. Today, nearly two million babies, children, and young adults in fourteen different countries have been rescued from both physical and spiritual poverty thanks to Compassion International. In tending to orphans, Reverend Swanson was following in a long line of Christian altruists going at least as far back as St. Nicholas of Myra (270–343), a.k.a. Santa Claus.

And we could go on about Christians serving in leper colonies, like Father Damien of Molokai, or in similarly deplorable conditions, like Mother Teresa of Calcutta; the Christian *invention* and staffing of hospitals and mental asylums; and the American Catholic invention of the largest independent health care system in the history of the world, and all with the nickels and dimes of struggling immigrants—but we must move on.

Who Really Cares: America's Charity Divide: Who Gives, Who Doesn't, and Why It Matters by Arthur Brooks (New York: Basic Books, 2007).

Christians and Government Programs for the Poor

The secular Left sometimes ignores Christianity's amazing track record with the poor and marginalized; instead, it has the temerity to accuse Christians, or at least conservative Christians, of being indifferent to the impoverished because of their opposition to welfare programs, universal health care, and so forth. There is no small amount of irony in all of this, since study after study shows what skinflints liberals are in comparison to conservatives when it comes to donating *their own money* to helping the disadvantaged.

But if conservative Christians really do want to help the poor, why do they object to government efforts to relieve poverty? There are several reasons.

First, they may not believe that the federal government has the authority to devote taxpayers' money to social services on the grounds that welfare is not one of the powers enumerated in the U.S. Constitution. This interpretation has a long and well-credentialed history. James Madison held that "charity is no part of the legislative duty of government," and Tennessee Congressman Davy Crockett recounted a story in which a backwoods constituent named Horatio Bunce chided him for voting in favor of a relief fund for victims of a local fire. Bunce was among the most Christian men Crockett had ever met. "If everyone who professes to be a Christian lived and acted and enjoyed it as he does," he recalled, "the religion of Christ would take the world by storm." But Bunce adamantly opposed Crockett's largesse with public monies on the grounds that it was unconstitutional, that it opened a wide door "for fraud and corruption and favoritism," and that it relieved one man by "drawing [money] from thousands who are even worse

Really Helping

"Through the establishment of Houses of Hospitality in the 1930s in cities throughout the nation, [Dorothy Day's Catholic Worker movement] demonstrated a commitment to a radical understanding of charity premised on the assumption of voluntary poverty and a willingness to be with the poor in the midst of their deprivation. The poor were treated as 'ambassadors of God' who brought with them the opportunity to perform the blessed act of charity, an understanding that shattered categories of 'deserving' and 'undeserving' and the hierarchies that separated giver from beneficiary. Day distinguished her commitment to personalism from her dedication as a Village radical to 'telescopic philanthropy' (borrowing a phrase Dickens used to describe a character in *Bleak House*), an imperative 'full of concerns for people everywhere' that tended to overlook the suffering nearer at hand. This work offered an alternative to bureaucratic, professionalized social service provision, whether provided by the state or private agencies; it also posed a fundamental challenge to the capitalist, consumerist order."

—Benjamin Soskis

off than he." If members of Congress were so concerned about the victims of the fire, Bunce noted, they could have taken up a private collection without abusing their powers and dipping into the public purse.

Second, even if the government has the power to help the poor, it may be unwise to exercise this power except in the rarest of circumstances. Centralized government is a large blunt instrument with clumsy standardized procedures, a lack of prudential flexibility, and a knack for inflating and perpetuating unaccountable bureaucracies—which is where so much of the money earmarked for the poor really goes. Thus it is ill-equipped to truly help the poor, something that is best done not by throwing money at the problem but by entering into the suffering of another individual before even beginning to answer the question, "How can I help?" Many conservative Christians agree with President Ronald Reagan: "There's very little that government can do as efficiently and economically as the people can do themselves." All told, private individuals

An Essay You're Not Supposed to Read

"Monogamy and Its Discontents" by William Tucker, in *Wing to Wing, Oar to Oar: Readings on Courting and Marrying*, edited by Amy and Leon Kass (South Bend: University of Notre Dame Press, 2000), 125–39.

and groups such as the Church are nimbler, more responsive, and better at charity than the State. Nor is State funding of the Church (such as President Bush's faith-based initiative) necessarily the answer, for government money comes with strings attached and over time creates a dependency that can hobble or compromise the Church's divine mission.

Third, if we truly care about the poor and marginalized, we should worry about the long-term effect that welfare has on the souls of its beneficiaries. Government programs often harm the very people they set out to help, eroding the family unit and creating a culture of servility and idleness. Much of this harm can be traced to the way in which guaranteed welfare increases "moral hazard," the risks a person is willing to take because of the assurance that someone else will bear the cost of those risks. State-funded generosity reduces the risks attached to sexual activity outside of marriage, for example. In a society without welfare payments, a single woman who conceives and bears a child without a husband is at a significant economic disadvantage; if she wants to be a mother, it makes sense morally, financially, and even psychologically (for her own wellbeing and that of her children) to get married first. But if she lives in a society which guarantees that the more children she has outside of marriage the more money the government will give her, and if she lives in a culture that no longer stigmatizes illegitimacy, she now has an incentive to stay single and continue bearing illegitimate children—even though, despite welfare, she is still confining herself to economic impoverishment and the heavy burdens of single parenthood. Before welfare, every woman had to weigh her desire for an attractive lover with her need for a good provider and to choose one man for a lifelong commitment

★ ★ ★

Moral Hazard

Children living apart from their fathers are two times as likely to be high school dropouts, two times as likely to go to jail, and nearly four times as likely to be poor as those with married parents. The children of single mothers are more aggressive; increasing single-parent families in a neighborhood by 1 percent drives adolescent violence up by 3 percent. Fatherless children have more trouble on math, reading and thinking skills tests, and in school generally. They make up 71 percent of high school dropouts and 71 percent of pregnant teens, 63 percent of youth suicides, 70 percent of the residents of state-operated institutions, 80 percent of rapists with "displaced anger" (using sexual assault as "a means of physically harming, degrading, or defiling the victim"), 85 percent of children diagnosed with behavioral disorders, 85 percent of young people in prison, and 90 percent of repeat arsonists. —statistics from the National Center for Fathering and the Fatherless Generation

(think of Elizabeth, Jane, and Charlotte in Jane Austen's *Pride and Prejudice*). The gravity of her decision often inspired a young woman to become a more mature and responsible adult. But in a welfare state, girls and women do not have to make these choices, and consequently they do not have to grow up. Women can hook up with one or more handsome cads who become "baby daddies," while the government stands in as the good provider and functions as the "sugar daddy." This arrangement is not good for the woman's character (*or* her economic prospects), and it is certainly not good for her children and the society they live in. As President Franklin Delano Roosevelt (no, that's not a mistake!) said in 1935, "The lessons of history, confirmed by evidence immediately before me, show conclusively that continued dependence on relief induces a spiritual and moral disintegration fundamentally destructive to the national fiber. To dole out relief in this way is to administer a narcotic, a subtle destroyer of the human spirit. It is inimical to the dictates of sound policy. It is a violation of the traditions of America... The Federal Government must and shall quit this business of relief."

Fourth, powerful welfare states tend to be socialist, and the attempts of socialist states to achieve economic equality weaken private property rights and thus puts the government at odds with the virtue of generosity, for one cannot be generous with one's possessions unless one first has possessions to be generous with. A truly Christian embrace of a right to private property is not for the sake of hoarding but for the sake of giving away, since freely sharing one's substance with others is one of the chief joys of the Christian life and the only arrangement that benefits both the giver and the recipient. Strictly speaking, states and bureaucracies and all such "gatherers and sharers," as the hobbits in J. R. R. Tolkien's *Lord of the Rings* call them, do not truly *give* but merely redistribute others' goods. After noting that there will always be poor people in the land, the Lord God commanded the Israelites "to open thy hand to thy needy and poor brother" (Deuteronomy 15:11). Liberals often use this verse against conservatives, but they are not reading it properly. God does not command that the Israelite government must be open-handed but that each and every Israelite *person* must be so. If the government taxed the Israelites in order to help the poor, it would not be fulfilling God's command. Voluntary obedience to God would be replaced by State compulsion—and there is no great virtue or moral merit in paying your taxes under compulsion and then assuming that the State will take care of the less fortunate for you. Judging from the donations in their tax records, this is precisely the assumption that prominent liberals like Andrew Cuomo, Ted Kennedy, Al Gore, and the Clintons appear to have made. No wonder Catholic bishop Aloisius Muench of Fargo, North Dakota responded to FDR's New Deal by saying "The poor belong to us... We will not let them be taken away."

CHAPTER FIVE

It's the End of the World as We Know It

One of the things that secularists really don't like about Christianity is its emphasis on the world to come. Marxists disdain talk about life after death because they think that it keeps workers indifferent to their current plight as they place all their hope in a heavenly reward. For Marx, religion was the opiate of the masses and its teaching on the afterlife was just "pie in the sky" (a phrase invented by socialist songwriter Joe Hill to mock a Salvation Army hymn) that keeps the downtrodden pacified. Similarly, radical environmentalists do not much care for belief in the ultimate destruction of the world on the theory that it discourages human beings from conserving the here and now.

We're not sure about the logic of either criticism. The historical record shows that Christianity has been an agent of enormous and beneficial social change, from the liberation of women to the abolition of slavery. As for not caring for the earth because we know it will be destroyed and recreated: just because you know that your father's car will one day be traded in and end up in a junk yard does not mean that you should treat it badly now, especially when he tells you not to.

Did you know?

- ★ Our souls will be judged twice after we die—kind of
- ★ Merely looking at God is bliss-inducing
- ★ Ghosts may be real
- ★ There will be no sea in the new Heaven and Earth

So let's take a fresh look at the final hope of the Christian disciple: the Particular Judgment, Heaven, Hell, Purgatory, Limbo, and the end of the world.

The Particular Judgment

Christians believe that when a creature dies its soul is separated from its body. Animals have mortal souls, which as far as we can tell cease to exist at the moment of their death. But human beings, being made in the image and likeness of God, have *immortal* souls: while our corpses decay, our souls live on to be judged by almighty God. Souls are not reincarnated, nor do they go into a kind of coma as they wait to be judged at the end of the world, as Muslims believe. Yes, Christians sometimes speak of our dead as having "fallen asleep in the Lord," but we do so not in order to deny judgment at the moment of death but to affirm that their dead *bodies*, which now look asleep, will rise up on the Last Day. Did you know that the word "cemetery" is actually Greek for dormitory or sleeping quarters and was first used by early Christians to signify their catacombs?

The Particular Judgment of the individual soul determines whether it will go to Hell or to Heaven. It is tempting to think of this event in terms of a brownie-point system, where if all your good deeds outweigh all your bad ones you go to Heaven and if the bad outweigh the good you go to Hell. But it is not quite like that. The Bible lists many criteria necessary for being saved and having eternal life: you must repent (Mark 1:14–15), you must be baptized in water and the Spirit (John 3:5, 22; 1 Peter 3:21), you must eat the Flesh of the Son of Man and drink His blood (John 6:35–36), you must believe in the Lord Jesus (Acts 16:31), you must have faith (Mark 1:14–15), you must have love (1 Corinthians 13:2), you must keep the Commandments (Matthew 19:16–17), you must perform certain works of mercy such as feeding the hungry, clothing the naked, and visiting the imprisoned (Matthew

25:31–46), you must avoid grave sin (1 John 5:17), and you must persevere to the end (Matthew 24:13).

All of these things can be summed up in one word: just as Jesus Christ is the *icon* or image of the Father (Colossians 1:15), we must become an *icon* or image of Christ. "Every Christian is to become a little Christ," C. S. Lewis writes in *Mere Christianity*. "The whole purpose of becoming a Christian is simply nothing else." If there is a laundry list in Christianity of right and wrong beliefs and right and wrong actions, they're there to prod us to resemble more and more the person of Jesus Christ, the God who became man in order to help men become like God. It is all quite simple: if you want to get into Heaven, you must first get Heaven into you. The devotion, the works of charity, the praying, the Sacraments, the Bible studies—all of them are ordered to this final end. The more Christ-like you are inside and out, the easier it will be for Christ the Judge to see Himself in the little mirror that is you and recognize you as one of His own.

Heaven

Heaven is the subject of many cartoonish portrayals involving clouds and harps—restful, but boring. The good news is that Heaven is where the soul is alive as never before. Consider the following:

- In Heaven we will see God face to face (1 Corinthians 13:13). And God, as we have already noted, is the Object of our soul's deepest yearning, "the joy of man's desire." Because our hearts are designed to run on God and nothing else, we will be thrilled when we finally unite with Him in a vision of His essence. Theologians refer to this immediate sight of God as the Beatific Vision, for merely looking at God is bliss-inducing or beatific.

Do All Good Dogs Really Go to Heaven?

"I think I can see how the higher animals are in a sense drawn into Man when he loves them and makes them (as he does) much more nearly human than they would otherwise be... It might be that when intelligent creatures entered into Christ they would, in that way, bring all the other things in along with them. But I do not know: it is only a guess."

—C. S. Lewis, *Mere Christianity*

- In the Beatific Vision, we not only see the Author behind every mystery, we see those mysteries solved as well. The answering of all of our questions will bring tremendous happiness. Do you know the "high" or delight you experience when you have a sudden insight? Think of Archimedes running out into the street buck naked after discovering the principle of water displacement and shouting ecstatically, "Eureka!—I have found it!" Well, as the theologian Bernard Lonergan puts it, "God is the unrestricted act of understanding, the eternal rapture glimpsed in every Archimedean cry of Eureka."
- Among the things we will know is what is happening on Earth. To quote Trent Horn, the New Testament in general and Hebrews 12:1 in particular speak of the saints in Heaven as "a cosmic stadium" cheering us on "to finish the race and 'keep the faith' (2 Timothy 4:7) lest we be disqualified by our sins (1 Corinthians 9:27)." The reality of this cloud of witnesses, incidentally, explains why many Christians do not think that praying to the saints is worshipping the dead. Those who die in Christ do not truly die (see Galatians 2:20), for they are part of Christ's mystical body, and ever since that first Easter Sunday morning, death has had *no* dominion over Christ (Romans 6:9): it will *never* again separate Christ from the members of His body. And because death cannot divide the members of Christ's Body,

there is essentially no spiritual difference between asking a pew mate for prayers and asking the same of a fellow Christian who passed away a thousand years ago.

- And don't worry about whether you'll get bored after seeing God and all the secrets of the universe, for there is no *after* in Heaven. As hard as it is to understand, Heaven is in eternity, and eternity is not infinity—one thing after another without end—but past, present, and future *as present*. It is the eternal NOW, an incredible intensification of presence. It is the highest high experienced in the ultimate present moment.
- And, of course, not only will ultimate knowledge be present; so too will ultimate love. The very sight of God in all His Triune glory, united to all the throngs of angels and saints, will flood the soul with love, and the soul will be united to God and His elect in perfect love and friendship.
- Finally, we will have eternal bliss because our wills at long last will be perfectly aligned with God's. Here and now, thanks to the lingering effects of original sin, our own bad habits, or even just our animalistic instincts and fears, we tend to wince or recoil from God's plan for us or for others, even though as believers we ardently wish to conform to whatever our Lord wishes. In Heaven we can finally say, both consciously and unconsciously and with 100 percent gusto, "Thy will be done." This total surrender to our loving Father will bring unspeakable peace and joy.

Better Than We Can Imagine

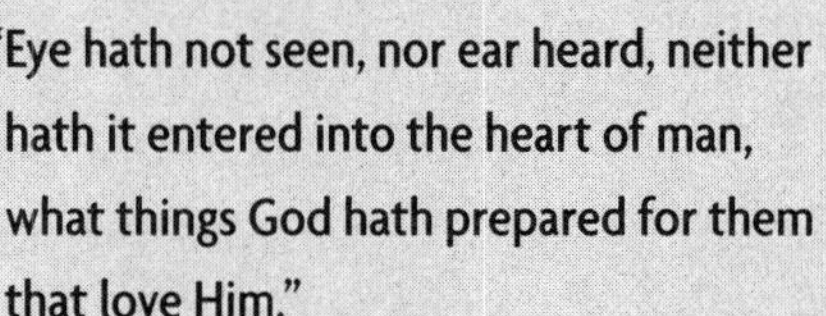

"Eye hath not seen, nor ear heard, neither hath it entered into the heart of man, what things God hath prepared for them that love Him."

—1 Corinthians 2:9

Hell

Just as Heaven is an extraordinary intensification of life, Hell is a "second death" (Revelation 21:8), an intensification of pain, sorrow, and every other bad thing surrounding death. Hell is described in the Bible as "the fires of Gehenna" (Matthew 5:22, 18:9): Gehenna or the Valley of the Son of Hinnom was a cursed place near Jerusalem where some kings of Judah had sacrificed children by fire to the god Moloch (see Joshua 15:8). Hell is also called a lake of fire (see Revelation 21:8) and a place where the "worm dieth not and the fire is not quenched" (Mark 9:44, 46, 48). Souls in Hell experience a kind of sensory pain through some agency that the Scriptures consistently describe as fire (see Matthew 13:50; Mark 9:43; and Luke 16:24). Whether Hell's unquenchable "fire and brimstone" (Revelation 14:10) are identical to the fire and sulphur we are familiar with in this earthly realm is unknown.

But the main source of agony will be the loss of God Himself. If our hearts are restless until they rest in God, then even when we reject God our hearts will continue to yearn for Him. Every soul in Hell hates God with a fiery passion, but it also can't help but love Him, and knowing that it has chosen to say No to the object of its love brings with it unparalleled grief. Hence the words of St. John Chrysostom: "The torments of Hell are awful; but if one were to heap a thousand hell-fires one on the other, it would be as nothing compared with the punishment of being excluded from the blessed glory of Heaven, of being hated by Christ, and of being compelled to hear him say, 'I know you not.'"

But is Hell fair? Of all of the Christian beliefs about the afterlife, the secular Left despises Hell the most—and it also despises all those people who so arrogantly and cruelly believe in the testimony of divine revelation that sinners are in danger of hellfire. Their critics' position is summed up by what Cuban dictator Fidel Castro said when he met with mostly liberal religious leaders in New York City in 1995. "The United Nations would not like the idea of Hell," he told them. "It would be a gross violation of human rights!" The room roared with laughter.

Of course, as an unrepentant (so far as we can tell) mass murderer, Castro had good reason to hope that there is no Hell, and we suspect a similar motive for many other Hell-deniers. Hell can be a troubling doctrine for sincere Christians as well. One atheist professor of mine flummoxed believers in his class when he said, "Strange that a God who is all love would inflict everlasting pain on anyone who refused to love Him."

So let's review the facts. First, in a weird way, whoever is in Hell is there because he wants to be there, that is, he has freely chosen some sin or some temporal good over God. Souls in Hell may regret being in Hell because of the suffering it involves, but they do not repent of their sins. They are fixed in eternal selfishness and defiance—remember, eternity is a single intense moment. God is love (1 John 4:8), and as such He loves everyone and does not want a single person to rot in Hell (see 1 Timothy 2:4): we can even say that God did not create Hell to put us into it but to keep us out of it. By letting us know about Hell through His divine revelation, He instills a healthy "fear of the Lord" as the beginning of our wisdom in order to help us steer clear of it—after all, God created Hell not for fallen humanity but for the Devil and his angels (Matthew 25:41). But God also respects free will. And if someone is adamant about going to Hell, even after he has received the grace to say Yes to the gift of Heaven, God respects that decision. To paraphrase Anne Graham, Billy Graham's daughter, God is a gentleman: He will not drag anyone kicking and screaming into Heaven.

Second, God is perfectly just. If a soul is in Hell, it is not because it was tricked or some mistake was made when God rendered the verdict. As one of my pastors once put it, "If you make it to Heaven, thanks be to God. If you end up in Hell, it's your own damn fault." We can even say that if there is such a thing as justice but there is no perfect justice in this world (a fairly obvious point), then there *needs* to be a Hell to address all of the incorrigible

> ### Better Not Count on It
>
> "To hope for all souls is imperative; and it is quite tenable that their salvation is inevitable. It is tenable, but it is not specially favourable to activity or progress. Our fighting and creative society ought rather to insist on the danger of everybody, on the fact that every man is hanging by a thread or clinging to a precipice. To say that all will be well anyhow is a comprehensible remark: but it cannot be called the blast of a trumpet... So Christian morals have always said to the man, not that he would lose his soul, but that he must take care that he didn't."
>
> —**G. K. Chesterton,** *Orthodoxy*

evildoers who have inflicted so much pain on others and gotten away with it. In 1984, National Public Radio's *All Things Considered* broadcast the now-legendary debate at Princeton University on the question, "Should there be a Hell?" The team arguing for the affirmative won.

Third, it is not unjust to condemn someone for all eternity for one or more sins. Even in our own judicial system, what matters is not how long the crime went on but how severe it is in nature. A murder can take only a second and you can jaywalk around town for hours, but the former can bring the death penalty and the latter a light slap on the wrist. And remember, souls in Hell do not seek forgiveness but seal themselves in their malice.

Fourth, we suspect that resistance to the doctrine on Hell is as strong as it is today because of the rejection of a more basic reality. We live in an age where the average American increasingly refuses to accept responsibility for his actions. Fat cat executives run their companies into the ground and expect a government bailout or a golden parachute; students rack up exorbitant debts and want them forgiven; chain smokers get lung cancer and clamor for socialized medicine; libertines lust for sexual gratification and are furious when their employers or their neighbors' taxes won't pay for their birth control devices and abortions (remember Sandra Fluke, the Georgetown law student preening before the cameras because a Catholic university would not fund her sterile fornication?); and activists demand a costly nanny state without caring about the danger it poses to the nation's solvency or the burden it places on future generations. These irresponsible disconnects from reality are symptomatic of the Left which, as we will see more closely in chapter ten, has recently taken to glorifying victimhood. There are genuine victims in this fallen world, but the problem with a victimhood *culture* is that it encourages *everyone* to see himself as innocent of wrongdoing and blame someone else for the consequences of his own decisions. As Steve Maraboli notes, "The victim mindset dilutes the human potential. By not accepting personal responsibility for our circumstances, we greatly reduce our power to change them."

Hell is a vivid reminder that man is responsible for his own actions, the consequences of which reverberate for all eternity, since God will render "to every man according to his works" (see Proverbs 24:12; Matthew 16:27; 2 Timothy 4:14; and Revelation 22:12). But precisely because it is such a sobering wakeup call, nobody wants to hear it.

Purgatory

If you're worried about not being pure enough to see God face to face because nothing unclean shall enter Heaven (Revelation 21:27), take heart. According to traditional Christian teaching, there is another realm in the afterlife, the function of which is to complete your transformation into a "little Christ." That transformation begins on earth, but unless you die replete with heroic virtue, chances are that your transformation is still a work in progress at the moment of your death. Enter "Purgatory," which is not really a permanent region of the afterlife but a temporary detox room where final debts are paid off and lingering stains are purged away. For more on the process of purification after death, see Corinthians 3:11–15, which, according to the interpretation of the early Church, indicates an intermediate state after death in which the dross of lighter transgressions will be burnt away "as by fire."

The good news is that every soul that makes it to Purgatory is saved: it knows that it is destined for Heaven and that every punishment it suffers is of the *remedial* variety rather than pure retribution. The bad news is that Purgatory can hurt like Hell, because of our need for further penance and reparation and because of the difficulty in letting go of our vices once and for all. (Like Hell, Purgatory is associated with fire, but unlike Hell, it is a temporary refiner's fire, removing the dross of imperfection.) That is why Christians pray for their dead, to relieve the suffering of those who may be in Purgatory. Because, think about it: prayers for the souls in Heaven are unnecessary, and prayers for the souls in Hell are in vain. Therefore, when a Christian prays for one's faithful departed—as the Apostle Paul did his for his dead friend Onesiphorus in 2 Timothy 1:6–18—one is implicitly praying that they get out of Purgatory and into Heaven as quickly as possible.

Not Ready for the Prime Time

"Our souls *demand* Purgatory, don't they? Would it not break the heart if God said to us, 'It is true, my son, that your breath smells and your rags drip with mud and slime, but we are charitable here and no one will upbraid you with these things, nor draw away from you. Enter into the joy.'? Should we not reply, 'With submission, sir, and if there is no objection, I'd *rather* be cleaned first.' 'It may hurt, you know'—'Even so, sir.'"

—C. S. Lewis, *Letters to Malcolm*

Nevertheless, Purgatory remains a controversial doctrine in contemporary Christianity. Catholics are fond of both the term "Purgatory" and the doctrine behind it, while the Eastern Orthodox aren't crazy about the term even though their understanding of what happens beyond the grave is not that different from the Catholic position. Protestants, on the other hand, have a range of reactions. For Martin Luther, the term evoked the sale of indulgences (the purpose of which was to get souls out of Purgatory) and was therefore suspect. Following Luther's lead, John Calvin acknowledged the need for purgation but speculated that it occurs during the transition from this life to the next. To the great apologist C. S. Lewis, on the other hand, Purgatory made perfect sense. Meanwhile there remains that curious verse about the soul being judged, cast into prison, and held there until it has paid the last penny (Matthew 5:26).

A Note on Ghosts

One advantage to the doctrine of Purgatory is that it may explain ghosts. Ghosts and demons are all thrown into the same Halloween stew, but they are utterly different: demons, as we have seen, are fallen and eternally wicked angels, whereas ghosts are the souls of deceased human beings that are not necessarily malevolent. Since the soul is judged immediately after death, it either goes to Heaven, Hell, or Purgatory. It is theoretically possible that a ghost from Heaven could, like an angel, be sent by God to communicate a message through a dream or apparition, but that would not explain the spookiness surrounding ghostly appearances. Limbo—see below—is another possibility. Indeed when King Saul had the Witch of Endor conjure up the ghost of Samuel in 1 Samuel 28:8–19, Samuel's soul was no doubt called from there. But as we will see shortly, the Limbo of the Fathers ceased to exist after Good Friday. Another possibility we can rule out is that a ghost is a *human soul* from Hell: in the Parable of the Rich Man and Lazarus (Luke 16:19–31), the deceased rich man is not permitted to leave Hell and visit his living brothers to warn them.

That leaves only Purgatory. The explanation would run something like this: by the mercy of God, souls in Purgatory are allowed to visit their old haunting grounds, so to speak, in order to shorten the painful purging process by getting people to pray for them. Some are more successful than others in communicating their wishes, and some (because of the gravity of the sins they committed) may be haunting a place longer than others. There is no Christian consensus on the matter, but for what it's worth, one of the more offbeat tourist destinations in the city of Rome is a small place called the Museum of the Holy Souls in Purgatory, which contains prayer books and furniture bearing scorched handprints and other burn-marks believed to have been left by souls begging their loved ones to pray harder for them.

Of course, if a ghost isn't from Purgatory, the other possibility (aside, of course, from possible error or hallucination on the part of the ghost-spotter) is that the alleged spook is actually a demon impersonating a deceased human. Both options are on the table in Shakespeare's *Hamlet*. When Hamlet first sees the ghost, he wants to know if he is from Heaven or Hell, if he is "a spirit of health or goblin damn'd." The ghost essentially replies that he is neither but someone suffering "sulphurous and tormenting flames" for a "certain term" until "the foul crimes done in [his] days of nature are burnt and purged away." In other words, he is claiming to be in Purgatory. But is the ghost telling the truth, or he is indeed a goblin damn'd, a deceitful devil making things more rotten in the state of Denmark? After all, the apparition preaches a Gospel of blood vengeance, not Christian forgiveness. The next time a ghost tells you to do something wrong, tell him to go to Hell.

Is Limbo in Limbo?

In the Apostles' Creed there is a curious line about Jesus Christ: that after "He suffered under Pontius Pilate, was crucified, died and was buried" and before He rose again on the third day, "He descended into Hell."

He did what now? What was Jesus Christ, the Son of God, doing among the damned? The answer is that He wasn't with them at all. Hell or *Helle* in old English simply means the netherworld (like the Hebrew *Sheol* or the Greek *Hades*), not necessarily the place of eternal torment. After meditating on certain Scriptural passages about Jesus Christ who, after He died, preached to "the spirits in prison" (1 Peter 3:18–19 and 4:6), the early Christians came to understand the underworld as consisting of two distinct realms: Hell proper, where the demons and the damned are confined eternally, and Limbo, which literally means edge or boundary in Latin. Thanks to the parable of the Rich Man and Lazarus, Limbo was also called "the Bosom of Abraham" because Abraham was there snuggling Lazarus like a kindly father. (But as we are about to see, because Abraham vacated Limbo when Christ harrowed it and eventually joined Christ in Heaven, the "Bosom of Abraham" can now be a term for Heaven. Whither Abraham goes, thither goeth his bosom.)

Only two groups have possibly resided in Limbo. The first is all the righteous souls who lived before the Incarnation. They did not deserve Hell but could not go to Heaven because Jesus had not yet opened the Pearly Gates to mankind with His own Precious Blood. Abel, Moses, David, Job, Elijah, and even Adam and Eve, who according to tradition felt awfully bad about the Fall and spent the rest of their lives in penance—all of them went to what is called the "Limbo of the Fathers" and all of them greeted their Lord when His soul descended to Limbo after dying on the cross on Good Friday. This event is traditionally known as the "Harrowing of Hell," and it is still a popular subject in Eastern iconography. Later (so the theory goes), when Jesus Christ opened the gates of Heaven during His Ascension, He allowed all the just souls He liberated from Limbo to enter the bliss of eternal life. At that point, the Limbo of the Fathers was empty, and from that point on adult souls would be sent immediately to Heaven, Hell, or Purgatory.

The Harrowing of Hell

"Well, when our Lord Jesus Christ had died on the Cross, and left his body in the tomb to wait till Easter morning, the first thing which his spirit did was—what? To explore his Father's lumber-room. He went to Limbo, and visited all the borderline cases of the old patriarchs who had been waiting so many centuries for him to come. How they must have crowded round him, and what a lot he must have explained to them which they hadn't been able to understand properly hitherto.... What a holiday that must have been for them all, when our Lord came and explained to them, at last, what their experiences in life had meant, and ended up, 'Now you are going home with me; it is time you went home!'"

—**Ronald Knox,** *The Creed in Slow Motion*

The "Limbo of the Fathers" is a fixed part of Christian teaching, but many Christians have also believed in a "Limbo of the Infants." The idea was that infants and children who have been baptized and who die before their faculty of reason and of moral responsibility kicks in (around the age of seven) go straight to Heaven: they have received sanctifying grace and have committed no sins of their own. *Unbaptized* infants, on the other hand, have not received the sanctifying grace of Christ through baptism, yet they have done nothing to merit the punishments of Hell. So what does God do with them? If you say that all unbaptized infants go to Hell, you are making God an awful meany, but if you say that all unbaptized infants go to Heaven, then what is the point of grace? It is quite a sticky wicket. One possible middle ground is that infants can be saved by the faith of their parents, much as they are baptized by their parents' consent. But the traditional speculation for centuries was that they went to the Limbo of the Infants, a place where there is no pain and indeed a state of natural happiness, but also no eternal bliss.

Catholics mostly believed in the Limbo of the Infants, but it was never officially defined as dogma. In 2007, an International Theological Commission, with the authorization of Pope Benedict XVI, issued the following statement: "Our conclusion is that the many factors that we have considered above give serious theological and liturgical grounds for hope that unbaptized infants who die will be saved and enjoy the beatific vision. We emphasize that these are reasons for prayerful hope, rather than grounds for sure knowledge. There is much that simply has not been revealed to us."

The End of Days and the Second Coming

One of the wildest areas of divergence among Christian communities concerns how Jesus Christ will fulfill His promise to come again. There used to be a consensus on the basic blueprint among Catholics, Protestants, and

Eastern Orthodox all over the world. But in the nineteenth century, an argument arose within American Protestantism over how to interpret Revelation 20:1–3 and 7–8, verses that tell of a millennium or thousand-year reign of Christ. Premillennial, postmillennial, and amillennial groups soon formed, depending on how literally they took the text. Complicating matters further was new speculation about a "Rapture" that was ostensibly based on 1 Thessalonians 4:16–17 and promoted by the premillennials: it ended up creating further subdivisions: pre-tribulation, mid-tribulation, or post-tribulation.

Rather than try to sort out this tangle, let's review the basic Christian consensus, which already offers much food for thought. According to traditional Christianity, we know the following: that Jesus Christ will come again; that we will be reunited with our bodies; that there will a general judgment; and that there will be a new Heaven and a new Earth.

In the First Coming, the Son of God, coeternal with the Father, assumed our human nature in the person of Jesus Christ and was born a babe in Bethlehem. It happened in humility and obscurity, so that even when Pontius Pilate was staring Truth Incarnate in the face all the hapless Roman could do was ask with unintentional irony, "What is truth?" (John 18:38).

Jesus' Second Coming will have considerably less ambiguity. Christ will return in the clouds with much power and majesty with His angels (Matthew 24:30–31) in the same way that He ascended into Heaven (Acts 1:11).

One interesting detail about the "Parousia" or Second Coming: the direction from which Christ will come will be the East (Matthew 24:27)—fittingly, because Christ is described as the Dawn from on high (Luke 1:78). All three of the great monotheistic religions have a tradition of praying in a particular direction: the orthodox Jew faces Jerusalem and the Muslim faces Mecca. But remember that Christianity is a transpolitical religion. So Christians have traditionally prayed facing not any earthly city but the East, in anticipation of the Second Coming. The early

Church, which aligned its centers of sacred worship on an east-west axis, took this orientation quite seriously: in the days when both the priest and the congregation prayed facing the same direction, they would all be ready for the Lord's coming as they expectantly celebrated the sacrifice of the altar. Similarly, in Christian cemeteries, the graves were often arranged so that the feet of the deceased are pointing east, in the expectation that they will rise and face Christ when He comes again from that direction. The term "orientation" actually comes from this hallowed tradition of facing the East, or Orient. It is ironic but oddly fitting that a word inspired by a profession of one's faith in the Second Coming should in our own day and age be used for one's sexual proclivities, the god of our postmodern times.

The Resurrection of the Body and the General Judgment

The graves will give up their dead and all souls, both in Heaven and in Hell, will be reunited with their bodies. Belief in bodily resurrection is complicated—the difficulties begin with a seemingly simple question: What is the body? Shakespeare plays upon this problem when Prince Hamlet describes how a king may go "through the guts of a beggar." A king dies, his body is eaten by worms, a beggar goes fishing with one of the worms, and then he eats the fish that ate the worm. Whose body is whose?

Paul chides doubters who ask, "How are the dead raised up?" by comparing the body to a seed that must die before it truly lives (1 Corinthians 15:35ff). That is a metaphor worth dwelling on. The human body, which is a magnificent creation, is a mere acorn in comparison to the oak tree it is destined to become. Acorns retain their substance when they grow into trees (they don't become butterflies), yet the difference between an acorn and an oak could not be more profound; the former is virtually nothing in comparison to the latter. If our bodies, impressive as they are, are mere acorns now, imagine what trees they will be on the Last Day.

Consider the four properties of a glorified body as identified in medieval theology: agility, subtlety, impassibility, and clarity. Agility is the perfect responsiveness of the body to the soul, which will allow it to move at the speed of thought. Subtlety is the power of penetrating solid matter. Impassibility is the impossibility of suffering or dying. Lastly, clarity is the total absence of bodily deformity and a "resplendent radiance and beauty." Our bodies will be like Christ's risen body.

The astonishing excellence of a resurrected body was described cleverly by a young colonial printer named Benjamin Franklin, who wrote his own epitaph at the age of twenty-two:

> The body of
> B. Franklin, Printer
> (Like the Cover of an Old Book
> Its Contents torn Out
> And Stript of its Lettering and Gilding)
> Lies Here, Food for Worms.
> But the Work shall not be Lost;
> For it will (as he Believ'd) Appear once More
> In a New and More Elegant Edition
> Revised and Corrected
> By the Author.

The resurrection of the body is a most fitting consummation of Christ's victory over death. The Passion, Resurrection, and Ascension of Our Lord open the gates of Heaven to our souls but do not immediately end our vulnerability to the effects of original sin. Those effects include a degradation of the body: every bodily deformity or disease, every violent injury

★ ★ ★

A Sure and Certain Hope

Forasmuch as it hath pleased Almighty God of his great mercy to take unto himself the soul of our dear brother here departed, we therefore commit his body to the ground; earth to earth, ashes to ashes, dust to dust; in sure and certain hope of the Resurrection to eternal life, through our Lord Jesus Christ; who shall change our vile body, that it may be like unto his glorious body, according to the mighty working, whereby he is able to subdue all things to himself.

—*The Book of Common Prayer*

or accident, every misuse or abuse, is a sad reminder that we still live east of Eden. And death remains what it always was, a literal humiliation for one and all, a return of the body to the ground (*humus*) or dust from whence it sprung.

As excellent as the Beatific Vision is, the human soul is naturally designed to rule a body, and thus there remains some unfinished business even for a saint in Heaven. How splendid, then, that the elect are promised not only eternal life in Heaven but a "reform" of "our vile body" into a body like that of our risen Lord, one that Saint Paul refers to as "glorified" and even "spiritual" (see Philippians 3:21 and 1 Corinthians 15:44). The body can be a pain to deal with this side of the grave, but once it is glorified it will become a luminous reflection of the soul's divinely given excellence. In Saint Augustine's words, "what was once [the soul's] burden will be its glory." And how fitting that this glory is part of God's ongoing transformation of creation until He becomes "all in all" (1 Corinthians 15:28).

It is also fitting, as St. Irenaeus (martyred in A.D. 202) points out, that the flesh which is nourished by the Body and Blood of our Lord will one day partake of His very life. The Eucharist is already, as Christian liturgy proclaimed throughout the ages, a "pledge of our future glory." And as Pope Benedict XVI preached, "The substantial conversion of bread and wine into his body and blood introduces within creation the principle of a radical change, a sort of 'nuclear fission,' to use an image familiar to us today, which penetrates to the heart of all being, a change meant to set off a process which transforms reality, a process leading ultimately to the transfiguration of the entire world, to the point where God will be all in all." In other words, Christ never abandoned His mystical body on Earth but remained with His Church sacramentally, continuing His work of redemption and transforming the world in preparation for its ultimate transformation when He comes again in glory.

Oh: and the souls in Hell will reunite with their bodies as well, but this reunion will not be "the resurrection of life" but the "resurrection of damnation" (John 5:28–29). The restored bodies of the damned will be disgraceful rather than glorious, hideous and repulsive like the demons. And as a result of being back in a body, the damned souls will suffer the added torment of physical pain.

Finally, after the resurrection of the dead, all will stand before the throne of God to be judged. "But wait!" you may be asking. "Wasn't the soul already judged at the moment of death?" Yes, it was. The Last or General Judgment is not so much a new court trial for the soul as a ratification of the first verdict, now made publicly. That is why the Last Judgment has been described as a "social judgment," one made with a view to manifesting to the whole human race God's mercy and justice. This manifestation will reveal not only each individual's good and evil deeds but the entire accumulated sweep of consequences resulting from them. We will then see how God has been just and merciful in dealing not just with us but with all of humanity. There will also

The Last Judgment

"When the Son of man shall come in His glory, and all the holy angels with Him, then shall He sit upon the throne of His glory. And before Him shall be gathered all nations, and He shall separate them one from another, as a shepherd divideth His sheep from the goats. And He shall set the sheep on his right hand, but the goats on the left. Then shall the King say unto them on His right hand, 'Come, ye blessed of my Father, inherit the kingdom prepared for you from the foundation of the world'... Then shall He say also unto them on the left hand, 'Depart from Me, ye cursed, into everlasting fire, prepared for the devil and his angels'... And these shall go away into everlasting punishment: but the righteous into life eternal."

—Matthew 25:31–34, 41, 46

be a general comeuppance. Christ and His Saints were spat upon and reviled by the world; now the world will see them in their true glory and bend the knee. Another difference from the Particular Judgment is that the soul will be judged as a whole person once again, body and soul.

Heaven and Earth 2.0

After the General Judgment, the world will be destroyed by fire (2 Peter 3:10–13; see also 1 Thessalonians 5:2 and Revelation 3:3, 16:15). As Prospero in Shakespeare's *Tempest* puts it,

> The cloud-capped towers, the gorgeous palaces,
> The solemn temples, the great globe itself,
> Yea, all which it inherit, shall dissolve,
> And, like this insubstantial pageant faded,
> Leave not a rack behind.

The bad news is that all that we hold dear will be going up in smoke—all the natural wonders, all the great works of art, and so forth. The good news is that God will then create a new Heaven and a new Earth that will be far superior. It will elicit the same awe and wonder as our glorified bodies. It should come as no surprise that creation itself should follow the example of Christ and His disciples in first dying in order to be born anew.

Think of it this way: it's as if, in the beginning, God created a computer program called "Heaven and Earth" and He saw that it was very good. One day the Devil dangled clickbait before Man, and he foolishly clicked on it. Ever since, the program has been plagued by viruses. God worked to fix the problem through remote access and sent various employees, but then He finally came in person. This office visit turned things around, to the extent that the viruses are no longer dominating the program. But before He left,

God said, "I am not fixing the problem entirely just yet. I want you to wrestle with a few of these issues until I return with a whole new version." Well, the Parousia is the return of the Divine Programmer, who will come to install a vastly superior 2.0 version of Heaven and Earth. After this version, there shall be no more tears nor viruses nor computer freezes nor blue screening; and everything that you loved about the old program will still be there, but in a far more amazing and user-friendly way.

What features Heaven and Earth 2.0 will have, Heaven only knows. We know that it will be a place "wherein dwelleth righteousness " (2 Peter 3:13). And we know that the New Jerusalem will descend from Heaven (Revelation 21:2), but don't expect a gilded Disney castle: the city will be made with precious stones (Revelation 21:19), but these could be the "living stones" that are the apostles and the saints (1 Peter 24). We also know that just as all of creation was adversely affected by the sin of Adam (Romans 8:19–21), so too will all of creation somehow profit from the new Adam's redemption of mankind. All animals, even the ones we know as carnivores, are described as vegetarian before the Fall (Genesis 1:29–30), and they are likewise prophetically described as vegetarian in the new Heaven and Earth: "The wolf and the lamb shall feed together, and the lion shall eat straw like the bullock" (Isaiah 65:25; see also Isaiah 11:7). But whether these accounts are meant to be taken literally or whether they point to a deeper mystery about a nonviolent cosmic order remains an open question. After all, why should animals in the new Earth eat *anything*—human beings won't be chowing down because we will have spiritual bodies with a whole new set of rules about space, time, and matter, to say nothing of intusseption and ingestion. Eating also requires a before, a during, and an after (before I eat the hamburger, while I eat it, after I ate it), but the end of the world means the end of time, which is the only realm in which befores, durings, and afters exist. C. S. Lewis hoped that as men become more Christ-like when they are drawn upwards into Him perhaps the same higher animals will be drawn into the new creation by their redeemed masters. This intriguing possibility would entail immortalizing animals' mortal souls just as our mortal flesh takes on immortality (1 Corinthians 15:53). But we really can't say for sure that God has this in store for our beloved cats and dogs.

Creation, St. Paul writes, "groans and travails" like a woman in labor (Romans 8:22), but to what will it give birth? All we can say is that creation itself will be delivered from "the bondage of corruption" and "into the glorious liberty of the children of God" (Romans 8:21).

There is one thing you may find missing from the new Heaven and Earth: the Book of Revelation states that there will be no sea (21:1). Surfers and other thalassophiles (that's ocean-lovers), however, can take heart. In Genesis 1:2, the waters represent a primordial soupy chaos, so the lack of a sea does not necessarily mean the obliteration of all things marine but the absence of any lingering chaos in God's perfected order. It is also not a coincidence that the seven-headed, ten-horned beast in Revelation comes from the sea (Revelation 13:1), so the sea's eradication also indicates a complete victory over evil and its sources.

Signs of the Times

And how will we know that the Second Coming is coming? The Scriptures offer some clues, but apocalyptic literature is exceedingly difficult to interpret because of its dense symbolism and because it often speaks of different events in the same breath: Old Testament prophets like Isaiah often conflate the First and Second Comings, and the Gospels often conflate the destruction of Jerusalem in A.D. 70 with the End of the World. But here are nine of the more salient clues:

1. There will be a general preaching of Christianity to the entire world (Matthew 24:14).

2. The Jews will convert *en masse* (Rom. 11:25–26).
3. Enoch and Elijah, who never tasted death (see Genesis 5:23–24 and Hebrews 11:5, Jude 14–15, 2 Kings 2:11, and Malachi 4:5–6) will return.
4. Entire nations will abandon the Christian religion in what Paul calls "the apostasy" or a "falling away" (2 Thessalonians 2:3; see also Luke 18:8).
5. A "man of sin" or "son of perdition" (2 Thessalonians 2:3), also identified as the Antichrist (1 John 2:18), will make himself an adversary of Christ and persecute the Church "at the last time" (1 John 2:18). But both St. Paul and St. John also state that the Antichrist was already around in their own day and age (2 Thessalonians 2:5–6; 1 John 4:3).
6. There will be many calamities such as war, famine, pestilence, and earthquakes (Matthew 24:6–8), as well as strange astronomical phenomena (Matthew 24:29; Luke 21:25–26).
7. The Church will be persecuted (Matthew 24:9) and there will be many false prophets and false Christs (Matthew 24:11, 24).
8. There will be (at least) two auditory indications for the dead to rise from their graves, the voice of the Son of God and an archangel's trumpet (1 Corinthians 15:52; 1 Thessalonians 4:15; John 5:28). From the latter sign comes the proverbial expression "till Gabriel blows his horn."
9. Immediately before Christ's appearance, there "shall appear the sign of the Son of man in heaven " (Matthew 24:30)—most likely, the appearance in the sky of the cross.
10. And my personal favorite: the hearts of fathers will be reconciled to those of their sons and vice versa (Malachi 4:5–6; Sirach 48:10). Truly a sign that the end is nigh!

It is worth noting that most of these signs, such as war and natural disasters and even strange astronomical phenomena, have been with us since the dawn of Christianity. This does not mean that these signs are worthless; on the contrary, we may go so far as to say that they indicate not that the end is nigh, but that the end is *now*. The Bible marks epochs by the different covenants that God made with man (the Noahic, Abrahamic, and so forth), and we are currently living in the final epoch, that of the New Covenant wrought by Jesus Christ. This epoch began with Christ's First Coming and will end with His Second. It is the "fullness of times" (Ephesians 1:10)—it was full at the Incarnation, it is full now, and it will remain full until the very end. If time were a gas tank, the needle would not move off "F" between the first Christmas and the Last Day. In one way, then, we are still living in the age of the apostles, for they lived and we are indeed living in the "last days."

Consequently, these signs remind us to remain ever vigilant and prepared. If there is one common theme about the end of the world in the Bible, it is to be in a constant state of preparedness. Basically, take everything that survivalists or preppers say about being ready for a nuclear attack or home invasion and apply it to your *spiritual life*, for the Lord will come like a thief in the night. (And He won't care if you have three months' worth of canned beans in your fallout shelter.) That way, should you die before the world ends, you'll still be ready to meet your Maker.

Still, Christians have had difficulty resisting the temptation to read the signs of the times and conclude that the Parousia is right around the corner. There was already a strong expectation in the New Testament that the Lord would return before the death of the last apostle—which the New Testament had to correct (John 21:21–23). The barbarian invasions of the western Roman Empire in the fifth century led to the next great wave of worry: with civilization as they knew it crumbling all around them, it certainly felt to the Christian citizens of Rome like the world was ending (in fact, it has been speculated that Ireland was evangelized in such a hurry because folks thought time was running out). Centuries later, many were convinced that A.D. 1000 would mark the end of the "millennium" mentioned in Revelation 12:1 and that Christ was on His way.

In the United States, the nineteenth and twentieth centuries gave rise to frequent and colorful apocalyptic speculation. My favorite example, although it's a bit pathetic: when a family of fundamentalist Christians first saw a Model T Ford, they concluded that the end was near, sold all their property, and waited all night on a hill for Jesus. When credit cards first came out, many thought that it was the 666 Mark of the Beast; today some people are saying the same thing about implanted RFID chips. And do you remember all the ominous emails about how Barack Obama's name was code for the Beast or the abomination of desolation?

Despite the beguiling puzzles in the Bible's apocalyptic literature, Christ and the apostles are insistent about the uncertainty of the day of judgment, the precise time of which is known only to the Father (Acts 1:6-7; Matthew 24:36; Mark 13:32) and that it will come unexpectedly (Matthew 24:27; Luke 21:34; Matthew 24:37). Better, then, to treat every day like it is our last and stop obsessing over a matter that Our Lord says is clearly none of our business.

CHAPTER SIX

How Do We Know? Christian Sources and Confirmations

We have outlined some of the central beliefs of Christianity, but how can we know that these teachings are true? The short answer is the Holy Spirit, who teaches us all things (John 14:26; 16:13). But the Spirit moves in different ways. Let us focus on a few specific witnesses of Christian truth: the Bible, the Church, miracles, the "cloud of witnesses"—that is, the saints—and beauty. Finally, we will take a look at the curious corroborating testimony of reason.

Did you know?

★ The Church determined the books of the Bible, rejecting the "Gospels" of Thomas and Peter

★ Every miracle is a supernatural act, but not every supernatural act is a miracle

★ Miracles occur in every era, but not with the same frequency

★ No religion can be proven true, but many—though not Christianity—can be proven false

The Bible

Dave was not happy. He had just read an op-ed piece in his local paper articulating the biblical critique of same-sex "marriage," and he was moved to post the following comment:

> The Bible supports a variety of antiquated and prejudiced views. It takes for granted throughout the Hebrew Scriptures that women are not equal, that slaves should obey their masters, that being anything other than a man is less than. The Bible was

> written by men in a patriarchical [sic] culture. Men wrote what allowed them to keep their privilege and power, which makes sense, because who wants to destroy societal norms which give you privilege and power? Of course, that is why we should be so thankful for Jesus. He did not consider equality with God as something to be grasped, but he came to dwell among us. He came to destroy racism, classism and homophobia. There is no longer male nor female, slave nor free... for we are all one in Christ Jesus. The redemptive trajectory of Scripture looks forward to a day when people matter more than doctrines, when humanity embraces others with the inclusive Spirit of the law, rather than the exclusive letter of the law.

Dave is confused. He thinks of Jesus as a hippie ushering in an Age of Aquarius in reaction to all that Dark Age stuff from the Old Testament (apparently, Dave hasn't read the New Testament very closely, or he would be just as upset about its statements on patriarchal authority, women, and homosexual acts). But if the Bible is as defective as he claims, how does Dave know that his understanding of Jesus, which is ostensibly derived from the same book, is correct? If the text is so unreliable, how can he speak with confidence about its "redemptive trajectory"?

So let's help Dave out. We'll start by correcting three common misconceptions about the Bible and then offer our own Ten Commandments on how to become a better reader of it.

Misconception #1: "The Bible is a product of its times."

Of course the Bible is a product of its times—in a certain sense. Its books arose out of particular historical, geographical, and linguistic contexts, which is why biblical scholars study history, geography, and Greek and Near Eastern languages. Unlike Muslims, who believe that Allah dictated the entire Qur'an to Mohammed through the angel Gabriel, Christians take a more historically accurate view of our sacred texts. The Bible is like the mystery of the Incarnation itself: as with the Word of God made flesh, so too with the words of God made written. Just as Jesus Christ is not half man and half God but fully human and fully divine, so too are the books of the Bible 100 percent human and 100 percent divine in their origins. That is to say, every word of the Bible was chosen by a human being for reasons all his own; he may not have even had the slightest clue that he was writing something of great significance, let alone something inerrant. At the same time, though, every author (or ancient redactor) of the Bible was somehow being guided or inspired by the Holy Spirit to get the right result. Just as divine providence operates in the world not despite human free will but paradoxically in and through man's freely made decisions, so too is there a hidden cooperation between the human authors of Sacred Scripture and its divine Author.

So Christians take into account human agency and historical context when interpreting the Bible. But because of the divine agency behind the Bible, Christians also recognize that the Scriptures are *more* than a product of their own times, that the Bible is a transcendent set of writings that are as relevant, as reliable, and as true today as the day they were written. (Consequently, Christians have always considered the Old Testament to be as much a part of their inspired canon as the books of the New Testament.) It is here that we see how Dave's assumptions fall woefully short of orthodox Christianity. Dave thinks that the Bible is "antiquated" because it was written "by men in a patriarchical [sic] culture" but he does not take into consideration that God Himself was the author of the Bible—and of the culture in which it was written. It was God who made Abraham the first patriarch, who made Abraham's descendants a great nation, who gave Moses a law for this nation, and who sent prophets to remind this nation of the covenant He had made with them. An ancient Semitic culture didn't create YHWH the Lord God and His law to justify their most powerful men; the Lord God YHWH created the law and this ancient Semitic culture (at least in its essential elements), and He did what He did for good reason. An atheist will, of course, reject this claim and dismiss the Scriptures as a masked play for power. But when a Christian does the same, he cuts himself off at the knees by rejecting a key pillar of his faith. Either his God becomes schizophrenic—first "prejudiced" in the Old Testament, then suddenly all about "people," not "doctrines" in the New—or *he* becomes schizophrenic, believing in an incoherent dualism like the second-century heretic Marcion, who accepted Jesus as Savior but rejected the God of Israel and the Old Testament because they were so despicably "Jewish."

Misconception #2: "The Bible is myth."

Another common misconception about the Bible is that it is a myth. As with the previous misconception, there is a sense in which it can be said to be true—depending on one's definitions. Classicist (and master of mere Christianity) C. S. Lewis knew that "myth" is the English version of the Greek *muthos* or "story." By that reckoning, the Bible is indeed a myth but a "true myth." Lewis converted to Christianity because he came to see that the biblical narrative is "to be understood as 'God's myth' where the great pagan narratives are 'men's myths.'"

But how does God's myth differ from men's myths? Let us begin with the Old Testament and consider how different it is from the world's other myths, especially on the questions of the creation of the cosmos and a lost Golden Age.

In men's myths, there are fantastic creatures such as griffins or dragons or giant turtles. In God's myth (Genesis, that is), there are only natural creatures such as cattle and creeping things and beasts of the field and fowls of the air. Yes, there are dragons here and there in the Bible, but they are usually in the apocalyptic (visionary) writings. And yes, there is a talking snake in the Garden, but it is still a snake, a recognizable animal as opposed to a minotaur. And yes, it is odd that a snake should be talking. It should not be forgotten, though, that the talking serpent is not really a serpent but Satan taking on the appearance of a natural creature. And one of the curious things about God's myth is that it incorporates distinctive elements of men's myths only to disparage them, casting them in a negative light. Men's myths, for example, typically tell the story of some kind of a lost age where the men or demigods were much bigger and stronger than the weaklings of today. You see this nostalgia in Greek mythology and in the epics of Homer. The Old Testament too has its giants, but what does it do with them? It wryly makes fun of them, lumping them with the inauspicious offspring of the "sons of God" and the "daughters of men" (probably the men from Seth's clan and the women from Cain's) who are grandly called "the mighty men of old, the men of renown" (Genesis 6:4). But if they are such men of renown, what are their names? What great feats did they do? Apparently, nothing worth writing down. God is certainly not impressed; on the contrary, He soon after resolves to destroy them all with a Flood.

The Myth That Actually Happened

"The heart of Christianity is a myth, which is also a fact. The old myth of the dying god, without ceasing to be myth, comes down from the heaven of legend and imagination to the earth of history. It happens at a particular date, in a particular place, followed by definable historical consequences. We pass from a Balder or an Osiris, dying nobody knows when or where, to a historical person crucified (it is all in order) under Pontius Pilate. By becoming fact it does not cease to be myth; that is the miracle."

—**C. S. Lewis,** *God in the Dock*

Which brings us to a second difference. In men's myths, the protagonists are great heroes, warriors who are brave, strong, or clever, and who usually meet a tragic but noble end. In God's myth, by contrast, the main human characters are noticeably lacking in martial and hunting skills and are more risible than awe-inspiring. Rather than possessing great strength or courage like the manly men of ancient Babylonian, Greek, and Roman lore, the leading figures in the Old Testament behave in a very imperfect way—creating a darkly humorous effect, rather than nostalgia for the demigods of old. When Prometheus stole fire from the gods, he was proud and defiant, owning up to his deed and accepting the awful punishment. When Adam stole fruit from the garden, he cravenly blamed his wife and was passive-aggressive towards God, showing himself to be anything but a macho man. "The woman whom thou gavest to be with me," he whined, "she gave me of the tree, and I did eat" (Genesis 3:12). Only moments earlier, Adam had been head over heels at the sight of Eve, calling her bone of his bone and flesh of his flesh. Now, he's basically saying that he didn't ask for this woman and that this is all God's fault. What a wuss.

All of the "heroes" of the Old Testament are more or less like this; they defy our worldly expectations of manliness (so much for "patriarchical culture"). Abraham's faith in the Lord is great, but he is a henpecked husband who does Sarah's bidding—resulting in the disastrous business with Ishmael—and who pusillanimously fails to tell the Pharaoh, who is attracted to Sarah, that she is his wife. When Moses is called to lead the Israelites out of Egyptian bondage, rather than gallantly accept his commission he demurs on the grounds that he has a stutter and isn't comfortable with public speaking. Moses sounds more like a fretful Woody Allen character than Hercules or Aeneas.

As for King David, what made him a "man after God's own heart" was not his military prowess or his way with the ladies (with which God was not pleased) but his love for and trust in God, as well as his willingness to repent when he had sinned. Don't be misled: Michelangelo's statue of David is magnificent artistically, but it would be a better portrayal of

Goliath than of David. The biblical David was probably a skinny kid who put his faith not in the might of his arm but in the Lord (that's what made the upset win so spectacular). As with the mysterious antediluvian giants, when "mighty men" like hunters or warriors are mentioned in the Old Testament, it is to put them in their place. Think of Nimrod (Genesis 10:8–9), whose name has become a byword for numbskullism, and the dumb redheaded jock Esau.

Whereas men's myths portray violence as part of the natural fabric of being, God's myth portrays it as a disruption of the original peaceful and intelligible order of creation. In cosmogenic myths such as the Babylonian *Enuma Elish*, there was a primordial battle between the mother goddess Tiamat and her consort Qingu on one hand and the warrior god Marduk on the other. After defeating them, Marduk used Tiamat's blubbery carcass to carve out the cosmos and the slain blood of Qingu to make mankind. The point of the story is to show that the universe and humanity have violence in their blood and that it is therefore natural for men to seek domination through imperial conquest (not to mention that, as we have already seen, this men's myth justifies violence against the feminine).

In the Book of Genesis, in contrast, God creates not through His sword but through His Word, imbuing His creation with an order that is intelligible, the product of wisdom rather than of power and tyrannical might. Moreover, violence is not even a part of God's original creation but a byproduct of human sin.

God's myth consistently upends men's myths and the things men find important. Perhaps that is why, whereas men's myths fall into the category of tragedy, God's myth is a divine comedy that, like a Shakespearean comedy, ends with a wedding (Revelation 19:6–9). The Bible does not fit into the genre of human myth. Indeed, if you define "myth" as men's myths and nothing more, then it may be said that the Bible is anti-mythical, a demythologizing agent that exposes the dark currents and dubious aspirations of human myth.

I See Satan Fall like Lightning by René Girard (Maryknoll, NY: Orbis Books, 2001).

As for the New Testament, since the nineteenth century it has been fashionable to see the Christ story as only one of many myths involving a savior figure or god who dies and comes back to life. But thanks to the work of French anthropologist René Girard, this theory is largely discredited. Girard discovered that ancient myths were designed to promote a sacrificial religion in which the community unites against a victim in an act of spontaneous killing. This act is the culmination of a growing tension within the community brought on by "mimetic contagion"—with more and more people vying for the same object of desire until their desires are united against a random and innocent victim, a "scapegoat" who is blamed for all the community's ills and subsequently murdered. "In this kind of religion," Girard explains, "the community is regarded as innocent and the victim is guilty. Even after the victim has been 'deified,' he is still a criminal in the eyes of the community (note the criminal nature of the gods in pagan mythology). But something happens that begins in the Old Testament. There are many stories that reverse this scapegoat process. In the story of Cain and Abel, the story of Joseph, the Book of Job, and many of the Psalms, the persecuting community is pictured as guilty and the victim is innocent. But Christ, the Son of God, is the ultimate 'scapegoat'—precisely because He is the son of God, and since He is innocent, he exposes all the myths of scapegoating and shows that the victims were innocent and the communities guilty."

The story of the Christ, then, does not repeat the scapegoating of men's myths but exposes it, exonerating the scapegoat (Jesus Christ) and showing the community to be guilty of gratuitous murder. The Gospels are the ultimate demythologizers. Notice that wherever Christianity spreads, bloody sacrifices end. The gig is up, and Satan, the evil force behind the scapegoating process, is exposed as the father of lies.

Misconception #3: "The Bible is full of errors."

Since Christians believe that the Bible is 100 percent inspired by the Holy Spirit, they also believe that it is 100 percent free from error, that it is "inerrant." But great caution must be exercised here. It is one thing to believe that every word of the Bible is true; it is another to claim to know what every verse *means*. In dealing with a series of texts thousands of years old written in different cultural contexts and in different languages, one must be careful not to mistake the meanings. Even the simplest of words can prove surprisingly elusive. Take the word "day." It usually denotes a period of time (divided today into twenty-four units called hours) measured by the earth's rotation around the sun. But in Genesis 1, the sun is not created until the fourth day (Genesis 1:14–19). What, then, is the intended meaning of "day" in these passages: a twenty-four hour period, a thousand-year period (for to the Lord a thousand years is like a day, as it states in 2 Peter 3:8), or simply an organizational unit by which to narrate the creation?

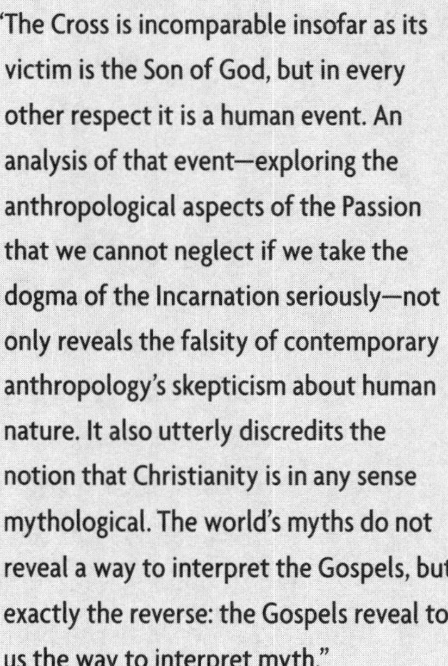

It's the Other Way Around

"The Cross is incomparable insofar as its victim is the Son of God, but in every other respect it is a human event. An analysis of that event—exploring the anthropological aspects of the Passion that we cannot neglect if we take the dogma of the Incarnation seriously—not only reveals the falsity of contemporary anthropology's skepticism about human nature. It also utterly discredits the notion that Christianity is in any sense mythological. The world's myths do not reveal a way to interpret the Gospels, but exactly the reverse: the Gospels reveal to us the way to interpret myth."

—René Girard

Another example: the Hebrew Bible portrays a universe with the earth at the center shielded by a giant dome in the sky called the firmament, through which water enters to form rain and above which the sun, moon, and stars rotate. Is this meant to be a scientific blueprint of the universe, or is it a map for understanding matters pertaining to our salvation? See the final book of St. Augustine's *Confessions* for the latter interpretation. As

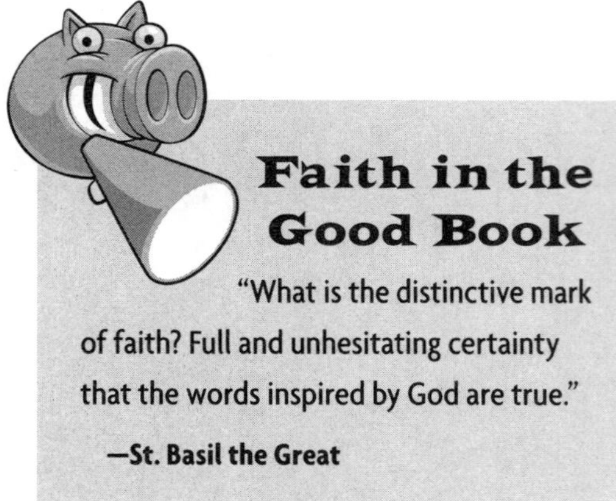

Faith in the Good Book

"What is the distinctive mark of faith? Full and unhesitating certainty that the words inspired by God are true."

—St. Basil the Great

Cesare Baronius once remarked to Galileo, "The Bible teaches us how to go to Heaven, not how the heavens go."

Ten Commandments for Reading the Bible

One of the more laughably naïve assumptions of the so-called Age of Reason, also known as the Enlightenment, is that a dispassionate observer can free himself of all presuppositions and scrutinize an object with complete impartiality. The truth about human knowing is far more complicated. There is no such thing as a self-interpreting text, and there is no such person as a completely neutral reader, since we always bring a lens of interpretation to bear upon what we are examining. The question is not *if* one should have an interpretive framework, but *what* interpretive framework one should employ to tease out what is really going on. The following is our list of Ten Commandments for Reading the Bible to help you bring out the hidden depths and genius of the Bible.

Everyone reads with a lens. The trick is not to despair of ever finding the truth but to find the right lens for the job, one that will magnify more than distort.

1. *Thou shalt read the Bible as a unity.* Treat the Bible like a unified story, because it is. Think of the Scriptures like a movie. A movie is the work of many hands: directors, producers, screenwriters, stagehands, actors, and film editors. Each will have his own opinion, and they may not always align. The movie itself may go through several rounds of edits that change its original meaning significantly. And yet when you sit down to watch a movie, you have only question in mind: Does it all hang together? Is it a good movie or not? It doesn't matter whether it took one person or one thousand to make

the final product; that product is to be judged on its own merits. The same is true of the Bible. Many biblical scholars wear themselves out with the impossible task of "unscrambling the omelet" in Robert Alter's immortal phrase, trying to figure out which author or community wrote this and which redactor did that; and although their work is not entirely without value, they are missing the big picture. Despite all its diversity, the Bible hangs together magnificently, and it has some rather important things to teach us. And if there are any apparent contradictions or inconsistencies, as with any other great work of art, human or divine, these hiccups are there for a reason. Perhaps it is to reveal something about the character who is speaking; perhaps it is to reveal a deeper truth hidden below the surface. Every detail in the Bible reveals a mystery, says Saint Gregory the Great, even and perhaps especially in the more puzzling details.

2. *Thou shalt appreciate development.* The Bible is consistent, but consistency does not mean a lack of change. Be attentive to a dialectical movement in the Bible, where the relationship between God and mankind develops or where God creates certain dispensations in history, permitting some things (divorce, for example) in one age but not in another. Some practices endorsed in one part of the Bible—the command to kill all the Canaanites down to the last man, woman, and child (Deuteronomy 7:1–5, 20:16–18)—can be quite shocking. We'll explain how to deal with the shocking parts of the Bible in our Fourth and Fifth Commandments. For now, it suffices to note that Christians can't (and don't) use passages to justify genocide today because they know that such verses are not a carte blanche for mass murder but a specific command uttered at a specific time for a specific reason, made before the game-changing and unsurpassable New Covenant. Indeed, in the Old Testament God often takes over a practice common at the time—polygamy, or the mistreatment of prisoners of war—not in order to perpetuate it but in order to wean His people off of it. Like it or not, Yahweh has much in common with supply-side Republicans: both

understand that excessive regulation of an industry or activity leads to its eventual demise.

One of the most significant differences between the Bible and the Qur'an (besides the fact that only one of them was authored by the Holy Ghost) is that the Bible has this dialectical quality whereas the Qur'an does not. As a result, a fervent Muslim can take the genocidal passages of the Qur'an and apply them to his jihad today whereas a fervent Christian cannot do the same thing with the Old Testament without first having to prove that this passage can be applied literally in light of the new and everlasting Covenant.

On the other hand, it is important to note that biblical development does *not* mean that everything from the earlier books is outdated. The ritual laws in Leviticus against the consumption of pork or physical impurity are no longer binding on Christians; the moral laws in Leviticus against theft, adultery, and homosexual activity still are (just ask St. Paul). Development does not mean evolution run amok, where a fish becomes a unicorn. There is continuity as well as change, with the essence of the thing (in this case, the natural laws of morality) remaining the same.

3. *Thou shalt recognize the different sections of the sacred library.* The Bible is a library of fascinating and truthful books. The word *Biblia* means "books" rather than "book," and this Book of books was written by different authors in different genres over a long period of time. And yet this sacred library with its great literary diversity still forms a single coherent story. *E pluribus unum*, you might say.

Recognizing that the Bible consists of different genres of literature is important because different genres demand to be read differently. A collection of poetry and a scientific textbook may both contain nothing but the truth, but a reader with half a brain does not read a poem in the same way as he reads scientific prose, for a poet does not present the truth in the same way as a scientist. Likewise, the Bible contains a variety of different kinds of literature: poetry such as the Psalms or the Song of Solomon, prophecy, apocalyptic literature like the Book of Revelation, legal literature, wisdom literature, epistles or letters, history such as the Gospels, and even apparently fictional stories like the parables Jesus tells. One must even be attentive to several genres within a single book of the Bible: the historicity of the opening chapters of Genesis may not be the same as the historicity of its later chapters.

4. *Thou shalt not read like a stick-in-the-mud.* Be ready for irony, understatement, overstatement, and disconcerting silence. The Holy Spirit sometimes has a wry and dark sense of humor and likes to surprise the reader by what He says and by what He doesn't say. When Adam and Eve eat of the fruit of the tree of the knowledge of good and evil in order "to be as gods," they immediately grow ashamed, make aprons out of leaves, and try to hide from the Lord God. After God replaces the leaf-aprons with clothes made out of animal skins, he says, "Behold, the man is become as one of us, to know good and evil" (Genesis 3:22). The joke, of course, is that man already knew good and evil before he fell; he knew that not eating the forbidden fruit was good and that eating it was evil. What he gained through his disobedience was a firsthand experience or taste of evil, but instead of making him godlike it made him a blushing, sniveling coward clothed like a beast. So when God says that man has joined the divine gang, He is being ironic, drawing attention to how far Adam has fallen.

No Generic Answer

"Christians sometimes get asked, 'Do you read the Bible literally?' But this is like asking, 'Do you read the Library literally?' Well, of course that would depend on what section I was in. If I were in the science section I might read rather literally and technically. But if I were in the poetry section I would read rather differently with an openness to allegory, hyperbole, and the like. Other interpretive modes would be operative in the history section, the computer and technical manual section, the science fiction section, philosophy, religion and so forth. When walking into a library we have enough sophistication to make distinctions as to the genre of a book, its historical period, its purpose and so forth."

—Monsignor Charles Pope

The Holy Spirit is also a master of understatement. After the Bible devotes an entire chapter to describing David's nefarious behavior in impregnating the married woman Bathsheba, trying to cover it up, and eventually having her husband killed, the narrator says tersely, "But the thing that David had done displeased the Lord" (2 Samuel 11:27). Classic.

Overstatement is also operative in the Scriptures. When the Israelites come to the Promised Land, the Lord God tells them to destroy all of the inhabitants. On the surface, this sounds like a green light for genocide, but hyperbole was a common device in war rhetoric at the time, much like the "wipe 'em out!" sports rhetoric of our own day and age. Joshua is said to have done everything the Lord wanted him to (Joshua 10:40) and yet there were Canaanites still living in Israel a generation later (Joshua 23:12–13), so it must not have been God's intention to see every Canaanite slaughtered. There is overstatement in the New Testament as well, as the Sermon on the Mount illustrates. Gouging out your right eye (Matthew 5:29) is not literally a good cure for lust—it would still leave the left eye for peeking and winking.

Finally, the biblical narrator will sometimes hold his tongue. In Genesis 19, Lot is hosting two male strangers when the men of Sodom surround his house and demand to "know" them (that's right: know in the biblical sense). In a very misguided application of the rules of hospitality, Lot offers the Sodomites his two virgin daughters instead. Infuriated, the men promise to do worse to Lot than what they were going to do to his guests. Fortunately, the strangers turn out to be angels who strike the intruders blind (4–14). After the destruction of Sodom, Lot's daughters think that their father is the world's last surviving male, and so to propagate the race they get him drunk and sleep with him. From their offspring came Israel's unfriendly neighbors, the Moabites and Ammonites.

One would expect a strident condemnation of this revolting act of incest, but there is nary a peep from the narrator. So does that mean that incest is okay, or there is no moral to the story? Look again. Lot was willing to have his daughters sexually violated out of his misguided reaction to the destructive behavior of the men of Sodom; not long after, he is sexually violated by his daughters out of their misguided reaction to the destruction of the men of Sodom. The sins of the father may be visited on his children, but the children may return the visit.

5. *Thou shalt know how to deal with the shocking.* Be sure to have good shock absorbers when reading the Bible, and know how to respond to the jarring bumps. Proper responses depend much on context and which section of the sacred library the passages are in, but here are three strategies to have at hand.

First, it may be hyperbole. As we saw with the example of God's endorsement of Canaanite genocide, the genre of war rhetoric may mean that God did not intend those statements to be taken literally.

Second, the shock may be there to warn us of divine judgment. To take the same example, God has allowed countless nations and peoples to be confined to the ash heap of history, often for their own crimes and corruption. He would have certainly been justified in such a judgment against the Canaanites, who were practitioners of adultery, homosexuality, transvestitism, pederasty, bestiality, and above all, infant sacrifice (archeological evidence suggests that children ranging from newborns to four-year-olds were burned by the thousands). God chooses many different means to execute His judgments, ranging from warring nations to bad weather. In this case, the only thing different is that He has singled out the Israelites to be His agent of judgment.

Third, the shocking passage may be a signpost for a deeper spiritual truth. Psalm 137 ends with the following jaw-dropper:

> O daughter of Babylon, who art to be destroyed; happy shall he be that rewardeth thee as thou hast served us; Happy shall

> he be, that taketh thy little ones and dasheth them upon a stone (8–9).

Now there is already a clue that the psalmist is not advocating infanticide: he has called the mighty empire of Babylon a "daughter," and hence her "little ones" are her adult citizens. But even so, is the psalmist praying for the annihilation of the Babylonians? Who knows the mind of the human author when he was writing it (we can only assume the best), but the text as it is presented to us has additional spiritual meaning when viewed in light of the rest of the Scriptures. Babylon, notes St. Augustine, is a biblical byword for sexual vice and other detestable things (see Revelation 17:5), and so when you plug in this meaning its "little ones" would be the inveterate lusts with which we are born and which we must quickly dash against the Rock that is Christ (1 Corinthians 10:4) lest they, as Augustine says, "gain the strength of evil habit." The right way to treat our lust is "when it is [still] little, dash it." Spiritual truths can be concealed behind the most striking of carnal images; to uncover those truths often requires connecting the dots to a broader biblical context.

Christianity's foes are well aware of the shocking parts of the Bible. The rabid Richard Dawkins latches on to these sections as proof that the biblical God is immoral (claiming the moral high ground while denying objective morality is one of the secular Left's most spectacular magic tricks). Personally, I find the Bible's troublesome parts the most fascinating: they wake me up from my dogmatic slumbers and force me to play the detective looking for a clue to their resolution, and in the process I become a better sleuth, not only of the Bible but of the reality around me. There are Christian fiction writers today who never use violence in their novels because they find it objectionable or impious. I thank God that the Holy Spirit never commissioned them to write for the Bible.

6. *Thou shalt recognize figurative meanings.* We have seen how "Babylon," "little ones," and "rock" are figurative expressions for vice, lusts, and Christ. The Bible is often written in a way accommodated to crude human perception. The greatest revelation of God's nature in the Old Testament is the meaning of God's holy name YHWH—"I AM THAT I AM" (Exodus 3:14). This astonishing definition affirms that God is pure and transcendent being outside all of our usual categories, especially the category of body. Yet this same Testament uses a variety of corporeal and anthropomorphic descriptions of the almighty and all-knowing God who walks in the cool of the day (Genesis 3:8), regrets a decision (Genesis 6:6), gets angry (Exodus 4:14), and so on. These descriptions might make the Bible seem schizophrenic, but in reality they are a condescension to a beginner's level of comprehension, starting with simple images in order to draw us into more advanced mysteries. The Bible is a good teacher, and like any good teacher it starts where the student is—not in order to confirm him where he is, but to lead him to where he has not yet gone. These bodily images also give greater delight to our learning, for they are vivid and memorable and effective at all stages of learning or aptitude.

Reading Literally

"People who take [biblical] symbols literally might as well think that when Christ told us to be like doves, He meant that we were to lay eggs."

—**C. S. Lewis,** *Mere Christianity*

This is the meaning of the famous verse about the letter of the law killing but the spirit giving life (2 Corinthians 3:6). Folks like our friend Dave use this passage to suggest that Jesus doesn't really care about the rules—especially the rules of morality or Church discipline—but Paul is not speaking here about rules or actions at all but about how to interpret difficult passages in the Old Law, such as the ones we have been discussing. For Paul, "letter" refers to a narrow literalism that takes primitive corporeal images at face

They Got It Back in the Fourth Century

"Regarding the things and names in the Bible: Some things have no existence but are spoken of; other things do exist but are not spoken of; some neither exist nor are spoken of, and some both exist and are spoken of. Do you ask me for proof of this? I am ready to give it. According to Scripture God 'sleeps' and 'is awake,' 'is angry,' 'walks,' has 'the Cherubim for His Throne.' And yet when did He become liable to passion, and when did you ever hear that God has a body? This, then, is not really a fact but a figure of speech. For we have given names according to our own comprehension from our own attributes to those of God. His remaining silently apart from us, and as it were 'not caring for us,' for reasons known only to Himself, is what we call His 'sleeping'; for our own sleep is such a state of inactivity. And again, His sudden turning to do us good is the 'waking up'; for waking is the dissolution of sleep, as visitation is of turning away. And when He punishes, we say He is 'angry'; for so it is with us that punishment is the result of anger. And His working, now here now there, we call 'walking'; for walking is change from one place to another. His resting among the Holy Hosts, and as it were loving to dwell among them, is His 'sitting and being enthroned'; this, too, is from ourselves, for God rests nowhere as He does in the Saints. His swiftness of moving is called 'flying,' and His watchful care is called His 'Face,' and His giving and bestowing is His 'hand'; and, in a word, every one of the powers or activities of God is depicted for us as something corporeal."

—Gregory of Nazianzus

value whereas "spirit" refers to a non-carnal level of meaning that points to the life of the soul or God.

7. *Thou shalt recognize types and antitypes.* A type (*typos*—see 1 Corinthians 10:6, 11) is a repeating pattern, figure, or image usually found in the Old Testament that serves as a foreshadowing of something in the New Testament, called the *antitype* (*antitypos*—see 1 Peter 3:21). To use Saint Peter's own example, the Flood, which brought death to many but life to the eight souls in Noah's ark, is a type for the waters of baptism (the antitype), which bring death to the old self and life in Christ Jesus. Types are all over

the Old Testament: types of baptism such as the Flood, baby Moses being saved in a rush basket floating in the Nile, and the crossing of the Red Sea; types of Jesus and His high priestly sacrifice such as Melchizedek and the Levitical offerings; types of the Eucharist such as manna in the desert, the shewbread in the Temple, and the unleavened bread during the Passover.

Recognizing the typological character of the Bible is not only important in appreciating the harmony between the two Testaments; it is also useful in delving the hidden meaning of troublesome passages. Consider the very disturbing commandment for Abraham to sacrifice his only son Isaac (Genesis 22:1–15). If we wanted to, we could spend a lifetime exploring the meaning of this shocking story. We could dwell on the back story of Isaac's miraculous birth and God's promise concerning it; on the possible motives and rationale behind the Lord's jaw-dropping command; on the motives behind Abraham's unquestioned obedience and the contrast between his reticence here and his vocal concerns about the destruction of Sodom and Gomorrah earlier (Genesis 18:16–33); on whether this test by God violates His own law; on the historical and social context of this sacrifice, and so forth.

But there is a second sense to this biblical story as well, a sense that only the hidden divine Author could have generated, and it is disclosed in the curious details of the narrative. Why, for instance, is this the sacrifice of an only son, born of a divine promise and a miraculous conception? Why is the location of the sacrifice a mount or hill? Why does Isaac, the sacrificial victim, carry the wood for the holocaust offering on his back? Why does Abraham, when his son asks where the victim is, answer that God Himself will provide the sacrifice? Why, after the angel stops Abraham, is a ram, whose horns are caught in a *thorn* bush, sacrificed in Isaac's place? What we see here is a type or a foreshadowing of Christ's sacrifice on the cross. Perhaps the sacrifice of Isaac will never fully make sense on its own, but if we recognize its typological character we can at least say that what God prevented Abraham from doing to his son He Himself would ultimately allow to happen to His own son out of love for fallen mankind.

8. *Thou shalt watch out for cultural peculiarities.* Numbers are a good example of how something so apparently precise can be conditioned by its native culture. When we say "thanks a million," we do not intend to offer exactly 1,000,000 thank yous: for speakers of American English, a million here symbolizes plenitude or abundance. Idioms of this sort are not universal: for the ancient Romans, the number 600 had the same significance as our 1,000,000—inflation, I guess. In Revelation 7:4, 14:1, and 14:3, the number of the elect is listed at 144,000, but this does not mean that only 144,000 souls from Adam to the Second Coming will be saved (let's hope not!). One hundred and forty-four is the sum of 12 x 12, a squaring of the twelve tribes of Israel, which is multiplied by 1,000, a number signifying completion or abundance.

Another example: when Jesus said that He will rise from the dead "in three days," He is not saying that the time between His death and His resurrection will be exactly seventy-two hours. Rather, He is using a Hebrew mode of counting, with the first day being the day on which He would die and the third being two days after.

9. *Thou shalt read with the Church.* For the ultimate takeaway, read the Bible with the Church and be on guard against private interpretation (2 Peter 1:20). The Bible, as we shall see, is the Church's book, and so it makes sense that the Church would have a leg-up on biblical interpretation. But is not following this Ninth Commandment a form of circular reasoning? Not necessarily. As we have already seen, there is no such thing as a self-interpreting text and no such person as a completely neutral reader. Atheists such as Penn Jillette and Richard Carrier claim that reading the Bible is a sure way to induce *atheism*; David Silverman, the president of American Atheists, has bluntly stated, "I gave a Bible to my daughter. That's how you make atheists." These men probably think that they are simply being rational and dispassionate, but

when your father is a prominent atheist who gives you a Bible and says "read it," do you really think that you will be able to do so utterly free of his bias? Atheists do not read the Bible from a detached and impartial point of view but with a hermeneutic or lens of exaggerated suspicion and an inquisitorial hunt for any "gotcha" evidence that might discredit divine revelation. This, we submit, is a distorted way to read *any* book, let alone the Bible. Since it is inevitable that some interpretive lens is involved in reading a text, it might as well be the most reliable lens available, the one least likely to overlook or misconstrue vital data.

Such a lens is especially important where the Bible is concerned, in order to clarify key points of biblical teaching. The early Arian heresy latched on to John 14:28, "the Father is greater than I," as proof that Jesus Christ is not consubstantial with (of the same stuff as) God the Father, whereas orthodox Christians latched on to John 20:28, where Thomas declares Jesus to be "My lord and my God," as proof that He is. Which party was right? It took the Council of Nicaea in A.D. 325 to declare that Jesus is indeed equal to and consubstantial with the Father as the Second Person of the Holy Trinity and "less than" the Father only with respect to His assumed human nature.

Conclusion: the ancient and unbroken creeds of the Church and its living authority today are not thumbs on the scales but a golden key that unlocks the door to the treasury of the Scriptures.

10. *Thou shalt be humble.* A corollary to reading with the Church is reading with humility. One of the reasons that the aforementioned atheists have gleaned so little from the Bible is that they are approaching it with pride. They are hardly the first to do so. In the fourth century a brilliant young man named Augustine who had been educated on the finest literature of the day tried reading the Bible on his own, but instead of falling in love with it, he was repulsed by its low style. The Scriptures "seemed to me unworthy to be compared with the majesty of Cicero," he later wrote. "My conceit was repelled by their simplicity, and I had not the mind to penetrate

Most Improved Reading Score

"Now that I heard them expounded so convincingly, I saw that many passages in these books which had at one time struck me as absurdities, must be referred to the profundity of mystery. Indeed the authority of Scripture seemed to be more to be revered and more worthy of devoted faith in that it was at once a book that all could read and read easily, and yet preserved the majesty of its mystery in the deepest part of its meaning: for it offers itself to all in the plainest words and the simplest expressions, yet demands the closest attention of the most serious minds. Thus it receives all within its welcoming arms, and at the same time brings a few direct to You by narrow ways: yet these few would be fewer still but for this twofold quality by which it stands so lofty in authority yet draws the multitude to its bosom by its holy lowliness. So I dwelt upon these things and You were near me, I sighed and You heard me, I was wavering uncertainly and You guided me, I was going the broad way of the world and You did not forsake me."

—Augustine of Hippo, *Confessions*

into their depths. They were indeed of a nature to grow in Your little ones. But I could not bear to be a little one; I was only swollen with pride, but to myself I seemed a very big man." The Bible's simple style and syntax make it easy for a haughty member of the elite to dismiss the sacred text as primitive or backwards. But in a sense this is God's plan all along. For just as God resists the proud but gives grace to the humble (see James 4:6 and 1 Peter 5:5), so too does He grant wisdom only to His "little ones." Think of biblical style as a screening mechanism in which the only people allowed to see the spectacular Gothic cathedral within are the ones willing to bend the neck to get through the low entrance. Years later, when St. Augustine picked up the Bible again, this time with a much humbler attitude, he marveled at how its "holy lowliness" drew both the simple and the educated into the truth, provided that both had checked their pride at the door.

Even if you are not convinced that the Bible's "lowly" style has a special screening quality ordained by divine providence, still a basic rule for reading any text is to approach it with an open and *modest* mind, that is, with a sincere resolve to give the work the benefit of the doubt and with a genuine willingness to learn from it. If you approach a work, any work, with the conviction that you will gain nothing from it, your wish will come true, for your prejudice will create a self-fulfilling prophecy and you will become impervious to whatever wisdom might be there. The inability to read a book properly is a virtual pandemic these days, especially where older works are concerned, since the average Westerner today thinks that he might be able to learn *about* the past but has little to learn *from* the past, which (he has been led to believe) is nothing but a parade of bigoted and ignorant dead white males who didn't have the Internet. An individual with that attitude is all but unteachable as long as he continues to marinate in this historicist arrogance.

An Authoritative Interpretation

"Then he said unto them, 'O fools, and slow of heart to believe all that the prophets have spoken! Ought not Christ to have suffered these things, and so to enter into His glory?' And beginning at Moses and all the prophets, He expounded unto them in all the scriptures the things concerning himself."

—Luke 24:25–26

The Church

The Bible, we have seen, is the Church's book. It was the Church that, guided by the Holy Spirit, sifted through all of the early writings that claimed to be inspired and recognized the ones that really were (the Gospels according to Matthew, Mark, Luke, and John were judged to be the real deal, for example, while the so-called Gospels of Thomas or of Peter were judged to be specious). Historical scholarship has confirmed the wisdom of the early Church in this regard, for all of the apocryphal literature that the Church rejected was later discovered to be written much later than the canonical Gospels and infected by the goofy heresy of Gnosticism. The Bible's Table

A Living Institution

"I have another far more solid and central ground for submitting to it as a faith, instead of merely picking up hints from it as a scheme. And that is this: that the Christian Church in its practical relation to my soul is a living teacher, not a dead one. It not only certainly taught me yesterday, but will almost certainly teach me to-morrow. Once I saw suddenly the meaning of the shape of the cross; some day I may see suddenly the meaning of the shape of the mitre. One fine morning I saw why windows were pointed; some fine morning I may see why priests were shaven. Plato has told you a truth; but Plato is dead. Shakespeare has startled you with an image; but Shakespeare will not startle you with any more. But imagine what it would be to live with such men still living, to know that Plato might break out with an original lecture to-morrow, or that at any moment Shakespeare might shatter everything with a single song. The man who lives in contact with what he believes to be a living Church is a man always expecting to meet Plato and Shakespeare to-morrow at breakfast. He is always expecting to see some truth that he has never seen before."

—**G. K. Chesterton,** *Orthodoxy*

of Contents did not fall out of the sky from Heaven; it is guaranteed by what Paul in his First Epistle to Timothy calls "the pillar and ground of the truth," the Church (3:15).

But beyond its role in establishing the canon of Scripture, the Church is an essential component of Christian identity, belief, and practice. The Bible calls it the Bride of Christ (Revelation 21:9), Christ's Mystical Body (Ephesians 4:12, 5:30) built upon the foundation of the Apostles and prophets (Ephesians 2:20), against which the jaws of death will not prevail (Matthew 16:18) and which the Holy Spirit will never abandon (John 14:16)—and all this despite the fact that Jesus Christ clearly chose imperfect human leaders to govern His Church (the Apostles weren't exactly to the manor born, and they made mistakes even after they received the Holy Spirit) and despite the fact that Jesus vividly described how His Church would be riddled with scandals and bad eggs until His return (Matthew 13:24–30 and 47–50).

Sadly, in our own day and age Christians must ask "which Church?" The first major split in Christendom occurred in A.D. 1054 when the Catholic and Orthodox Churches parted ways; five hundred years later, the Protestant Reformation led to the proliferation of numerous new ecclesial communities. It is beyond the scope of this little PIG to identify which of these contenders is the true Church founded by Jesus Christ; we can only stress that it is the duty of every believer and every seeker to raise this question and answer it with the utmost care. In his Preface to *Mere Christianity*, C. S. Lewis reminds his readers that although his goal is "to explain and defend the belief that has been common to nearly all Christians at all times," he does not want to give the impression that someone can believe in this pure or "mere" Christianity without belonging to a church. Mere Christianity, he continues, "is more like a hall out of which doors open into several rooms. If I can bring anyone into that hall I shall have done what I attempted. But it is in the rooms, not in the hall, that there are fires and chairs and meals. The hall is a place to wait in, a place from which to try the various doors, not a place to live in."

But how does one choose the right door? Again we can do no better than quote Lewis: "In plain language, the question should never be: 'Do I like that kind of service?' but 'Are these doctrines true: Is holiness here? Does my conscience move me towards this? Is my reluctance to knock at this door due to my pride, or my mere taste, or my personal dislike of this particular doorkeeper?'"

Miracles

In Christianity, miracles are a funny thing. On the one hand, Jesus gently chides those who need miracles to confirm the truth about Himself (John 4:48); on the other, Jesus performs miracles in order to confirm the truth about Himself (John 4:46–54). Jesus is aware of our human weakness and graciously condescends to it by authenticating His message with miraculous deeds, even though the entire point of His message is to be moved by love and faith and not razzle-dazzle displays of power. Perhaps it is to keep the central focus on individual belief and not awe over the miraculous that God performs some miracles from time to time but not too many of them.

What exactly is a miracle? It is an extraordinary action of God truly beyond the power and order of created nature (not just beyond our current knowledge of nature and its causes). Miracles are the result of a supernatural intervention on God's part. Not everything supernatural is miraculous (sanctifying grace, for example) but everything miraculous is supernatural. And a miraculous intervention is by definition out of the ordinary: God saves or sanctifies countless souls every day, but He does not heal people of incurable diseases every day. Further, the ultimate author of the miracle must be God, either working directly or through the agency of an angel or a human being. Demons cannot perform miracles but only manipulate phenomena so that it appears that their actions are miraculous. Whereas Moses performed genuine miracles wrought by God, the Pharaoh's magicians were practicing "their enchantments" (Exodus 7:22)—either cleverly similar parlor tricks or a more sinister dabbling in demonic deceit (Exodus 7:8–8:19). Either way, even the magicians could tell the difference between a genuine miracle and their own handiwork; when they were unable to replicate the plague of gnats, they informed Pharaoh, "This is the finger of God" (Exodus 8:19).

A miracle can be "beyond" nature's power or order in a number of ways. It can be something that nature could never have produced on its own, like our glorified bodies at the end of time. Or it can be something quite natural in itself, like eyesight, marvelously coming to the pupil-less eyes of a blind person, as was the case with seven-year-old Gemma di Giorgi when she was healed by Padre Pio in 1946. (Gemma, who is still alive today, can see fine despite the fact that her eyes continue to have no pupils.) Finally, it can be something natural like rain or lightning ("fire from Heaven") but coming at the command of a prophet (see 1 Kings 18:36–38). By this strict definition, things that we often call miraculous, like the normal birth of a baby or healing from an illness are wonderful things indeed but not miracles.

A common objection to miracles is that they are a "violation" of nature. But an operation that occurs above or beyond nature is not necessarily a violation of it. When a farmer plants corn, he controls nature and gets more out of it than if it had been left alone, but he is not violating it. So too with God and miracles. Even some of the more spectacular miracles, such as bringing the dead back to life, stay within certain natural boundaries. Note that reanimating a corpse involves reuniting it with its soul and hence *restoring* nature's prior arrangement. In Greek mythology, one creature is often changed into another without the slightest regard to the laws of nature. In Christianity, there are no such metamorphoses; a human corpse becomes a human being once again, not a camel or a salamander. And in those cases where one thing is turned into another (such as water into wine at the Wedding of Cana), God accelerates a natural process whereby water is absorbed into grapes and grapes are fermented into wine.

There are four basic possibilities in the case of any claimed miracle. First, it could be an honest mistake—for example about the severity of the disease cured or the problem solved, or about what actually cured or solved it. Second, it could be a case of fraud, an attempt to deceive either by a chiseler (like some of the 1980s televangelists) or a demon. Third, the alleged miracle could be the result of the placebo effect, in which a person so sincerely believes that good is going to happen that in fact it does. Such events would not be miraculous strictly speaking, but we should still thank God for them, just as we thank God for aspirin when we have a splitting headache. And fourth, the miracle could be real. How the authenticity of a miracle is verified depends on the investigators. The Catholic Church has a clear list of criteria and a strict vetting process for judging miracles, usually in connection with the canonization of a saint. For a healing to be miraculous, a committee of theologians and scientific experts must determine through various testimonies and medical records that 1) a patient had an illness for which no cure was known, so that there was no medical or natural chance of recovery; 2) the patient was fully cured; 3) the cure was spontaneous, instantaneous, complete, and enduring; and 4) physicians have no natural or medical explanation for the recovery.

Miracles occur in every Christian age (including our own) but not always with the same frequency. When the Church was still young, numerous miracles confirmed the preaching of the Apostles and their claim that they were carrying out the mission of Christ. Today, miraculous healings continue to occur throughout the Christian world, along with Eucharistic miracles and the incorruption of saints' bodies in the Catholic and Eastern Orthodox Churches. Some miracles have been instrumental in helping an entire people to recognize the truth of the Gospel, as when the apparitions of Our Lady of Guadalupe led to mass conversions of Native Americans in Mexico. Other miracles seem to have a more private purpose, providing an individual with consolation or hope in a dark hour.

But God also uses different "signs and wonders" besides miracles in the strict sense. As the Church grew over the centuries, other kinds of testimony to God's greatness became more prominent: in the fourth and fifth centuries, for instance, instead of lepers being cured, crowds of men and women were living holy lives of extraordinary charity and chastity as monks and nuns. In our own time, the "miracle" of Mother Teresa of Calcutta is not that she worked supernatural cures but that she provided natural aid to the poorest of the poor with a superhuman loving kindness.

And as Thomas Aquinas noted, perhaps the greatest miracle in Christianity is that it spread at all. It really is quite remarkable that a tiny offshoot of Judaism preaching meekness and sexual purity should have not only survived three centuries of Roman persecution but triumphed over an empire and a culture that prided itself on military valor and worldly conquest—and all through peaceful persuasion. This new religion, moreover, was led not by well-educated or well-placed men but simple fishermen who were flawed vessels. And the same wonder repeated itself in the spread of Christianity among the barbarian tribes of Europe. How on earth did some monks with funny haircuts who had foresworn all violence convince the medieval vikings to stop their murderous piracy and embrace Christ? To paraphrase the French poet Paul Claudel, who had probably listened to one too many lackluster sermons, surely the greatest miracle of Christianity is that it spread through preaching.

Sociologists often point to certain conditions in a native culture that help create fertile soil, so to speak, for the seeds of the Gospel. Fair enough, but Aquinas's point still stands: the peaceful spread of a nonviolent, almost effeminate religion with extremely high moral standards among warlike peoples east and west, north and south, is impossible to explain without divine providence. It is as "miraculous" as the preservation of the Jews, who have survived historical depredations suffered by no other people in world history—and survived. Moreover, neither the spread of Christianity to the four corners of the globe nor the survival of the Jewish people happened by chance; both were prophesied long before the fact in the Sacred Scriptures. By contrast, Aquinas notes how the rise of Islam is no great mystery, but rather something that can be explained in completely human terms. It spread largely at the point of a sword and succeeded largely because it let macho men do the two things they most want to do: copulate and fight. Islam offers polygamy on earth and the promise of a harem in Heaven, and instead of admonishing them to turn the other cheek, it gives its adherents a green light to subdue the world by force.

Compare and Contrast

"This wonderful conversion of the world to the Christian faith is the clearest witness of the signs given in the past; so that it is not necessary that they should be further repeated, since they appear most clearly in their effect... On the other hand, those who founded sects committed to erroneous doctrines proceeded in a way that is opposite to this. The point is clear in the case of Muhammad. He seduced the people by promises of carnal pleasure to which the concupiscence of the flesh goads us. His teaching also contained precepts that were in conformity with his promises, and he gave free rein to carnal pleasure. In all this, as is not unexpected, he was obeyed by carnal men. As for proofs of the truth of his doctrine, he brought forward only such as could be grasped by the natural ability of anyone with a very modest wisdom. Indeed, the truths that he taught he mingled with many fables and with doctrines of the greatest falsity. He did not bring forth any signs produced in a supernatural way, which alone fittingly gives witness to divine inspiration; for a visible action that can be only divine reveals an invisibly inspired teacher of truth. On the contrary, Muhammad said that he was sent in the power of his arms—which are signs not lacking even to robbers and tyrants! What is more, no wise men, men trained in things divine and human, believed in him from the beginning. Those who believed in him were brutal men and desert wanderers, utterly ignorant of all divine teaching, through whose numbers Muhammad forced others to become his followers by the violence of his arms."

—**Thomas Aquinas,** *Summa contra Gentiles*

Miracles are a powerful reminder of God's sovereignty over nature and of His triumphant care for us. They confirm believers in the Faith as well as lead nonbelievers to it. That said, although every true believer assents without hesitation to the existence of miracles, the prudent believer approaches specific claims that such-and-such an event is unequivocally a miracle with healthy skepticism—at least until the claim is evaluated by a competent authority. Nor is it ideal to base one's faith on miracles personally observed. After Thomas saw the risen Lord with his own two eyes and presumably placed his finger in His still open nail holes, Jesus said to him, "Thomas, because thou hast seen Me, thou hast believed: blessed are they that have not seen, and yet have believed" (John 20:29).

So Great a Cloud of Witnesses

So there are many reasons for believing in the truth of Christianity, or at least for respecting it as reasonable. But at the end of the day people become Christian not because of rational argument but because of an encounter with the person of Jesus Christ. This can happen dramatically, as when Saul of Tarsus was struck down on the road to Damascus, heard the voice of Christ, and went on to become St. Paul the Apostle. But more often than not it happens indirectly, through recognizing the truth, beauty, and goodness of Christ through agents such as the Bible, solid preaching, or His Church.

Two other such agents are the communion of saints and beauty. Before becoming Pope Benedict XVI, Cardinal Joseph Ratzinger wrote, "I have often affirmed my conviction that the true apology of Christian faith, the most convincing demonstration of its truth against every denial, are the saints and the beauty that the faith has generated."

The example of the saints, referred to in the Epistle to the Hebrews as a great cloud of witnesses (12:1), is a powerful thing. Cicero spoke of a "moral beauty" that he called *honestum*; Christians speak of an even more compelling beauty that they call holiness. Think about it: Isn't there something beautiful about a person who is radiant, loving, patient, kind, and joyful? Doesn't someone like that have an aura of beauty that can dwarf any physical defects? Such is the magnetic beauty of holy men and women, a beauty that is as palpable and as wonderful as the greatest natural wonders of the world. The lives of the saints—whether

Difficult, but Not Impossible

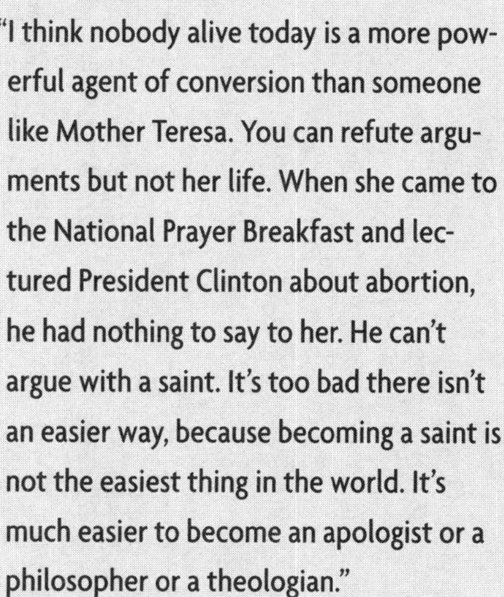

"I think nobody alive today is a more powerful agent of conversion than someone like Mother Teresa. You can refute arguments but not her life. When she came to the National Prayer Breakfast and lectured President Clinton about abortion, he had nothing to say to her. He can't argue with a saint. It's too bad there isn't an easier way, because becoming a saint is not the easiest thing in the world. It's much easier to become an apologist or a philosopher or a theologian."

—attributed to Peter Kreeft

they have been officially recognized by a church as such or have gone largely unnoticed—are a vital confirmation of the truth of the Gospel. As St. Philip Neri said, "Words cannot express the beauty of a soul which dies in the grace of God."

But doesn't this argument cut both ways? Aren't bad Christians proof of the falsity of the Gospels? Many people certainly think they are. Father Józef Tischner, the first chaplain of the Solidarity trade union in Poland, said that he knew no one who had lost his faith by reading Marx or Lenin but many who had after meeting their own parish priest. But let's consider the following three points:

1. Christianity has never claimed that it would turn every sow's ear into a silk purse. On the contrary, in the Parable of the Wheat and the Tares (Matthew 13:24–30) and in His warning about wolves in sheep's clothing (Matthew 7:15) Jesus warned about bad Christians and false Christians. Rejecting Christianity because of the bad example of its nastier members is like refusing to drink life-giving spring water in a desert oasis because the people surrounding it happen to be too stupid to use it properly.
2. As we'll see in chapters seven through nine, when all is said and done, Christianity has done far, far more good in the world than ill. And a lot of that has to do with its Christ-like saints.
3. When Christians act badly, their actions can be easily understood in human terms, but when they act superlatively well, their actions can only really be understood as divinely inspired. Christians' hurting themselves or their neighbor, even in the name of their religion, is no different from other groups' hurting themselves or their neighbors either out of egotism or for the

sake of some cause. At their worst, Christians are generally no worse than anyone else; indeed, the greatest monsters in history were *anti*-Christians such as Nero, Hitler, and Stalin. To understand bad Christian behavior is simply to understand bad human behavior. But when a Christian warmly forgives those who are about to murder him (like St. Stephen or St. Thomas More), when a Christian kisses the sores of lepers and helps the marginalized (like Damien of Molokai or Mother Teresa), when a Christian laughs lightheartedly in the midst of extreme torture (as St. Lawrence on the grill), when a Christian heroically stands up to totalitarian tyranny (like the Lutheran Dietrich Bonhoeffer or the Catholic Cardinal Clemens August von Galen), and when a Christian gladly meets death for sheltering Jews from the Nazis (like Blessed Sister Sára Salkaházi), it is more difficult to explain without some recourse to the divine. Yes, there are also commendable non-Christians such as Gandhi, but there is nothing quite like a Christian saint.

★ ★ ★

A Terrible Beauty

The beauty of holiness explains why Jesus Christ is surely "fairer than the children of men" (Psalm 45:2) as well as the one in whom "no form nor comeliness... no beauty that we should desire him" (Isaiah 53:2). During the Passion, Christ looked terrible: bruised, disfigured, and bloody. But as His supreme act of love for mankind, the Passion shows forth the beauty of God's love for us, a love that knows no bounds but goes to the bitter end. Not everyone understands this divine and beautiful mystery. The famous Zen Buddhist teacher D. T. Suzuki felt uncomfortable being in a room with a crucifix; he saw the ugliness of a brutal execution but not the beauty of sacrificial love shining through it.

The Rays of Beauty

The second thing that Cardinal Ratzinger singled out as a testimony to the truth of Christianity is the beauty that the faith has generated. Beauty is not

The Divine Archer

"When men have a longing so great that it surpasses human nature and eagerly desire and are able to accomplish things beyond human thought, it is the Bridegroom who has smitten them with this longing. It is he who has sent a ray of his beauty into their eyes. The greatness of the wound already shows the arrow which has struck home, the longing indicates who has inflicted the wound."

—fourteenth-century Byzantine theologian Nicholas Cabasilas

empty aestheticism or sensory titillation; rather, it gives a healthy emotional shock that draws a man out of himself. "The encounter with the beautiful," Ratzinger writes, "can become the wound of the arrow that strikes the heart and in this way opens our eyes, so that later, from this experience, we take the criteria for judgement and can correctly evaluate the arguments." As an example Ratzinger mentions attending, along with the Lutheran Bishop Johannes Hanselmann, a Bach concert conducted by Leonard Bernstein. When the last note of one of the great Thomas-Kantor-Cantatas triumphantly faded away, Ratzinger and Hanselmann looked at each other and said, "Anyone who has heard this, knows that the faith is true."

Beauty is an arrow that wounds in a good way, and the Archer, so to speak, is Christ, the Bridegroom of our hearts who is calling us to Him. You can experience this beauty in sacred works of art great and small, from Constantinople's Hagia Sophia to the Sistine Chapel to a small group of Baptists singing "Praise God from Whom All Blessings Flow" in four-part harmony. The Romanesque, Gothic, and Baroque churches; the compositions in Gregorian chant, classical music, and Christian hymnody; the statues of Michelangelo and Bernini; the icons of Giotto and Rublëv and the paintings of Raphael and Murillo; and the English writings from the early medieval poem *Beowulf* to the twentieth-century novels of Evelyn Waugh—all bespeak a beauty, terrifying at times but beautiful nonetheless, that is greater than this world. (And, of course, let us not forget the awesome beauty of solemn liturgical worship.) Christianity is not only the most beautiful religion in the world, it produces the most beautiful people and the most beautiful things in the world.

Reason Nods and Shrugs

We conclude with another confirmation, not of Christianity's truth, but of its lack of provable falsehood. Knowing that something is not proven false is not necessarily the same as knowing that it is true. Centuries ago Augustine of Hippo began to have doubts about the Manichean religion of which he was a part. He came to the realization that Manicheism included elements that could clearly be disproven—in this case, the fanciful Manichean astrology rubbed up against what Augustine knew to be true from his study of the science of astronomy. But when Augustine looked into Christianity he found nothing that could be proven false. You can't prove that the Trinity exists but neither can you prove that it doesn't; it doesn't contradict any known facts, and it involves no intrinsic contradiction like the concept of a square circle. You can't logically prove that the Resurrection happened but neither can you prove that the Resurrection didn't happen. Augustine concluded that Christianity was reasonable and consistent with known facts. And Christians did not claim to be able to *prove* their beliefs by rational proofs; on the contrary, being a Christian called for an act of faith. After all, if a belief can be logically demonstrated, it's no longer belief but knowledge.

Beauty in the Crucified Heart

"Beauty will save the world."

—Fyodor Dostoevsky

"The beauty that will save the world is the love of God. This love is both human and supernatural in character, but it germinates, flowers, and comes to fruition only in a crucified heart. Only the heart united with Christ on the Cross is able to love another as himself, and as God loves him. Only such a heart can pass through the narrow gate of the Cross and live in the light of Resurrection. The good news is that this resurrection begins here and now."

—Michael D. O'Brien, writer and artist

Who Ya Gonna Believe?

"I remembered many truths that [the astronomers] had spoken of the created world itself, and I saw their theories justified by numbers and the order of time and the visible evidence of the stars. I compared all this with what Manes had said, for he wrote at great length upon such matters and quite wildly: but I did not find in him any explanation of the solstices or the equinoxes or the eclipses of sun and moon; nor any of such things as I had learnt in the books of worldly philosophy. I was commanded to believe [what the Manicheans taught], yet it did not harmonise with the principles I had arrived at by mathematics and indeed by my own eyes, but was far otherwise... From this time on I found myself preferring the Catholic doctrine, realising that it acted more modestly and honestly in requiring things to be believed which could not be proved—whether they were in themselves provable though not by this or that person, or were not provable at all—than the Manichees who derided credulity and made impossible promises of certain knowledge, and then called upon men to believe so many utterly fabulous and absurd things because they could not be demonstrated."

—**Augustine of Hippo,** *Confessions*

That said, we have already seen that there are some Christian beliefs, such as the existence of God, that *can* be proven true. You can know that murder is wrong either by faith in the Ten Commandments or by rational reflection since both faith and reason come to the same conclusion about the wrongness of murder. It makes sense that this should be so, since the God who made a rationally coherent universe and endowed us with the gift of reason that can tell the difference between right and wrong is the same God who gave Moses the Law.

In sum, we may say that unlike false religions and ideologies, *Judaism and Christianity are above reason but not against reason*: the religion of the God of Abraham, Isaac, and Jacob (and Jesus Christ) teaches things that reason can confirm and it teaches things that reason cannot confirm, but it never teaches things that reason can deny or refute. That may not sound like a big deal, but it is. Reason *can* prove false religions to be false, as

Augustine's reasoning did with Manicheism. Reason, therefore, is useful in weeding out the false alternatives and leaving us the possibly true options. For those on the journey back to God, that's a step in the right direction.

Another way to put this point is to say that Christianity is not always rationally demonstrable but that does not mean that it is unreasonable. The teachings of Christianity are like the irregular and unexpected contours of a key that fit the lock of reality perfectly but could not have been rationally predicted. One could never deduce a doctrine such as original sin by reason alone, yet once it is revealed, one realizes that it is the only teaching that adequately accounts for man's greatness and wretchedness. And one could never have predicted that God would solve the problem of original sin by becoming a human being and allowing sinful man to abuse and crucify Him, but when we learn about the Incarnation and Crucifixion, there is an "Ah!" moment in which we recognize the awesome fittingness of God's solution to our sinfulness. It is this familiar strangeness or strange familiarity of Christianity, its combination of "all the fascinating terrors of going abroad combined with all the humane security of coming home again," that has attracted converts like G. K. Chesterton to the faith.

If the Key Fits

"When once one believes in a creed, one is proud of its complexity, as scientists are proud of the complexity of science. It shows how rich it is in discoveries. If it is right at all, it is a compliment to say that it's elaborately right. A stick might fit a hole or a stone a hollow by accident. But a key and a lock are both complex. And if a key fits a lock, you know it is the right key."

—**G. K. Chesterton,** *Orthodoxy*

But what about Galileo and evolution? Hasn't Christianity often been at odds with science? We'll go into this issue in more detail in chapter nine. In the meantime, keep in mind the general rule that there cannot be a contradiction between the true faith and sound reason. If it looks like there is, then one of two things has happened: you have either mistaken the claims of faith, or you have mistaken the claims of reason. Scientists often misinterpret or exaggerate the significance of their findings, and religious believers often fail to distinguish between what the Bible says and what the Bible means.

One thing is certain: sometimes reason nods yes to certain aspects of the faith, and sometimes it shrugs its shoulders in uncertainty, but the one thing it never does is shake its head no.

CHAPTER SEVEN

The Battle of the Sexes

In "9 of the Biggest Lies Christianity Tells Us about Sex and Marriage" at everydayfeminism.com, bisexual activist Eliel Cruz bemoans Christianity's historic "monopoly on Western conversations about sex and marriage," which has "ended up perpetuating patriarchy, rape culture, and [gasp!] heteronormativity." Eliel seems blissfully unaware that the statistics on rape show a spike in sexual assault after the Sexual Revolution rather than after the Incarnation. But he can swing wildly and still be cheered because he has tapped into a nerve; his article reinforces the bedrock conviction that biblical patriarchy is little more than a mask for men's will to power. In this chapter, we will see if this is true by looking at the timeless Christian teaching on the relationship between men and women and setting the historical record straight.

Did you know?

★ Christians have always believed that women are equal to men

★ "Subject" does not mean "inferior"

★ Restricting liturgical roles to men is not on account of male holiness—it's to transform the male propensity for violence

Christian "Gender Relations"—Backwards or Upwards?

Among the embarrassing revelations by WikiLeaks during the 2016 presidential election were emails from Hillary Clinton's staff deriding Protestants for

A Grosser Subordination?

"We believe firmly in the equality of the sexes, and we agree, moreover, that to use woman merely as a wooden idol is as bad as to use her as a wooden broom. But, in the interests of equality, we must say that we doubt whether the mere equalisation of sports and employments will bring us much further. There is nothing so certain to lead to inequality as identity. A mere struggle between the sexes as to who will make the best tinkers, tailors, or soldiers, is very likely indeed to result in a subordination of women infinitely more gross and heartless than that which disgraced the world up to now. What we really require is a revised and improved division of labour. Whatever solution may be best (we do not pretend for a moment to have decided) it must emphatically not be based upon any idea so paltry and small-minded as the idea that there is anything noble in professional work or anything degrading in domestic. Woman must not be elevated as the worst type of working man is elevated, merely (to use the silly phrase) 'to a better kind of work,' to choke the memory of his own class in a stick-up collar. If this is the only end of the noble promise of female emancipation, the intellectual woman's lot will certainly be an ironic one, for she will have toiled to reach the haughtiest eminence from which she can look down upon the housemaid, only to discover that world has become sane and discovered that the housemaid is as good as she."

—**G. K. Chesterton,** "Woman and the Philosophers"

wanting to baptize their children in the River Jordan and lambasting Catholics for being "extremely backwards on gender relations." We're sure that if Hillary's team had thought about it more they would have extended the jab to all morally conservative Christian churches, but perhaps they were too busy coming up with other deep thoughts such as the one about Muslims being "just like us."

The bias of the Clinton coterie came as no surprise to the faithful. When the secular Left is not trying to shame Christians into abandoning the Gospels of Matthew, Mark, Luke, and John for those of the LGBTQQIAP2 (that's the ever-growing Lesbian, Gay, Bisexual, Transgender, Queer, Questioning, Intersex, Asexual, Pansexual, Two-Spirit Alliance), it is accusing Christianity of oppressing women and treating them as second-class citizens. (Islam, despite a notorious track record of "honor killings" and adulteress stonings, is given a free pass.) Even liberal Christians have hopped onto the bandwagon, bemoaning the fact that the Bible was written during "patriarchal times" and then cherry-picking the Scriptures to conform the Word of God to their radically egalitarian agenda. Their favorite verse is Galatians 3:28—"There is neither Jew nor Greek, bond nor free, male nor female, for you are all one in Christ Jesus." Their least favorite is Ephesians 5:22—"Wives, be subject to your husbands."

But as these two passages—from the same author, no less—suggest, the Christian teaching on the sexes has nuances that elude the mind of modern man. On the one hand, Christianity affirms the full spiritual equality of the sexes; on the other, it speaks of a division of labor or a hierarchy of responsibility within the family and in divine worship. Modern man, who worships the idol of equality, loves the former teaching but despises the latter.

Nuptial Meaning

In chapter three, we noted how Christianity teaches that the human person is a nuptial animal, a man or a woman whose sexuality is ordered towards a complementary union that mirrors the relationship between Christ and His Church. This "great mystery" (Ephesians 5:32) will never be fully plumbed, at least not this side of the grave, but two things at least are clear. The first is spiritual equality. On the natural level, both men and women are equally made in the image and likeness of God, and since the image of God has to do with the human soul rather than the body, it may be said that the souls of men and women are completely equal (for example, in their rational capacities and in their dignity). On the supernatural level, men and women are also equal. Jesus called both women and men to be His disciples and even broke social convention in order to reach out to the Samaritan women at the well and to St. Mary Magdalen. Accordingly, St. Peter calls men and women "coheirs of grace" (1 Peter 3:7).

But men and women are not disembodied souls floating about in the ether; their personhood takes shape in the different bodies they animate. And if we're honest with each other, these different bodies have all sorts of natural inequalities making one sex or another superior with respect to a particular function. Men, for instance, usually have more upper body strength than women, and women usually have a higher pain tolerance than men and are uniquely privileged to bear new life. Thus, in the same sentence in which he calls women "coheirs of grace," St. Peter commands husbands to honor their wives "as the weaker vessel." (If his thoughts had turned to the fragility of the male ego instead of to men's physical strength, he could have just as easily used the same term to describe husbands when giving advice to wives.) Looking over the accumulation of these natural differences, we may say that the bodies of men and women have different "nuptial" meanings that are not interchangeable, with a woman's body oriented to motherhood and its virtues and a man's body oriented to fatherhood and its virtues.

Now a truly just and ideal society would be one that honors both the equal dignity of the sexes and their unique complementarity, a society that shouts *égalité*! and *vive la différence*! with identical gusto. Of course, that is not an easy balancing act. An overemphasis on equality can warp both women and men. In radically egalitarian societies women are made to feel that they must imitate men in order to claim the same recognition, and they feel compelled to insist to their own detriment that they be treated no differently than men; thus they lose some of the radiant genius and unique privileges of their femininity. Meanwhile men in such societies react by either exaggerating or diminishing their masculinity in unhealthy ways—becoming a Mr. Sensitive Ponytail Man or a preening fitness buff or an extreme sports fanatic or perhaps worst of all a "guy," who is not a man but a boy in a man's body wearing the same clothes as a boy (jeans, t-shirt, and baseball cap), enjoying the same entertainment as a boy (video games and gross-out movies), and bearing the same responsibilities as a boy (neither will take out the trash unless threatened). On the other hand, an overemphasis on the differences between the sexes can make men brutish or vain and women manipulative and controlling. One need only think of machismo cultures, which despite appearances to the contrary are matriarchal in crucial respects—slick hotheaded young men strut about in the piazza like feckless peacocks while termagant babushkas rock the cradle and rule the roost.

And this already difficult balancing act is complicated by innumerable variables of culture, history, political constitutions, economic conditions, and so forth. Because of this complexity, traditional Christianity wisely refrains from dogmatic assertions regarding "the role of women" in political or professional life. Indeed, Church history is peopled with powerful Christian queens and empresses, and the Old Testament has the wise female judge Deborah (Judges 4:6–7). And according to some historians, women in medieval Christendom were freer and more active than women in the nineteenth century, when the Industrial Revolution put both sexes in soulless factories and took the production of homemade goods away from women.

Subject versus Inferior

Where we do see the Scriptures speak up more explicitly is with respect to domestic life, namely, with the admonition that a wife is to be subject to her husband (see Ephesians 5:22 and 1 Peter 3:1). That language sends shivers down our egalitarian, democratic spines today, so it is important to retrieve its original meaning. To say that one person is *subject* to another is not to say that one person is *inferior* to another. To be "subject" or "subordinate" is simply to be placed under the authority of another; it is a statement concerning a distribution of rank or responsibility within a team, not of worth or excellence. A person who is subordinate in rank can at the same time be superior in character or talent or essence, and vice versa. Jesus, who is vastly superior to Mary and Joseph both as the Son of Man and as the Son of God, nevertheless goes down from Jerusalem after being found in the Temple and is "subject unto them" (Luke 2:51). Did you read that? Jesus, the Creator of the Universe and the King of Kings, is *subject* to two measly human beings. So when the New Testament speaks of a wife's subjection to her husband, it is not implying that she is an inferior specimen. On the contrary, there is a way in which she is called to a nobler task than her husband, for she is called to something far more important than career or politics or money—she is called to be the life and center of a home. As Chesterton asks, "How can it be a large career to tell other people's children about the Rule of Three, and a small career to tell one's own children about the universe? How can it be broad to be the same thing to everyone, and narrow to be everything to someone? No. A woman's function is laborious, but because it is gigantic, not because it is minute. I will pity Mrs. Jones for the hugeness of her task; I will never pity her for its smallness" ("The Emancipation of Domesticity").

Take a Knee

"The lover is always on his knees; the beloved must always be on a pedestal. Whether it be man or woman, the one must always consider himself or herself as undeserving of the other. Even God humbled Himself in His Love to win man, saying He 'came not to be ministered unto, but to minister.' And man, in his turn, approaches that loving Saviour in Communion with the words: 'Lord, I am not worthy.'"

—**Fulton J. Sheen**

Now that we have a better sense of what it means for a Christian to be "subject," we can add three other points:

First, subjection may involve obedience, but it is not servitude. The model is not that of a slave being beaten by his master but of a duke collaborating with the prince to whom he has pledged fealty. The early Church—which, contrary to rumor, was not an awful patriarchal institution that hijacked Hippie Jesus' free love movement—understood this well. As St. Ambrose of Milan (340–397) solemnly warned new bridegrooms, "You are not her master but her husband; she was not given to you to be your slave but your wife."

Pyrrhic Victories

"[Feminism] is mixed up with a muddled idea that women are free when they serve their employers but slaves when they help their husbands."

—**G. K. Chesterton,** "Social Reform versus Birth Control"

"Ten thousand women marched through the streets shouting, 'We will not be dictated to,' and went off and became stenographers."

—**attributed to G. K. Chesterton**

Second, natural subjection does not mean that the husband will be in charge of every decision and that his wife will be mousy and mealy-mouthed. The portrait of an ideal wife in the Book of Proverbs, for example, is far from the 1950s television stereotype of the perfect housewife: she is a self-starting entrepreneur and bread-winner, a resourceful mistress of a teeming household, and a speaker of wisdom (31:10–31). The biblical model is a basic template that admits of numerous variations, with no two successful marriages being alike; much depends on the chemistry of the couple and what each brings to the table. At the very least, it behooves a Christian husband with half a brain to delegate authority to a wife who surpasses him in certain areas. And it behooves a Christian wife with half a brain to know that the Roman Empire was in decline when it thought that it could have two simultaneously presiding emperors.

Third, natural subjection properly exercised is a good thing in itself, but when transformed by grace (the whole point of Christian discipleship) it becomes a marvelous instance of "mutual subjection," in which the husband understands his leadership, such as it is, as a form of service that puts the genuine needs of his wife and children ahead of his own. It's like the police departments in our democratic society, which have certain powers over civilians but which are commanded to exercise this authority, as the sides

Back in the Bad Old Days

"The wife... possesses real authority and equality of dignity while the husband still retains the role of headship; the welfare of the household is thus maintained."

—**John Chrysostom (c. 349–407),** "Homily 20 on Ephesians 5:22–33"

of their squad cars announce, "to protect and to serve." This servant-leader model is completely different from both the oppressive Neanderthal chauvinism of yesteryear and the contemporary "baby man" mentality with its puerile "man cave" and avoidance of self-sacrifice. The Christian husband's self-emptying is so Christ-like and oriented towards the gift of his wife and children that, to modify St. Augustine's generic advice on ruling and serving, he rules in such a way that it is a delight to serve him. And the wife is so attentive and prudent that she serves in such a way that it would be embarrassing for her husband to rule her. After all, in the very next verse after Paul tells wives to be subject to their husbands, he tells husbands that they have to lay down their lives for their wives. "Husbands, love your wives, even as Christ also loved the church, and gave himself for it" (Ephesians 5:25). This model certainly sets the bar high and is impossible by purely human means, but it is precisely the possibility opened up by the sanctifying grace of the Cross and the example of the Savior, who restores the right relationship between the sexes by His self-offering on behalf of His bride the Church, putting her own needs far ahead of His own. And this, ladies and gentlemen, is the meaning of Ephesians 5.

Sacred versus Holy

The Bible is also explicit about service in the Church, specifically divine worship. Paul commands that women's heads be veiled while praying or prophesying and that they not speak up *in church* (1 Corinthians 11:6–10 and 14:34). Even though he never explicitly defines it in these terms, Paul is implicitly relying on one of the distinctions least understood today within Christianity or without, the distinction between the holy and the sacred. Contrary to sloppy usage, "holy" and "sacred" are far from synonymous. To be holy is to be filled with the breath of the Holy Spirit, whereas to be sacred is to be consecrated for special use. The opposite of "holy" is "wicked," but the opposite of "sacred" is "profane," a word that literally means "outside the temple" and has no necessarily negative connotations. In Christianity, "holiness" first and foremost describes persons and their souls, while "sacred" refers to specially designated things: spaces, objects, times and, as we shall see, the body.

The Privilege of Being a Woman by Alice von Hildebrand (Sapientia Press, 2002).

The Old Testament has a robust sense of the sacred (see the laws concerning ritual purity) whereas the New Testament emphasizes holiness. Nevertheless, the New Covenant does not abolish the sacred but fulfills it (see Matthew 5:17). And one of the areas where we see a sense of the sacred fulfilled in mere Christianity is with respect to the sexes.

Simply put, both Christian men and women are equally called to holiness, but they are also called to different roles regarding the sacred. These different roles do not prejudice the ability of one sex to become holy. As all the bad popes writhing in Dante's *Inferno* amply attest, having a particular access to the sacred and becoming holy are two entirely different matters. One way of describing the difference is that men are called to be protectors or keepers of the sacred, whereas women are called to be an embodiment of the sacred. Alice von Hildebrand has written eloquently on how the female body is sacred in a way that a man's isn't. A woman's body is a tabernacle capable of bearing immortal lives, a fact that explains why it is typically more adorned with clothing than a man's—for like the curtain in the Holy Temple, we only veil what is sacred. Or to dumb things down a bit, as Elaine notes in *Seinfeld*, a woman's body is beautiful like a work of art; a man's body is practical like a Jeep. And beauty is more sacred than practicality.

The distinction between holiness and sacredness also explains how the same St. Paul who declares that there is neither male nor female in Christ (Galatians 3:28) could also prescribe different kinds of comportment for men and women in divine worship regarding headdress, preaching, and so forth. (1 Corinthians 11:3–12, 14:34–35). Contrary to popular arguments dismissing Paul's admonitions as products of the patriarchal era in which he lived, they are a practical instantiation of the perennial distinction between holy and sacred.

Male custodianship of the sacred also appears to be linked to sacrifice. Although offering oneself as a sacrifice is equally incumbent on both sexes (Romans 12:1), men are the only ones in the Bible who offer physical immolations—that is, they are the only ones who put a knife to a sacrificial victim like a lamb or a bullock and slit its throat. Scripture doesn't say why, but we may hazard a guess. Ever since Cain, men are the more violent sex, likelier to have recourse to bloodshed as a means of obtaining what they want. While this fact does not deny that women can also be violent, it does explain the causes of war, the population of our prisons, and the consumer demographic of video-game players.

God's strategy appears to have been to channel the fallen male's propensity for violence away from murder toward animal sacrifice as a way of helping him recognize his devious impulses and repent. "God in his seeming bloodthirstiness," writes Patrick Downey in his superb *Desperately Wicked*, "is actually more concerned with curing us of our own." This strategy culminated in the New Covenant, when its High Priest, rather than committing violence, allowed Himself to be victimized by it. God's final solution to the problem of man's deicidal heart was to give him exactly what he wants.

Which brings us to those awful churches that dare to deny some ministerial positions to women in our egalitarian age. Is this a rank act of chauvinism, or is it fidelity to the distinction between the holy and the sacred? In Churches such as the Catholic and the Orthodox that have a priesthood (that is, an ordained ministry, the central act of which is understood as a real sacrifice), men alone are called to preside in the liturgy not because they are superior in holiness but because they are the bloody sex. In these churches, the sacrifice of the altar (Holy Mass or the Divine Liturgy) is a re-presencing of the sacrifice of the Cross. Thus, it remains linked not only to the darkness of the human heart but to the specific problem of male violence. Serving at the altar in these churches is actually a healthy form of humiliation for men and boys, for it constitutes a confession of their wicked hearts; God's restriction of sacrifice to males in the Tabernacle, Temple, and beyond is in decisive respects a back-handed compliment. And remember, the tradition of only men serving in the sanctuary of God is four thousand years old, beginning before Moses. Nor was it simply a reflection of the *zeitgeist* at the time, but a marked rejection of the priestess practices of Israel's and the Church's pagan neighbors.

And in those Protestant churches that do not have female ministers there remains a fidelity to the Word of God, which explicitly enjoins that women not speak up (that is, formally teach) during the church service (1 Corinthians 14:34). Often these same churches, though, have women who prophesy or speak in tongues during worship, which is also in keeping with St. Paul, who assumes that women will continue prophesying in church (see 1 Corinthians 11:5). Neither the sacrificial-sacramental churches nor the evangelical churches are necessarily claiming that males are superior, and neither are saying that women cannot exercise religious leadership—some of the most powerful leaders in the Middle Ages were abbesses and prophetesses. But *liturgical* leadership involves a mirroring of the Wedding Feast of the Lamb, a re-presenting of the marriage of Christ and His Bride. The stand-in for the Groom is the unworthy male and his unworthy groomsmen (the priest or preacher and his assistants), while the Bride is signified by the receptive hearts of the congregation and by the womb-like sanctuary itself, from which Eucharistic life is born.

Small side note: this distinction between the holy and the sacred may explain Christendom's general aversion to women serving in active combat. It is one thing for a hardy pioneer woman to grab her Winchester at the sound of whooping Comanches or for Grace Kelly to swallow her Quaker convictions and shoot the bad guy about to kill her beloved Gary Cooper—to say nothing of Jael nailing Sisera (literally—see Judges 4:17–22 and 5:24–26) or Judith beheading Holofernes (Judith 12–13:10). It is another thing to say that as a matter of routine in a civilized society, a sacred and potential tabernacle of new and innocent life should practice a mode of life steeped in the destruction of life, even for a just cause. The sacred is to be protected from violence, not the executor of it. At the very least, excluding women from the violence of war gives men an incentive to stop seeing themselves as playboys or predators and to start seeing themselves as protectors of their mothers, sisters, and wives.

The Emancipation of Women

Today's secular liberals like to portray the Christian religion as the enemy of women's progress, but they do not always define their terms. If "progress" means the abolition of woman—that is, the denial of anything essentially unique or special about womanhood and the treatment of a woman as if she were indistinguishable from a man—then, yes indeed, Christianity opposes this androgynous and nihilistic idea of progress (and so, incidentally, do some feminists).

But if progress means the fair treatment of women, the appreciation of their unique genius, the affirmation of their equality before God and the law, and the commitment to protect them and their children from injustice, then Christianity is not opposed to women's progress; on the contrary, it is the chief champion of that progress. Consider the following history.

When Christianity spread throughout the Greco-Roman world, it attracted a disproportionate number of female converts in part because, as Rodney Stark has explained, "women in the early Christian communities were considerably better off than their pagan and even Jewish counterparts." Roman fathers had the right to force their wives to expose their infant children (which they overwhelmingly did when daughters were born to them); Christianity's opposition to abortion and infanticide defended both mother and daughter from this practice. Christianity also dramatically curtailed the phenomenon of child brides and ended the double standard regarding sexual promiscuity, which was enshrined in the laws (Roman courts only recognized the adultery of a married woman as a crime and as grounds for divorce; men were culpable only if they slept with another man's wife or were conspicuously indiscreet in their extramarital affairs). By and large, Christian women married later in life, enjoyed the loving fidelity of their husbands, and were spared the abortionist's knife. Indeed, if more of the Roman Empire had become Christian sooner, the Empire might not have fallen. The Romans would not have had the population crisis that led them to make the fateful decision to import "barbarians" to work the land and serve in the army.

Wherever Christianity has spread—Europe, the Americas, Africa, Asia—it has raised the status of women and eliminated as many prejudicial practices as it could. The Christian prohibition of divorce gave women more power in their marriages, as did the prohibition of polygamy and of marriages arranged without the consent of the spouses. In parts of West Africa,

A Book You're Not Supposed to Read

The Triumph of Christianity by Rodney Stark (New York: HarperOne, 2011).

Saints and Suffragettes

"The Church would just as soon canonize a woman as a man and I suppose has done more than any other force in history to free women."

—Flannery O'Connor

mothers of twins were often the first to convert to Christianity because under the old religion one of their children would be killed (apparently, twins really spooked people out). In medieval Europe, laws were designed to protect widows from getting shafted by their husband's families, and numerous guilds protected women in trade.

Feminism often portrays paganism as a golden age for women and Christian heretics as early champions of women's rights, but this revisionism is ludicrous. As we have noted in chapter one, the earliest cosmogenic myths involving goddesses were misogynistic, portraying the feminine as fodder for male violence and domination. And simply because Greece and Rome had priestesses and vestal virgins does not mean that women had power: inhaling hallucinogenic vapors from a volcanic crack at the Oracle of Delphi and spouting "prophecy" is a far cry from being respected as an intelligent, rational agent. As a general rule, women in the Roman and Hellenic worlds did not play any significant role in religious life—unlike their Christian counterparts, who were valued members of the evangelical team. Finally, one of the most prevalent heresies in the early Church was Gnosticism, which deplored women as inferior and unclean beings. And yet despite the historical record, authors like Elaine Pagels prattle on as if Gnosticism were feminism *avant la lettre*. Sigh.

Finally, if Eliel and his liberal friends are looking for causes of "rape culture," they should take a look in the mirror. It is not biblical patriarchy but the vacuum created by its loss that leads to a culture of rape; for as we see in the *cries-de-coeur* lyrics of rap and hip hop, when fathers stop being fathers, their sons do not know how to act as real men and can turn violently misogynistic (for a fascinating analysis of this trend, read Mary Eberstadt).

And, of course, the breakdown of the American family is for the most part the result of LBJ's Great Society and the Left's embrace of sexual libertinism in the 1960s. In the words of George Weigel, "Women asking for the Sexual Revolution is like turkeys asking for more Thanksgivings." The Left loves to create problems and then blame the Right for it.

An Essay You're Not Supposed to Read

Mary Eberstadt, "Eminem is Right" (December 2004), Hoover Institution

CHAPTER EIGHT

Intolerance

"Atheists Aren't the Problem, Christian Intolerance Is the Problem," declared Richard Dawkins and Robyn Blumer in *Time* magazine. Although their 2014 article failed to provide much evidence for their assertion, it did reflect a common stereotype held by the politically correct Left: that Christians are bigoted zealots who fail to have the same care and compassion as their far more tolerant secular counterparts. Of course, it is debatable whether the secular Left is as tolerant as it thinks it is—as I write these words, a Google employee has just disseminated a coherent argument critical of Google's "ideological echo chamber," and the leftist tech giant has ironically confirmed the employee's critique by firing him. Hence the following summary by wry observer Kevin Clark: "It is only when all of us think exactly the same thoughts that we can achieve perfect diversity." There is an old story that Louisiana governor Huey Long was once asked whether fascism would ever come to the United States. "Of course it will," the Kingfish replied, "only it will be called Anti-Fascism." Something similar can be said by the secular Left's Orwellian practice of totalitarian toleration. (And can we call Huey Long a prophet for predicting Antifa?)

Did you know?

★ Popes issued more than a hundred documents condemning Christian scapegoating of Jews

★ The Crusades were attempts to re-take Christian lands from Muslim conquerors

★ Planned Parenthood kills more people every six days than the Spanish Inquisition killed in 350 years

Intolerant?

"The Church is intolerant in principle because she believes; she is tolerant in practice because she loves. The enemies of the Church are tolerant in principle because they do not believe; they are intolerant in practice because they do not love."

—French theologian Reginald Garrigou-Lagrange

"If you are Christian you do not have to believe that all the other religions are simply wrong all through. If you are an atheist you do have to believe that the main point in all the religions of the whole world is simply one huge mistake. If you are a Christian, you are free to think that all these religions, even the queerest ones, contain at least some hint of the truth. When I was an atheist I had to try to persuade myself that most of the human race have always been wrong about the question that mattered to them most; when I became a Christian I was able to take a more liberal view. But, of course, being a Christian does mean thinking that where Christianity differs from other religions, Christianity is right and they are wrong. As in arithmetic—there is only one right answer to a sum, and all other answers are wrong: but some of the wrong answers are much nearer being right than others."

—C. S. Lewis, *Mere Christianity*

Nevertheless, the hypocrisy of the Left does not automatically make Christianity right. Historical events such as the Crusades and the Spanish Inquisition seem to many to provide proof of Christian intolerance. It therefore behooves us to revisit the historical evidence.

The Jews

Of all the anti-Christian spaghetti thrown at the wall, the charge that Christians have persecuted the Jewish people sticks the most.

Christians and Jews have had a complicated relationship from the beginning. The Jewish leadership of first-century Palestine, jealous of Jesus' popularity and worried that His Messianic message would upset the delicate political balance between the subjugated people of Israel and the conquering Roman Empire, incited a mob to shout for His death at the hands of the Roman governor Pontius Pilate. Pilate, afraid of a Jewish rebellion, acquiesced. Many Jews did not like the new "Way," as Christianity was then called (Acts 9:2), and some of them persecuted the early Christians. Forms of persecution included:

- Expulsion from the synagogue
- Scourging. On five different occasions St. Paul received the "forty lashes minus one" (2 Corinthians 11:24)
- Death. Herod Agrippa murdered St. James the Apostles and, when he saw that this was pleasing to the Jews, tried to do the same to St. Peter (Acts 12:1–19); similarly, St. Stephen was stoned to death after chewing out the Sanhedrin (Acts 7:54–60).

In the wake of the eventual legalization of Christianity, the tables were turned and Christians gained the upper hand. By A.D. 438 Jews in the Roman Empire were barred from civil and military service and from the practice of law. Around the fourth century when several heretical sects within the Church attempted to "Judaize" Christianity with some kind of return to the Mosaic Law, their efforts had the effect of heightening the anti-Jewish rhetoric of Church Fathers such as St. John Chrysostom (such rhetoric was later lifted from its original context to justify anti-Jewish discrimination in the Middle Ages). Jews and not Romans were held responsible for Jesus' death, and the term "deicide" was coined to describe their murder of the God-man Jesus Christ. Other Church Fathers such as St. Augustine, however, exonerated the Jews from the charge of deicide on the grounds that had they known Jesus was God, they would not have killed Him.

In the Middle Ages, legal and cultural discrimination against Jews continued, along with atrocities including massacres, pogroms, and expulsions.

Much of this behavior can be explained in terms of fallen human nature and political crises. Through no fault of their own, minorities become lightning rods for scapegoating, especially when there is some illness festering in the community that requires catharsis (other historic examples of this phenomenon include black lynchings in the South, the Salem witch trials, and the burning of the Catholic Ursuline convent in Massachusetts in 1834). The Christian critique of Judaism provided an all too convenient window-dressing to hide the ugly reality of political scapegoating; Jews were blamed for calamities such as the plague even though the pope at the time denounced this conspiracy theory as outrageous. Most of the violence against the Jews in the Middle Ages was the result not of the law but of a breakdown in the law (again, like lynchings in the Jim Crow South). The popes in particular tried to protect Jewish minorities from unfair treatment, issuing over one hundred papal bulls and letters on that subject, some of which, such as Innocent III's *Constitution for the Jews*, promised excommunication to anyone who injured Jews, took their property, disturbed their feasts, or desecrated their cemeteries.

The early modern period was arguably worse for the Jews than the Middle Ages. Martin Luther's venomous *Against the Jews* makes the medieval critiques pale in comparison (although his attitude apparently softened shortly before his death), while Jews were often caught in the crossfire of seismic changes in European politics. It did not help that Jewish intellectuals were often the most radical politically, since they weren't exactly happy under the old regime of Christian kings.

Fortunately, in the twentieth century great strides were made in reconciling Christians and Jews and in eliminating polemical excess. The Second Vatican Council (1962–1965), Pope St. John Paul II, and the Vatican's 1985 "Notes on the Correct Way to Present the Jews and Judaism in Preaching and Catechesis in the Roman Catholic Church" were instrumental in mending fences between the Catholic Church and the Jewish community.

Similarly, many Protestant denominations have issued statements reformulating their theology about the Jews in a more positive light and denouncing anti-Semitism as sinful. Evangelical Protestants are particularly well-known for their Judeophilia: many of them subscribe to premillennial dispensationalism, which foresees an earthly Jewish state as an important sign of the end times (hence the alliance between American evangelicalism and Zionism), and most, according to evangelical author Joe Carter, have a "truncated view of Jewish history" in which "the Jewish people exited the stage of history after the destruction of the temple in A.D. 70 and only reemerged in the 1940s with the Holocaust and the birth of modern Israel." This historical outlook conflates ancient Hebrews and modern Jews and encourages Evangelicals to have a special affection for the latter-day children of Abraham.

The Holocaust

Where controversy continues is on the extent to which Christians are responsible for the Holocaust, which took the lives of six million Jews. At one extreme, critics of Christianity charge that Nazi anti-Semitism differed only in quantity but not in quality from Christian anti-Jewish sentiment and that a straight line can be drawn from the New Testament passages against the Pharisees and the Jews to the death camps of Dachau and Auschwitz. At the other end of the spectrum, defenders of Christianity declare it to be completely innocent of the Holocaust, pointing to the profound differences between Nazi ideology and Christian teaching and to heroic Christians who saved Jews during World War II such as Pastor André Trocmé, Irena Sendler (who saved 2,500 Jewish children and was allegedly passed over for the 2007 Nobel Peace Prize in favor of Al Gore), the Protestant village of Le Chambon-sur-Lignon in France in collaboration with nearby Catholic monasteries and convents, the 6,706

Christian Poles awarded the title of Righteous Among the Nations by the state of Israel (far more than those of any other nation), and above all, Pope Pius XII.

The truth lies somewhere in between. On the one hand, there is a profound difference, rarely acknowledged, between anti-Semitism and anti-Judaism. The former is a modern racist ideology: in its most virulent form, it combined Darwinism, Nietzscheism, and German nationalism to label the Jewish people biologically subhuman and call for their extermination. Anti-Judaism, by contrast, is focused not on a race but on a religion, and thus it calls for conversion rather than genocide. Jews in the Middle Ages were forced to hear sermons arguing that their Torah was fulfilled in Jesus Christ (many simply plugged their ears with wax); and in Spain after the Reconquista, Jews were given the option of converting or leaving the country. These are heavy-handed tactics, to say the least, but seeking the eternal salvation of someone's soul in a bullying and demeaning manner is not the same as seeking the annihilation of an entire people. There was no possibility for conversion under the Nazis; if you were "tainted with Semitic blood," you were marked for enslavement and death. Initially the Nazis spared Jewish converts to Christianity, but only as a tactic to mute Christian outrage; when it suited them, they rounded up converts like Edith Stein (a.k.a. St. Teresa Benedict of the Cross) and sent them to the gas chambers along with all the other so-called Semites. The difference between anti-Semitism and anti-Judaism was illustrated by the words of Pope Pius XI, who as early as 1928 saw the evils of the new ideology: "Anti-Semitism is unacceptable. Spiritually, we are all Semites."

On the other hand, it can be said that Christian anti-Judaism, especially in Germany, created some of the conditions that allowed anti-Semitism to take root. The challenge for Christians today is to acknowledge with sorrow and regret this connection and to proclaim the good news that salvation comes only through Jesus Christ in such a way that those conditions are never, ever again recreated.

Slandering Pius XII

If a moment ago you read with surprise the claim that Pope Pius XII did more than just about anyone else to help the Jews during WWII, then you have most likely come under the spell of one of the most pervasive politically correct lies of the last half century. Fortunately, you are reading a *Politically Incorrect Guide®*, and our specialty is breaking such spells.

As Rabbi David Dalin has pointed out, even before Eugenio Pacelli was elected to the papacy, he had condemned the Nazis as "false prophets with the pride of Lucifer," with forty of Pacelli's forty-four speeches on German soil containing "attacks on Nazism or condemnations of Hitler's doctrines." When Pacelli became pope in 1939 and took the name Pius XII, the Nazi newspaper *Berliner Morganpost* expressed its displeasure: "The election of Cardinal Pacelli is not accepted with favor in Germany because he was always opposed to Nazism."

Pius XII's first encyclical was *Summi Pontificatus*, which rejects Nazi ideology and its attempt to destroy "the unity of the human race" (the Allies would print eighty thousand copies of the encyclical and drop them over Nazi Germany in an effort to rally resistance). During the war, the pope's activities on behalf of the Jews included, but were not limited to:

- Forging thousands of baptismal certificates and other documents for Jews
- Instructing monasteries, rectories, and convents to shelter Jews

A Book You're Not Supposed to Read

The Myth of Hitler's Pope by David G. Dalin (Washington, DC: Regnery, 2005).

- Using a wide array of diplomatic measures to delay or halt deportations
- Hiding, feeding, and sheltering between 4,000 and 7,000 Jews in the 180 known places of refuge in Vatican City, including the pope's summer residence of Castel Gandolfo
- Evacuating Jews from Axis-occupied territory. The pope took personal responsibility for the evacuation of Italian Jewish children; and
- Facilitating opposition to Hitler, including hosting conspirators plotting to assassinate the *Führer* (in the meantime, Hitler was planning to invade Vatican City and kidnap the pope. But the pope, anticipating the attempt, had signed a letter stating his abdication from the papacy in the event of kidnapping)

In the Pope's Own Words

"For centuries the Jews have been most unjustly treated and despised. It is time they were treated with justice and humanity. God wills it and the Church wills it. St. Paul tells us that the Jews are our brothers. Instead of being treated as strangers, they should be welcomed as friends."

—Pope Pius XII

Pius XII had also planned to follow the Dutch Catholic bishops in explicitly mentioning the Jews when condemning deportations. But less than a day before he was to issue his own statement, the Pope learned that 40,000 Dutch Jews were being rounded up in retaliation for the bishops' letter (that figure would eventually include Jewish convert Edith Stein). The pope immediately had his own statement burned, saying, "If the protest of the Dutch Bishops has cost the lives of 40,000 people, my intervention would take at least 200,000 people to their deaths." The loud protestations of the Church in Holland did not stop the Holocaust but accelerated it: 79 percent of the

Jewish population in the Netherlands was wiped out, more than anywhere else in the West.

All told, Pius XII's success in saving Jews was extraordinary. According to Israeli diplomat and scholar Pinchas Lapide, "The Catholic Church, under the pontificate of Pius XII, was instrumental in saving the lives of as many as 860,000 Jews from certain death at Nazi hands." This figure, Lapide added, "far exceeds those saved by all other Churches and rescue organizations combined." At least one other person was equally impressed. Israel Anton Zolli, Chief Rabbi of Rome, was so moved by the pope's love for the Jews that he converted to Catholicism after the war, taking Eugenio as his baptismal name in honor of the pope.

Pius XII continued to treat the Jews with love and courtesy after the war. He once received a large delegation of Roman Jews in the Vatican, ordering that the Imperial Steps, which were reserved only for crowned heads of state, be opened for them. Upon noticing that his Jewish visitors felt uncomfortable in the Sistine Chapel, the pope came down from his throne and greeted them warmly, telling them to feel completely at home and adding, "I am only the Vicar of Christ, but you are His very kith and kin."

Yet despite this amazing legacy, Pius XII is widely derided today as a stooge for the Third Reich who "kept silent" when he could have denounced the Holocaust and ended it with a magic wave of his crosier. How did things come to such a pass? To answer that question is to pass into a twilight zone where truth is stranger than fiction.

Exploiting the Holocaust

"The anti-papal polemics of ex-seminarians like Garry Wills and John Cornwell... of ex-priests like James Carroll, and or other lapsed or angry liberal Catholics exploit the tragedy of the Jewish people during the Holocaust to foster their own political agenda of forcing changes on the Catholic Church today."

—**Rabbi David Dalin**

Contemporary Testimony

"The voice of Pius XII is a lonely voice in the silence and darkness enveloping Europe this Christmas. . . . he is about the only ruler left on the Continent of Europe who dares to raise his voice at all."

—*New York Times* editorial, December 25, 1941

"The people of Israel will never forget what His Holiness and his illustrious delegates, inspired by the eternal principles of religion which form the very foundations of true civilization, are doing for us unfortunate brothers and sisters in the most tragic hour of our history, which is living proof of Divine Providence in this world."

—Chief Rabbi of Jerusalem, Isaac Herzog, to Pope Pius XII on February 28, 1944

After World War II, Pius XII was hailed by all, including the World Jewish Congress, the American Jewish Committee, the Italian Hebrew Committee, then–Israeli foreign minister Golda Meir, and the Chief Rabbi of Jerusalem. The one major power that did not join the chorus of praise was the U.S.S.R. Angry at the Catholic Church in Eastern Europe for its resistance to communism, the Soviets sought ways to discredit the Church.

One trick regularly employed by the Soviet propaganda machine was to besmirch the reputation of the deceased, who aren't around to fight back. And so five years after the death of Pius XII, a first-time German playwright named Rolf Hochhuth published a tendentious and historically absurd play called *The Deputy* (1963) that portrayed the pope as Hitler's right-hand man. In 2007, Ion Mihai Pacepa, a defector and Romanian spymaster, revealed to the world that the outline to the play had been provided to Hochhuth by none other than the KGB.

Historians are divided about the veracity of Pacepa's testimony, but two things are clear: *The Deputy* fit perfectly with Communist disinformation goals, and it was highly successful, deeply influencing even the non-Communist Left. In the 1990s, liberal dissident Catholics repeated and expanded upon Hochhuth's lies in an effort to discredit the papacy of John Paul II. With the publication of works like John Cornwell's *Hitler's Pope*, the situation had become so outrageous that it inspired a new generation of Jewish scholars like Rabbi David Dalin to defend the honor of the Catholic pontiff.

A Book You're Not Supposed to Read

Disinformation: Former Spy Chief Reveals Secret Strategies for Undermining Freedom, Attacking Religion, and Promoting Terrorism by Ion Mihai Pacepa (Washington, DC: WND Books, 2013).

The more historians research the Second World War and the more access they gain to primary documents in the Vatican Archives, the more evidence they find that exonerates the actions and decisions of Pius XII. Nevertheless, the secular Left continues its smear campaign, partly to defame the Catholic Church, partly out of a naïve activist faith in the power of virtue-signaling and grand public denouncements, and partly to deflect criticism away from liberal leaders like FDR who did next to nothing to stop the Holocaust. "When the legend becomes fact, print the legend"—or so goes a famous quote. Hochhuth's notorious legend has become fact in the liberal media, which is only too happy to print and reprint it.

The Crusades

The Crusades were a series of military campaigns to retake the Holy Land after it had been conquered by the Seljuk Turks in the eleventh century. The name "crusade" comes from the Latin word for cross, as the Christian warriors who participated in these campaigns wore a red cross over their armor. There were a total of eight crusades initiated by various popes and other European leaders between 1095 and 1270. Some of them, such as the First Crusade (1095–1101) were spectacular military successes against the odds; others, such as the Fourth Crusade (1204), were a clustercuss from beginning to end.

But were the Crusades evil, the product of power-hungry Europeans or, as Ridley Scott's 2005 hit-job of a movie *Kingdom of Heaven* would have us believe, of religiously motivated maniacs? Let us consider four points that help answer this question.

Imperialist Colonization versus Self-Defense

If the Crusaders weren't religious fanatics forcing innocent Arabs to accept Jesus or die, then they were imperial colonists interested in the same things as all colonizers: plunder, power, and property. That is the common canard about the Crusades.

But the idea of the Crusaders as imperial colonists is laughable. To be imperial, you need to have an empire, and to colonize, you need to have far-reaching logistical skills, effective lines of communication, and a modicum of national discipline. God bless 'em, the Crusaders had none of the above. Medieval Europe was not a military and economic powerhouse seeking to expand into other geographical regions or exploit other markets, and it was not well-organized or effectively united. On the contrary, Europe was a divided Third-World David in comparison to the wealthier and more powerful Goliath of Muslim lands. When the Crusaders recaptured land taken by Muslim aggressors, they did not set up colonies or plantations that sucked wealth from the natives and sent it back to the mother country; they set up military outposts to defend the Holy Land from invaders and to make it safe for pilgrims. The Crusaders' homelands received a few cool things from the Middle East, such as spices not seen in Europe since the fall of the Roman Empire, but they never profited economically from the Crusader kingdoms in the Holy Land, as Spain did from New Spain or Great Britain from India. Instead of taking from conquered territory, the Crusaders ponied up at great personal cost: nobles sold off so much of their own property to finance the Crusades that they caused inflation in Europe, and the mortality rate of

Europe's noblest sons in the Crusades was as high as 75 percent. Perhaps if the Crusaders *had* been imperialistic they would have been more successful in holding onto the spoils of their military victories. Instead, after the success of the First Crusade, most of the Crusaders eagerly returned home, and with little plunder to show for it; within decades, a good portion of their territorial gains had disappeared.

The motive for the Crusades was not economic, nor was it a violent effort to convert Muslims to the Christian faith. It was largely a defensive action. After the prophet Muhammad seized control of his native Mecca in A.D. 630, Islam embarked on an amazingly successful military expansion. Only one hundred years after the conquest of Mecca, Muslims had taken most of Spain and Portugal; most of the Middle East, including all of the Arabian Peninsula, Iraq, and the once-mighty Persian Empire in Iran; virtually all of Egypt and North Africa; and parts of India. Christian Europe suddenly found itself outflanked to the West, South, and distant East, with Muslims gobbling up all of the historic sees of Christianity in Jerusalem, Alexandria, and Antioch and then invading France (they were defeated by Charles Martel at the Battle of Poitiers in A.D. 732). Later, when the balance of power in the Muslim world shifted from the Arabs to the Seljuk Turks, things grew even worse for Christians in the Middle East. After the Turks took the Holy Land from the Egyptian caliphate, they blocked all Christian access to the sacred sites and attacked the (Christian) Byzantine Empire. Finally, after several defeats, the Byzantine Emperor Alexius I appealed to Pope Urban II in 1095 for military aid. The pope responded by calling the First Crusade.

Dogged by a lack of logistical preparedness and military discipline, by disease and poor lines of communication, and by just plain bad luck, the Crusades were ultimately a failure. Nevertheless, they were eminently justifiable from both a moral and a geopolitical perspective. Morally, it is permissible to defend oneself or one's allies from an unjust aggressor, and the Arab and Turkish Muslims were indeed unjust aggressors, having attacked and conquered Christian land after Christian land without provocation. And as for geopolitics, put yourselves in the shoes of a medieval European. A highly motivated and highly bellicose foe has conquered two-thirds of Christendom in a relatively short period of time and is now attacking Europe's sole remaining ally. That ally desperately asks for help. Do you do nothing and wait for the enemy to attack European soil? (Oh wait, he already did—most of Spain and Portugal have fallen, France almost did, and Muslim pirates have sailed up the Tiber River and raided St. Peter's Basilica in Rome). Do you wait until the Byzantine Empire falls to the enemy? (By then, you will be the only ones left, and you are militarily and politically weaker than the Turk.) Or do you strike while you can? Sometimes the best defense is a good offense. The Crusades did not ultimately retake the Holy Land or save the Byzantine Empire, but they did buy Europe enough time to grow and prosper, so that Christendom was eventually able to repel the Moors from the Iberian Peninsula and withstand the onslaughts of the Ottoman Empire.

Just Cause versus Just Conduct

The Crusades as a whole qualify as a just, morally defensible series of wars, even if atrocities occurred during them. Moral theologians make a useful distinction between the *jus ad bellum* (it being right to go to war) and the *jus in bello* (the right conduct *in* the war). A warring party may score high marks in one but not the other. The United States was morally justified in declaring war on Japan and its Axis allies after the surprise attack on Pearl Harbor, but that does not mean that everything the United States did during World War II (the bombing of civilian populations, for example) was morally justifiable—and it certainly does not mean that every action of every G.I. was right. Similarly, if Crusaders did bad things during the war (either officially as a group or unofficially as individuals), those actions concern the *jus in bello* and do *not* affect the verdict on the *jus ad bellum* question. They are two separate issues.

But did the Crusaders commit atrocities during the Crusades? Undoubtedly they did (like soldiers in just about every other army in the history of warfare), but it is not always easy to identify them. Many of the sensational accounts of massacres and the like were written either by the Crusaders' adversaries or by people who weren't there. In addition, an action that qualifies as a war crime today may not have qualified as one at the time.

Consider the sacking of Jerusalem on July 15, 1099, during the First Crusade. Most accounts were written twenty years after the event, and none by an eyewitness. And many of these rely on the testimony of a cleric named Fulcher of Chartres, who arrived in Jerusalem five months after the sacking and who was prone to exaggerate the carnage in order to demonstrate the city's "purification." Fulcher made physically impossible claims, such as that the entire city was ankle-deep in blood; later chronicles, as in the game of "telephone," turned these puddles into a river of blood flowing up to a horse's bridle. That consummate moderate Bill Clinton, when he all but laid the blame for 9/11 at the feet of the Crusaders in a November 2001 speech at Georgetown University, settled for knee-deep.

Did the Crusaders really slaughter every man, woman, and child in Jerusalem after their siege of the city? Recent scholarship indicates that they did not, but even if they had, it must be remembered that it was an accepted practice from the days of Homer on that "a city which resisted capture was utterly forfeit." As historian Thomas Madden explains, "The property and lives of the citizens belonged to the victorious forces. That is why all cities had to consider whether they believed they could withstand a siege or should surrender." In 1268, Christian Antioch peacefully surrendered to the Egyptian ruler Baibars, only to see him bolt the gates of the city and have every man, woman, and child slaughtered. Baibars then wrote to "the absent lord of the city describing in gruesome detail what he had missed."

One final consideration. Enemies of Christianity often point to atrocities committed during the Crusades as if they show the true nature of Christianity, while conveniently overlooking the fact that many of these atrocities were condemned *at the time*. The Sack of Constantinople (1204) was a reprehensible act in which Crusaders, after being drawn into Byzantine infighting to help one claimant to the throne overthrow another and then getting gypped on their pay, attacked the capital of Constantinople; to this day, the Greek Orthodox still bear a grudge against the Catholic Church as a result. What is never mentioned, though, is that the Crusader army that did this was mutinous: they had disobeyed the pope's orders, and after the sack the outraged pope excommunicated them all. The situation is roughly comparable to the 1968 My Lai Massacre during the Vietnam War, which drew outrage from America and its allies as soon as it became public knowledge.

Unfortunately, atrocities occur in war. When they do, what must be weighed is not only the atrocity itself but how the nation and leaders of those guilty of the atrocity respond to it. The fact that Pope Innocent III and the American public were horrified by the mass murders at Constantinople and My Lai are to their credit; their condemnation of the wrongs done in their name separates them from the Soviet, Maoist, and Nazi officials who delighted in their henchmen's most nefarious deeds.

Holy War versus Jihad

Leading liberals such as Bill Clinton and Barack Obama have suggested a moral equivalence between the Crusades and contemporary Islamic terrorism, and their words are listened to because of a general aversion today to the very concept of a "holy war." We agree that the idea of a "holy war" is disturbing, but then again so is just about any war. How different is killing in the name of God from killing in the name of liberty (the

American Revolution) or killing in the name of national unity (the Civil War) or killing in the name of democracy (World War I, at least according to Woodrow Wilson) or killing in the name of compassion (that is, killing people because they are killing innocent people, as in Rwanda)? Any "killing in the name of X" is bound to elicit a negative response even when X is something noble; this reaction may well be a good thing lest we take the business of killing too lightly, but we should be aware of it nonetheless.

A Book You're Not Supposed to Read

Il Jihad e La Crociata [The Jihad and the Crusade] by Marco Meschini (Edizioni Ares, 2007).

But not all wars are inherently immoral, even if they are all horrible and wasteful. So let's reboot and try to distinguish between the Crusaders' concept of holy war and the Islamic concept of jihad. Our guide will be history professor Marco Meschini.

According to Meschini, a holy war has two elements. The first is that, according to believers, "it is a war willed by God and promoted by his legitimate representatives; secondly, participating in this war opens the gates to paradise." Regarding the first element, the Crusades qualify as a holy war. The battle cry of the Crusaders was "God wills it!" and the Crusades were launched or blessed by popes and preached by saints such as Bernard of Clairvaux.

It is with the second element that we begin to see significant differences between the Christian Crusades and Islamic jihad emerge. On the one hand, the pope did grant a plenary indulgence to all who participated in the Crusades. A plenary indulgence, however, is not a "Get into Heaven Free" card but only a remission of temporal punishment for sins *already forgiven*; it also requires complete repentance and spiritual purity. Catholics believe that indulgences do not open the gates of paradise directly but are one element among several in a process of genuine conversion and

Two Books You're Not Supposed to Read

The Politically Incorrect Guide® to Islam (and the Crusades) by Robert Spencer (Washington, DC: Regnery, 2005).

The Crusades, Christianity, and Islam by Jonathan Riley-Smith (New York: Columbia University Press, 2008).

spiritual transformation. With the Islamic notion of jihad, on the other hand, the holy warrior or *mujahid* is automatically sanctified by his martial activities. His access to Heaven and the seventy-two virgins who await him is simple and direct.

Further, the Crusades were *not* an instrument of evangelization or proselytization but, as we have already noted, a defensive measure with a limited purpose: to recover land unjustly seized by Muslim aggressors. Jihad, by contrast, authorizes the spread of Islam through violence.

Finally, and most important, the Crusades or any other Christian holy war is not and never has been essential to Christianity. Christianity got along fine for a thousand years without a holy war and it will, God willing, get along fine for another thousand years without one. Jihad, however, *is* essential to Islam; according to some Sunni scholars, it is the sixth pillar of Islam, one of the precepts that define the religion.

Today there are very good prudential reasons for Christians to avoid talk about a "holy war," as such talk tends to blur the line between holiness and violence, which have always been sharply distinguished in Christian theology and practice. But our modern-day reticence does not make the holy war of the Crusades evil, nor does it put the Crusades on par with Islamic jihad.

Memories Then and Now

We have already made mention of that deep student of history, President William Jefferson Clinton, and his assertion that the 9/11 attacks can be traced to the First Crusade and the sack of Jerusalem. After giving a highly skewed summary of the sack, Clinton concluded, "I can tell you that that story is still being told today in the Middle East, and we are still paying for it." Clinton and others like him would have us believe that the experience of the Crusades left on the Muslim psyche a deep resentment of the Christian West and a justifiable desire for vengeance that would culminate in the Islamic terrorism all too common today.

Jihad: The Holy War at the Heart of Islam

"Fight those who do not believe in Allah and who do not take as illicit what Allah and his messengers have declared to be illicit."

—the Qur'an

"Know that paradise is in the shade of the sword."

—a hadith (saying) of Muhammad

Rubbish. The oldest Muslim memory of the Crusades was actually positive; after all, *they* won. For centuries, the Crusades did not stand out in the Islamic mind as exceptional acts of animosity between Christians and Muslims; they were simply part of a long history of armed conflicts that Muslims had initiated in the name of Allah (there's that "in the name of" again). The Arabic language did not even have a word for the Crusades until the mid-nineteenth century, and when one was coined, it was coined as a term of approval by Arab *Christians*. And there was not even a Muslim history of the Crusades until 1899.

When the Crusades finally did become "a thing" in Muslim consciousness, it was through a strange synergy between liberal Western self-hatred and Arab nationalism. Anti-Christian Westerners such as Voltaire and Gibbon, aided and abetted by the novels of Sir Walter Scott, had wrongly portrayed the Crusaders as crude and greedy pilferers attacking a peaceful and civilized people, and their distortions filtered into the Middle East through European colonization of the region and through the education of wealthy Arabs at elite European schools. As Arabs began to chafe under their colonial masters, they connected the dots and portrayed the secular

The Christian Resistance

"Wherever the Mohammedans have had complete sway, wherever the Christians have been unable to resist them by the sword, Christianity has ultimately disappeared. From the hammer of Charles Martel to the sword of Jan Sobieski, Christianity owed its safety in Europe to the fact that it was able to show that it could and would fight as well as the Mohammedan aggressor."

—Theodore Roosevelt, *Fear God and Take Your Part*, 1916

European colonial powers as latter-day "Crusaders." At first their critique was more secular than religious, but starting in the 1950s a militant pan-Islamic fundamentalism began to replace Arab nationalism. By the time the Myth of the Crusades was filtered through the addled brain of Osama bin Laden, the *Jews* were Crusaders as well and the Crusades a permanent fixture of the West since 1095. So if liberals want someone to blame for the contemporary Muslim animus against the Crusades, they should take a good look at the family album and at their own ideological forebears and the lies that they spread.

There is no moral equivalence between the Crusades and the terrorist activities of modern Muslim fanatics such as al-Qaeda or ISIS, nor did the Crusades cause these strains of contemporary Islam to be weaponized against the West. Some of the events of the Crusades are tragic, some are just downright embarrassing, and some, like the deeds of Godfrey of Bouillon or Richard the Lionheart or Baldwin IV the "Leper King" or St. Louis IX King of France, are inspiring examples of Christian chivalry. And as for the hand-wringers who decry these holy wars, Chesterton knows them well when he writes: "They seem entirely to forget that long before the Crusaders had dreamed of riding to Jerusalem, the Moslems had almost ridden into Paris."

The Spanish Inquisition

It would be inappropriate for *me* to begin a discussion on a serious topic like the Spanish Inquisition with a joke, so let me instead mention some of the jokes *other* people have told about it. In *My Fair Lady*, the misogynist Henry Higgins sings a little ditty about not wanting to get married, which includes these lines:

> I'd prefer a new edition
> Of the Spanish Inquisition
> Than to ever let a woman in my life.

Not to be outdone, Mel Brooks has a rousing musical number on the Inquisition ("what a show") in *History of the World, Part I*:

> We know you're wishing
> That we'd go away
> But the Inquisition's here and it's here to stay.

And finally, who can forget the Monty Python sketches featuring the punchline, "Nobody expects the Spanish Inquisition"? They include such memorable quotes as, "Amongst our weaponry are such diverse elements as fear, surprise, ruthless efficiency, an almost fanatical devotion to the pope, and nice red uniforms."

What all of these pop culture references reflect is the reputation of the Spanish Inquisition as one of the most horrible chapters in human history. In the words of the historian Henry Kamen, "No institution in Western history has so fearful a reputation as the Spanish Inquisition." Think about that for a moment. Western history is crowded with evil organizations including the KGB, the Gestapo, the SS, the KKK, and Planned Parenthood—which kills more people every six days than the Spanish Inquisition did in three hundred fifty years. Yet in this crowded list, the name that evokes the most fear and distrust is that of the Inquisition. According to dictionary.com, the very word "inquisition," which originally meant nothing more than "inquiry," has now come to mean "a rigorous, harsh interrogation" that "violates the privacy or rights of individuals."

And, of course, the Spanish Inquisition has become a favorite bludgeon to use against the Catholic Church in particular and against Christianity in general—to "prove" that Christians who care about sound doctrine (Titus 2:1) are repressive, bloodthirsty, and insanely power-hungry.

It's time for another PIG intervention. Let's start by busting six prominent myths about the Inquisition and then get to the bottom of all this.

Myth #1: The Inquisition was motivated by religious fanaticism—Although it was authorized by the Holy See, the Spanish Inquisition was begun by the Spanish royal *court* in response to a dire *political* crisis.

Most Americans do not know that for approximately 780 years the Christian country of Spain was under Muslim control and that the last Islamic state on the Iberian Peninsula did not fall to the Christian Spaniards until 1492, right before the discovery of the New World. As the Christian kingdom of King Ferdinand II and Queen Isabella expanded, more and more Muslims and Jews fell under their jurisdiction. The Christians had engaged in a protracted winner-take-all war, and because the Ottoman Empire was waxing strong and capable of invading the Iberian Peninsula, their position was precarious. And the Turks played for keeps. When they invaded the south Italian city of Otranto in 1480, they killed nearly every resident who refused to convert to Islam (twelve thousand people) and enslaved the rest. Every cleric in the city was slaughtered and the archbishop sawn in half. Because it was clear that the Turks could do the same to any coastal city in Spain, Ferdinand and Isabella instituted the Inquisition to ensure the sincerity of the Spanish Muslims and Jews who had converted to Christianity. The king and queen were worried that those who had only pretended to convert might open the gates of Spanish cities to the Turks.

The Spanish Inquisition thus began as a form of surveillance during a wartime crisis when the stakes were very high; it was more of a political than a religious overreaction (which explains why the pope at the time actually tried to stop or at least curtail it). In some respects the early years of the Inquisition may be compared to the United States' internment of Japanese citizens during World War II; at the time each seemed a reasonable way of dealing with a suspect population in the midst of total war and uncertainty.

Myth #2: The Inquisition targeted Jews and Muslims—The Inquisition was strictly an in-house affair, comparable to an Internal Affairs investigation. Hence its jurisdiction was limited to baptized Christians. No Jew who said he was a Jew was ever brought before the Inquisition. Rather, the Inquisition initially focused on former Jews and Muslims who had converted to Catholicism (they had been given the choice of converting or leaving the country). As mentioned above, the Crown's chief concern was crypto-Muslims who might aid and abet the enemy. But converted Jews came under suspicion as well since it was believed that they had allied themselves with Muslims during the Christian reconquest of Spain. Although this may sound like the makings of a witch hunt, as Rodney Stark has reported, "nearly all of the Jewish and most of Muslim converts were sincere," and the Inquisition did not fan the flames of bigotry against the newly converted but instead quelled them by replacing chronic outbreaks of scapegoating mob violence with bureaucratic due process.

Myth #3: The Inquisition used horrific tortures—All European courts at the time used interrogation techniques inherited from the Romans, and the tribunal of the Spanish Inquisition was no exception. But reports of its atrocities are greatly exaggerated. Indeed, the methods of the Inquisitors were more humane than those of any contemporary secular court, as there were strict parameters within which they had to work. A doctor was required to be present during the interrogation, which was limited to fifteen minutes. No blood was allowed to be shed, and no permanent bodily damage done. One historian has compared the level of brutality of the Spanish

Inquisition's interrogation methods to American police departments in the 1930s. And leather blackjacks are hardly the stuff of iron maidens.

What is more, because the clerical authorities were skeptical of its efficacy, torture was used rarely. Of the 44,701 Inquisition cases on record, only 2 percent involved the use of torture. (Or should we call it "enhanced interrogation"?) Moreover, only 1 percent of all cases involved torture applied twice, and never was it applied a third time. In other words, 1 percent of all Inquisition cases involved fifteen minutes of torture, 1 percent involved thirty minutes, and 98 percent involved *no torture whatsoever*. The Inquisition puts Jack Bauer to shame.

Myth #4: The Inquisition was draconian and harsh—In general, most secular governments despised the ecclesiastical courts at the time because both their methods and their sentences were too *light*, and this was true of the Spanish Inquisition as well. The Inquisition was a model of due process: acquittals were common, sometimes with entire investigations being thrown out, and it was also possible to appeal to a higher authority such as a synod or the Vatican. The same goes for Inquisition prisons, which were not the dismal dungeons of our macabre imagination. On the contrary, they were so comfortable that criminals in secular jails purposely blasphemed in order to be transferred there.

Myth #5: The Inquisition was a bloodbath—The Spanish Inquisition never executed a single individual: as a Church tribunal, the most it could do was declare someone guilty of a capital crime and then hand him over to the State, which wielded the power to execute. This did indeed happen, but far less frequently than is commonly imagined. Only 1.8 percent of the trials conducted by the Spanish Inquisition resulted in an execution. Indeed, fewer people died from three and a half centuries of the Spanish Inquisition than "the thousands of English Lutherans, Lollards, and Catholics (in addition to two of his wives) that Henry VIII is credited with having boiled, burned, beheaded, or hanged," as Rodney Stark points out in *The Triumph of Christianity.* And in a great many of the Inquisition cases the death penalty was only doled out to repeat offenders. Popular images of mass burnings at weekly *autos-de-fe* are pure poppycock.

Burning at the stake sounds like a horrible way to go, but it was probably more merciful than the English practice of hanging, drawing, and quartering, as the person condemned to the stake would suffocate from the smoke before actually being burned alive, and in many cases the executioner would mercifully strangle the condemned before he even lit the pyre. Nor was such a punishment the sadistic invention of the Inquisition: it was another inheritance from the ancient Romans, who had replaced crucifixion with burning in the fourth century.

Myth #6: The Inquisition burned books and was against scientific and cultural progress—Like other Catholic countries after the Reformation, Spain had an Index of Forbidden Books, and some of these books (such as Lutheran treatises) were burned during the Inquisition. However, very few of these were scientific (Galileo was not even on the Spanish Index), and the vast majority of them were pornographic, a genre that proliferated after the invention of the printing press. All told, the censorship was not that severe. Many books simply had sections crossed out rather than being consigned to the flames, and scholars could get permission to study banned books for their research.

One indication of how different the censorship of the Inquisition was from that of a truly repressive society is that, unlike the totalitarian regimes of Hitler, Stalin, and Mao, the Inquisition indirectly *fostered* cultural and intellectual creativity. The height of the Spanish Inquisition coincides with the "Golden Age" of Spanish literature and arts, the age of great writers such as Miguel de Cervantes, Lope de Vega, and Pedro Calderón, renowned painters such as El Greco, and celebrated composers like Tomás Luis de Victoria. If that strikes you as counterintuitive, consider this fact: the "Golden Age" of Hollywood (1930s–1950s) roughly coincides with the Hays Code, the motion picture industry's internal censorship that kept morally unacceptable content from making it to the big screen. (The Hays Code, incidentally, was the result of an early ecumenical collaboration. It was first drafted by a Jesuit priest and a Catholic layman and enforced by a Presbyterian elder, the eponymous William B. Hays.) Filmmakers from that era complained about the restrictions (a very natural human reaction), but some of them also admitted that fencing with the censors made them better artists, goading them to find more subtle and artistic ways to get what they wanted across. Alfred Hitchcock was particularly adept at circumventing the rules, and one senses a similar wryness in Cervantes' *Don Quixote* regarding the Inquisition. Light censorship brings out the best in an artist, like sand irritating an oyster to make a pearl.

The great Russian author Fyodor Dostoyevsky bought into the caricature of the Inquisition and gave world literature the unforgettable and frightening figure of the Grand Inquisitor in his *Brothers Karamazov*, but ironically Dostoyevsky had more trouble with the czar's censors than Cervantes did with Spain's.

"The Black Legend"

It should be clear by now that there is an enormous discrepancy between the myth of the Spanish Inquisition and the reality, a discrepancy so great that historians speak of the accumulation of lies and gross exaggerations about the Inquisition as "the Black Legend." That legend was begun by English and Dutch propagandists in the sixteenth century in an effort to discredit Spain, which at the time was their main rival on the high seas and in colonizing the New World. The English in particular were masters of misinformation. In the late seventeenth century, for example, they created a propaganda display called the Spanish Armoury that, according to an exhibit currently on display at the Tower of London, was "designed to show the Spaniards' planned persecution of the English—and England's moral superiority over Spain." The display ostensibly included torture devices taken from the remains of the Spanish Armada, but the truth was far more domestic: some of them had been borrowed from the Royal Navy! Even as late as World War I, the English invented wild stories about Germans boiling down the corpses of their own soldiers to make machine oils and pig food, stories disseminated (ironically) by the British government's Department of Information.

As for the Black Legend, it first reared its ugly head in 1567, one year after the English defeat at the Battle of Mühlberg. Over time, contributors to the tale invented absurd statistics about millions of people being burned at the stake and created fantastic accounts of sadistic, sodomite hooded clerics with red hot pokers, iron maidens, and so forth. Underlying these calumnies was a subtle and sometimes not so subtle current of racism: the fair-skinned English with their Anglo-Saxon virtue saw themselves as superior to the oily, dark-skinned, and sexually deviant Hispanics to the south. Another factor was an ignorance of the Continental judicial system. Anglo-American law is based on an "adversarial" system of criminal justice in which two advocates argue against each other in court before an impartial judge or jury. European criminal justice, on the other hand, is an "inquisitorial" system in which judicial officers "perform a critical investigative, even prosecutorial, function" themselves, as Notre Dame law professor Gerard R. Bradley has explained. There is nothing wrong with the European model—indeed it was based on that of ancient Rome, which gave mankind the gift of the concept of the rule of law—but to Anglo-American eyes it appears sinister.

And, of course, the Black Legend was fueled by anti-Catholicism. The pump had already been primed by John Foxe's *Book of Martyrs*, which contained colorful accounts of Protestants being tortured and killed under the reign of "Bloody Mary" and which conditioned the British public to

A Book You're Not Supposed to Read

Spain's Long Shadow: The Black Legend, Off-Whiteness, and Anglo-American Empire by Maria DeGuzman (Minneapolis: University Of Minnesota Press, 2005).

view Catholic authorities as fanatical, cruel, and twisted. The Black Legend capitalized on this stereotype and ran with it.

Hispanophobia, racism, ignorance of foreign judicial systems, anti-Catholicism—all of these explain the origins of the Black Legend, but they do not explain how such an outrageous misrepresentation continues to this day. The answer to that question is quite simple: the secular Left finds it very useful for excluding Christian morality from the public square, for their goal is not a mere institutional separation of Church and State but the reduction of Christian influence on civic law to nil. We see this today in the debates on same-sex "marriage," where not only are arguments based on the Bible or divine revelation dismissed out of hand, but even arguments based on natural law theory are rejected on the grounds that they are "inherently theological" and thus automatically unconstitutional. (See the Affidavit of Martha Nussbaum in the 1993 Colorado case *Evans v. Romer*.) The de-Christianizing of American society is aided and abetted by the Myth of the Inquisition because we have all now been trained to think that there are only two alternatives: a totally secular public square where Christianity has no impact and human rights are respected, or the evil Inquisition in which religious fanatics micromanage all aspects of our lives and barbeque dissenters. What began as an anti-Catholic myth perpetuated by English propagandists has morphed into an anti-Christian myth that discredits all religious believers. Take, for example, a recent rehashing of the Black Legend, Jonathan Kirsch's 2008 *The Grand Inquisitor's Model: A History of Terror in the Name of God*. The subtitle says it all, with Kirsch linking just about every dark chapter of history in the last five hundred years—including atrocities of the Gestapo, Stalin's show trials, McCarthy's communist witch hunts, and George W. Bush's Guantanamo Bay—to "the friar-inquisitors who set up the rack and the pyre." No agenda there, I'm sure.

Adolf Hitler once asserted that if you tell a big enough lie often enough, it will be believed. Exhibit A of the sad truth behind this statement is the lie of the Black Legend. But where does this leave Christians today? On the one hand, we must be truthful about the abuses that occurred during the Spanish Inquisition and own up to them. As Pope Leo XIII once said, "The Church has no need of any man's lie." On the other hand, those abuses must be studied in their proper historical and political context and the outlandish caricatures about them put to rest once and for all. Achieving that goal, however, will not be easy, since Christianity's enemies have a vested interest in keeping the Black Legend alive and well.

CHAPTER NINE

Christianity and Science

The Library of Alexandria is famous for having been one of the greatest repositories of knowledge in the ancient world and famous also for having been burned to the ground. The trouble is that no one is sure who lit the match. Suspects range from Julius Caesar, Coptic Pope Theophilus, to Caliph Omar after the Muslim conquest of Egypt. Later authors quote the Caliph as saying, "If the books in this library contain things contrary to the Qur'an, they are evil and must be burned. If they contain only the doctrine of the Qur'an, burn them anyway, for they are superfluous."

Historians do not know if Caliph Omar said these words, if he started the fire, or indeed if there ever was a fire. (So, what are we paying historians for?) But the Caliph's logic about non-Qur'anic knowledge is something typically associated these days with Christianity rather than Islam. When critics think of Christianity and the intellectual life, they think of the Bonfire of the Vanities, Spaniards burning the Maya codices, and Bostonians burning Quaker and anti-Puritan books—as if all church history were lit by a series of *Fahrenheit 451* moments.

Every now and then one does indeed come across a misologist Christian, usually because he is uneducated. But to tar all Christians with the

Did you know?

★ Educated people in Columbus's day knew the earth was round

★ Devout Christians were founders of myriad branches of science, from chemistry and bacteriology to genetics and microbiology

★ Science was stillborn everywhere outside the Christian West

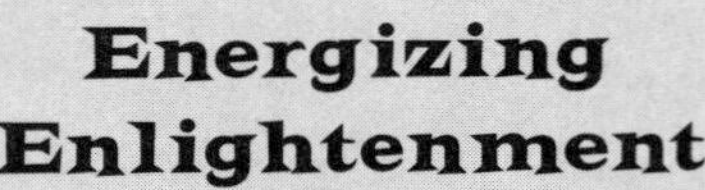

Energizing Enlightenment

"Christianity... was never intended to replace or supersede the ordinary human arts and sciences: it is rather a director which will set them all to the right jobs, and a source of energy which will give them all new life, if only they will put themselves at its disposal."

—**C. S. Lewis,** *Mere Christianity*

same brush is to be deceived by yet another politically correct myth (slander is more like it) and to miss out on one of the most fascinating stories in human history—the role that Christianity has played in increasing the world's knowledge. For more than burn, Christianity waters, baptizing what is best in human thought and even prompting new intellectual discoveries and whole new fields of science. Let's start by debunking some myths about Galileo and evolution and then get to the heart of the matter.

Galileo—and a Side Note on Columbus and Magellan

Galileo's head was on the block
The crime was lookin' up the truth...

So sing those great students of history, the Indigo Girls. Of course, Galileo's head was never close to being put on a block; the worst he got was house arrest at a villa in Italy—would that we were all so unlucky. Secular liberals love to brandish caricatures of the past and use them to bludgeon Christian conservatives in the present. My other favorite example, which I have seen as the email signature of an angry leftist, is: "The Church says that the earth is flat, but I know that it is round. For I have seen the shadow of the earth on the moon and I have more faith in the shadow than in the Church —Ferdinand Magellan."

Magellan? It is hard to keep a straight face when others can't keep their lies straight. This bizarre statement from the nineteenth-century "Great Agnostic" Robert Green Ingersoll is a lame combination of two falsehoods. First it confuses Ferdinand Magellan with Christopher Columbus, and second it associates the Church with a belief that the world is flat. Before Magellan got thrown into the mix, the original lie was that the pious king and queen of Spain, together with the nefarious Spanish Inquisition, were reluctant to fund Christopher Columbus's expedition because they all thought the world was flat and that Columbus would sail off its edge. But the truth is that no educated Westerner or sailor at the time thought such a thing; the only point of contention was the size of the earth's circumference, which Columbus had vastly underestimated. The Crown's geographers advised Queen Isabella against backing Columbus's voyage not because they were superstitious ignoramuses but because they had calculated that Columbus could not reach China in the manner he proposed (and they were right). The flat-earth yarn was invented out of whole cloth by the novelist Washington Irving in 1828 and adopted by anti-Catholic polemicists such Andrew Dickson White—the founder of Cornell University—as "proof" that clerical religion was inherently hostile to rationality. Then, as we have seen more than once in this PIG, what started out as anti-Catholic propaganda was later weaponized against all Christians.

As for Magellan, the notion that he had more faith in a shadow than in the Church would have come as quite a surprise to him. He was an eager proselytizer in the Philippines, credited with introducing the Christian faith to those islands. "Magellan's Cross," which is believed to have been planted in Cebu by the famous explorer, is still a symbol of Catholicism in the Philippines.

But back to Galileo Galilei (1564–1642), the Italian astronomer whose theory that the earth revolves around the sun was condemned by the Roman

Inquisition as "foolish and absurd in philosophy, and formally heretical since it explicitly contradicts in many places the sense of Holy Scripture." What is the truth about this notorious affair? Well for one thing, it is not proof that the Church felt threatened by scientific knowledge in general or even by heliocentrism. The Polish cleric Nicolaus Copernicus had already advanced the same theory a century earlier, and instead of being condemned he was encouraged by several prominent Church prelates to publish his ideas, ideas that went on to become the basis for Pope Gregory XIII's reform of the calendar in 1582. If the Galileo affair was only about heliocentrism, then why didn't the Church condemn Copernicus?

The answer is that the Galileo case was complicated by various political and religious crises and by the following two factors:

1. In addition to heliocentrism, Galileo made metaphysical claims about "primary and secondary qualities" that *were* wrong, both scientifically and theologically;
2. Galileo was asking for trouble when he betrayed his old friend Pope Urban VIII, who had simply asked him to make it clear in his writings that the conclusions of empirical science are not absolute truth but plausible hypotheses. Instead Galileo wrote a dialogue that put the geocentric opinion in the mouth of a character named Simplicio or "simpleton." Ouch!

Even though Church authorities explicitly condemned only the heliocentric part of Galileo's thought, it is likely that they were influenced by the whole stew. And it should be noted that insofar as the Roman Inquisition was reacting against Galileo's opinions about primary qualities and heliocentrism as absolute truth, it was siding *with* science. Galileo may have been a great astronomer and physicist, but he did not understand the full significance of the scientific method and precisely what that method does and does not disclose. For as any good scientist will tell you, science does not deliver metaphysical verdicts on "primary qualities," and it certainly does not make pronouncements that are absolutely true. On the contrary, it delivers highly probable *hypotheses* that are empirically verifiable and subject to further revision based on new discoveries and new explanatory models. The Roman Inquisition was right to suspect that there was something "off" about Galileo's ideas but they were wrong to pinpoint heliocentrism as the culprit. Fortunately, the condemnation did little to stop Christian work in heliocentric research, astronomy, or any of the other sciences. To this day the Vatican Observatory remains one of the most prestigious astronomical institutions in the world. Even at the time some Church officials held an opinion different from the Inquisition's verdict: as the esteemed Cardinal Cesare Baronius reportedly said to Galileo: "The Bible teaches us how to go to heaven, not how the heavens go."

Two Books You're Not Supposed to Read

Inventing the Flat Earth: Columbus and Modern Historians by Jeffrey Burton Russell (New York: Praeger, 1991).

Galileo, Science and the Church by Jerome L. Langford (Ann Arbor: University of Michigan Press, 1992).

There's no doubt about it: the Church blundered when it condemned Galileo. But harping on this one decision and ignoring the Church's otherwise stellar record with astronomy and all other science (see below) is like saying that Muhammad Ali was a lousy boxer because he once lost to Joe Frazier.

Evolution

Anytime the alleged War between Science and Religion is brought up, you can be sure that mention of evolution is not far behind. Since the publication of Darwin's *Origin of the Species*, there has been a lively debate about the compatibility of evolutionary theory and biblical faith. At the dawn of the twentieth century, a good number of American Christians strongly opposed Darwin's ideas (hence the famous Scopes Monkey Trial in 1925), and as the twenty-first century marches on, a good number still do. But other Christians equally committed to biblical inerrancy and doctrinal orthodoxy, men like John Henry Newman, take a different approach. When a worried friend wrote to Newman less than ten years after the publication of *Origin of the Species*, the famous English scholar replied, "As to the Divine Design, is it not an instance of incomprehensibly and infinitely marvellous Wisdom and Design to have given certain laws to matter millions of ages ago, which have surely and precisely worked out, in the long course of those ages, those effects which He from the first proposed? Mr. Darwin's theory need not then to be atheistical, be it true or not; it may simply be suggesting a larger idea of Divine Prescience and Skill...I do not [see] that 'the accidental evolution of organic beings' is inconsistent with divine design—It is accidental to us, not to God."

Note Newman's phrasing. Evolution can be used as ammunition by atheists but there is nothing intrinsic to it that is antithetical to Christian doctrine. Instead Newman posits that evolution can just as easily suggest a "larger idea" of Divine Providence, a "bigger picture" of God's wonderful workings in the universe.

Indeed, given what we said about the right way to read the Bible in chapter six, it is eminently possible to reconcile the theory of evolution *properly understood* and the doctrine of creation *properly understood* on the grounds that the Book of Genesis, which is entirely true and contains no errors, is written in a certain literary mode that should not be confused with scientific data. Think of it this way: the verse declaring that "the Lord God formed man of the dust of the ground" (Genesis 2:7) may be shorthand for *the Lord God providentially formed human beings out of a primordial ooze using trillions upon trillions of intermediary causes over a long period of time and without in any way violating nature's integrity.* Jesus Christ employs a similar shorthand in the Sermon on the Mount when He says: "Behold the fowls of the air: for they sow not, neither do they reap, nor gather into barns; yet your heavenly Father feedeth them" (Matthew 6:26). Is Jesus claiming that God the Father is an old man on a park bench feeding all the world's birds? Not quite. God feeds the fowls of the air through a countless multitude of secondary causes, but He feeds them all the same.

Yet note our caveat: both evolution and creation must be *properly understood.* Atheists often assume that the coherence and intelligibility of the natural world are a mark against the doctrine of creation, as if the more that nature can be understood on its own terms, the less need there is for a Creator. And some Christians unwittingly fall into the same trap. Pointing to gaps in our scientific understanding about evolution, they argue that only God's intervention can explain these missing links. Or, they point to "irreducible complexities" in nature and argue that only God could have jump-started them.

The problem with this "God of the gaps" approach is that it sets one up for a fall if or when science does eventually provide an answer to a puzzle. It also inadvertently portrays God as a computer programmer who designs his software and then comes back only when something breaks down or needs an upgrade (I know: we used a similar metaphor in chapter five, but that was only to describe the end of the world!). Seeing God as the occasional fixer, however, is hardly the Christian view of an omnipresent God who forever exercises His Providence over all of creation, both immediately and through a vast network of intermediate causes. In other words, contrary to what atheists and God-of-the-gaps Christians think, nature's intelligibility is not an argument against God; it is an argument *for* Him. The very fact that we can investigate nature at all, that it is capable of being understood by scientific inquiry because it contains consistently knowable patterns—it is this and not the blank spots in our understanding that elegantly points to a God who creates intelligible laws for His universe, just as He creates intelligible essences in His creatures. Remember what we said in chapter one when discussing God's existence: things in this world are not partly caused by nature and partly caused by God, so that when we can't explain something in nature we then ascribe it to God. Rather, their causes are *wholly* natural and *wholly* divine, but on different planes. When we say that this author wrote this sentence and that this pen wrote this sentence, we rightly attribute the same effect (the sentence) to both causes (the author and the pen), only not in the same way. The same goes with God and His creation.

And as for properly understanding the scientific theory of evolution, it must first and foremost be carefully distinguished from "Darwinism," an all-encompassing explanation of reality that is both monstrous and unscientific. Darwinists have the same religious fervor as so-called Creationists without seeming to realize that evolution may not necessarily be true. Evolution is a scientific explanation of the development of animal and plant life, and scientific explanations are subject to sometimes radical revision in light of new breakthroughs. It should also be pointed out that evolution is a currently incomplete scientific explanation, for while there is scientific proof for microevolution (change within a species) there is not the same level of proof for macroevolution (change from one species to another). There are also philosophical problems with the theory of evolution, such as the fact that if one species can evolve into another, then there is really no such thing as a species, for everything is then on a continuum.

Properly understanding the difference between evolution and Darwinism is more than just wordplay: much is at stake. Of all of the scientific theories advanced in the last half-millennium, evolution is the one that has been used to justify the greatest moral evils. Social Darwinism, the political application of the biological theory of survival of the fittest, has led to a laundry list of horrifying atrocities that includes neglect and forced sterilization of the poor and disabled, a ruthless national aspiration to world domination (German National Socialism), eugenics, and racial genocide (the Holocaust). The racist element of Darwinism, which is particularly odious, goes back to the very beginning: the full title of Darwin's book is the *Origin of Species by Means of Natural Selection, or The Preservation of Favoured Races in the Struggle for Life* (emphasis added); and Darwin's sequel, *The Descent of Man*, is even more blatantly racist. Most nineteenth-century evolutionists held racist views on the grounds that Asians and blacks were not as evolved as the "favoured" Caucasians, having come from different subhuman stock. The racist strains in Darwinism went on to have a noticeable impact on Adolf Hitler, who incorporated elements of evolution in his autobiography *Mein Kampf*.

Similarly, Darwinism (again, as opposed to evolution properly understood) claims that *all* reality can be explained by evolutionary changes to matter. But if this is true, then not only is Darwinism an enemy of faith, it is also an enemy of science, for scientific knowledge is itself a reality that cannot be explained in a purely materialistic manner. Put simply, if Darwinism is true, then reason is impossible, for if man is no more than a dumb animal, man could not possibly have come up with a theory of evolution. This conundrum tripped up Charles Darwin himself who, like so many scientists before and after him, was unable to fathom the full significance of his own scientific breakthroughs. In a letter to a friend, Darwin defended the idea of a divine plan to the universe, but then added, "With me the horrid doubt always arises whether the convictions of man's mind, which has been developed from the mind of the lower animals, are of any value or at all trustworthy. Would anyone trust in the convictions of a monkey's mind, if there are any convictions in such a mind?"

Note Darwin's reasoning and its unintentional corollary. Man can't know God because man has a monkey's mind. But if man has a monkey's mind,

How Can You Think That?

"Evolution is either an innocent scientific description of how certain earthly things came about; or, if it is anything more than this, it is an attack upon thought itself. If evolution destroys anything, it does not destroy religion but rationalism. If evolution simply means that a positive thing called an ape turned very slowly into a positive thing called a man, then it is stingless for the most orthodox; for a personal God might just as well do things slowly as quickly, especially if, like the Christian God, he were outside time. But if it means anything more, it means that there is no such thing as an ape to change, and no such thing as a man for him to change into. It means that there is no such thing as a thing. At best, there is only one thing, and that is a flux of everything and anything. This is an attack not upon the faith, but upon the mind; you cannot think if there are no things to think about. You cannot think if you are not separate from the subject of thought."

—G. K. Chesterton, *Orthodoxy*

then how can man even know the theory of evolution? Darwin the scientist has just denied the possibility of science.

Christians may believe that God created man's body quickly from the slime of the earth or that He created man from the same slime through a gradual process involving trillions upon trillions of domino-effects which He foresaw and arranged perfectly. Whatever option God chose, it does not detract one iota from His role as Creator. The key question is not *how* human beings came to be, as if the hand of God and natural processes were mutually exclusive agencies, but *why we came into existence at all*—and *what* we are.

Christianity: The Enemy of Science or the Reason for It?

To listen to Richard Dawkins and folks like him, you would never have guessed that Christians have made significant contributions to every branch of science. Here are just a few examples:

- Johannes Kepler (1571–1630), the father of modern astronomy who discovered the laws of planetary motion, was a devout Lutheran.
- Robert Boyle (1627–1691), the father of modern chemistry, was motivated by his Christian faith to pursue scientific research. In addition to Greek, Boyle learned Hebrew, Syriac, and Chaldee just so he could read the Scriptures in their original languages. Like Saint Augustine, he was a firm believer in the complete compatibility of science and the Bible; apparent contradictions only mean that you have misunderstood one or the other.
- Louis Pasteur (1822–1895), the celebrated microbiologist and founder of bacteriology, was deeply motivated by his Catholic faith to find ways to end the suffering of children through his research.
- The father of modern genetics was an Augustinian monk named Gregor Mendel (1822–1884), who proved that hereditary traits are transmitted through genes. Mendel conducted a number of experiments involving peas in the gardens of his monastery and discovered that traits were passed on according to a particular pattern, by what today we call dominant and recessive genes.
- George Washington Carver (1860s–1943), the son of a slave and one of America's greatest scientists, discovered hundreds of uses for the peanut, greatly aiding impoverished blacks in the South. Carver called his laboratory "God's little workshop" and prayed every day at 4:00 a.m. for guidance. Once he prayed to be shown the secrets of the universe. "Little man," God is said to have replied, "you're not big enough to know the secrets of My universe, but I'll show you the secret of the peanut."

- The Belgian priest and astrophysicist Georges Lemaître (1894–1966) came up with the Big Bang Theory in 1927. After almost a century and a minor revision by George Gamow, it remains the leading theory of cosmology.

Three Books You're Not Supposed to Read

Scientists of Faith: Forty-Eight Biographies of Historic Scientists and Their Christian Faith by Dan Graves (Grand Rapids: Kregel Publications, 1996).

Men of Science Men of God by Henry M. Morris (Green Forest, AR: Master Books, 1982).

1000 Years of Catholic Scientists by Jane Meyerhofer, 6th edition (Ye Hedge School, 2016).

And that is just the tip of the iceberg. From aeronautics to zoology, Christians have contributed to existing branches of learning and created entire new disciplines in their search for knowledge. If that weren't enough, we have an even bigger bombshell to drop: Christianity made science possible in the first place. That's right. Were it not for the Christian belief in an intelligible order created by a supremely intelligent God who also created human reason, there would have been no faith *in* reason. And without faith in the power and reliability of reason, there can be no science. As Guy Consolmagno, director of the Vatican Observatory, once pointed out, every scientist, Christian or not, relies on *some* form of faith, hope, and love: faith that there is an objective reality, hope that one's instruments will work properly and that one's observations will not be tainted, and the love of discovery.

Don't believe us? Then read the works of renowned physicist and priest Stanley L. Jaki, who argues that it is no coincidence that modern science took root and flourished only in the Christian West. Christians believe in a rational and orderly universe governed by consistent laws and principles since all things are made by the *Logos* or Word of God (John 1:3) and bear a reliable trace of God's logic. Christianity also believes in the capacity of human intelligence to gain knowledge, and it respects philosophical inquiry. Other cultures, such as the Arabic, Babylonian, Chinese, Egyptian, Greek, Hindu, and Maya, also produced great moments in the history of science, but they did not last long because, Jaki argues, they lacked one or more of these elements. Thus, while the rest of the world produced "stillbirths" in science, the Christian West alone gave birth to a healthy and self-perpetuating scientific tradition. You're welcome, Richard Dawkins.

A Book You're Not Supposed to Read

The Savior of Science by Stanley L. Jaki (Grand Rapids: Eerdmans, 2000).

Christianity has long supported education and the advancement of knowledge, and indeed it was Christian doctrine that gave skeptical, fallible, and frail human beings the confidence and the framework to become great scientists. Even though it is not in the business of making eggheads but of saving souls, Christianity became the world's greatest catalyst for scientific inquiry, thus providing a nice example of the Scripture verse: "Seek ye first the kingdom of God and His righteousness; and all these things shall be added unto you" (Matthew 6:33).

Yet old canards die hard, especially when they are so useful to the secular Left. Ever since the late seventeenth century and the so-called Age of Enlightenment, Western intellectual elites have pilloried the great medieval period that lay the foundation for science and gave us the university as the "Dark Ages." And even though historians have repeatedly demonstrated the fallacy of this anti-medieval bigotry, the secular Left continues to repackage the same lie that for a millennium, doctrine ruled and reason became heresy until reason was supposedly rescued by modern secularism. Once again Chesterton deserves the last word: "How can we say that the Church wishes to bring us back into the Dark Ages? The Church was the only thing that ever brought us out of them."

CHAPTER TEN

The War against Common Sense, or the Seven Deadly Sins of Modern Thought

As you may have gathered, many of the accusations against Christianity are based on a misconstrual of its teachings or its historical legacy. Fulton J. Sheen once observed that there are not "one hundred people in the United States who hate the Catholic Church, but there are millions who hate what they wrongly perceive the Catholic Church to be." What Sheen said over fifty years ago about the perception of Catholicism in America can now be said about Christianity in much of Western society today.

But there is another set of accusations against Christianity that has less to do with misunderstanding the claims of the Christian faith or its track record and more to do with rejecting sound judgment. Put simply, we live in a world that is increasingly at war with common sense, and since Christianity is paradoxically yet ultimately common sense incarnate, it is inevitable that the world would also be at war with Christianity. What really gets today's haters hopping mad are not the distinctive beliefs of Christianity, such as that there are three Persons in one God, but the common beliefs that have been held by virtually everyone in human history, such as that men are men and women are women—and each should know which restroom to use. The core of the Christian teaching on the sexes is not unique to Christianity; little boys and girls in our own

Did you know?

★ If materialism is true, all rational thought is nonsense—including the thought that materialism is true

★ The Myth of Progress is secularism's way of compensating for the loss of Truth and Goodness

★ Christianity, which first taught the world to value victims, is now the victim of a victimhood culture

Trickle Down Inanity

"For among the evils that afflict man, none is graver than the erroneous beliefs which at once distort his mind and make systematic the aberrations of his conduct."

—**Bernard J. F. Lonergan,** *Insight*

day and age still know it, too, until the truth is drummed out of them. That a belief is universally held does not prove it to be true, but that is not our point here: we are merely observing that when people deride "heteronormativity" or an unwritten moral code or the principle that the same thing cannot be and not be in the same place at the same time in the same way, they are repudiating not only religious authority but a common consensus shared by virtually all of humanity past and present. Today's Western elite is in rebellion not only against Christianity but against the wisdom of the ages—because that wisdom gives the lie to their increasingly fantastic agenda.

So let the curly tail of our PIG be a closer look at the current war against common sense, since that war accounts for so much of the present-day animus against Christianity. Lurking behind the secular Western elite's rebellion against both age-old wisdom and divine revelation are seven false presuppositions. They could be characterized as meta-errors or erroneous meta-narratives because they are big-picture false stories that, once accepted, lead to scads of bad judgments about specific issues. But let's just call them the Seven Deadly Sins of Modernity. Understand these sins, and you will understand the spirit of our age and why it does not mix well with belief in the God of our fathers.

The First Deadly Sin of Modernity: Attacks on Truth Itself—Subjectivism, Scientism, and Materialism

There are three things for which man yearns—truth, goodness, and beauty—and modernity has basically rejected all three. Let's start with the truth. Common sense holds that truth is a standard independent of the human mind that the mind seeks to discover and to which it is subordinate. We don't judge the truth, we judge *according to* the truth, which is objective and separate from our personal fears, desires, or ambitions.

Now, how much truth we can know this side of the grave has always been a vexed question (after all, the great philosopher Socrates claimed that the one thing he knew was that he knew nothing). But in modernity, skepticism is jacked up on crack. What started off as a denial of the relevance of truth to our daily lives (a kind of pragmatism) ended up becoming a denial that truth even exists. No longer does the so-called educated Westerner believe in objective or absolute truth; he thinks that the sophisticated view is that all truth is either relative or nonexistent and that every quest for truth is merely a masked "will to power." All that is left is subjectivism, the subject's limited viewpoint and his desire to control others by making truth claims.

The Great Divide

"The fundamental cleavage is not the West v. Islam or the West v. the rest, but within the West itself: between those who recognize the values of Judaeo-Christian Graeco-Roman culture and those who use terms like 'democracy,' 'values,' 'rights' but pervert the latter. So it means democracy of the elites, values of secularism, rights to kill Charlie Gard, marriage that has nothing to do with sex, sex that... is a 'private' matter to be funded by the confiscatory state and your duty to support this incoherence...."

—Polish philosopher Zbigniew Stawrowski

Ah, but there is a snag. The person who says there is no truth is saying that it is true that there is no truth. But if it is true that there is no truth, then there is something true after all. Strictly speaking, subjectivism can be proven false on the basis of what philosophers call self-referential incoherence.

Of course, modern people still cling to the truths discovered by modern science, but there are problems there too. First, the embrace of scientific discovery can be largely self-serving and opportunistic. Leftists tend to cling to the latest findings that support their prejudices (for example, on

More than Matter

"When philosophers have subdued their passions, what material substance has managed to achieve this?"

—**Blaise Pascal**, *Pensées*

"Materialism has more restrictions than spiritualism... The Christian is quite free to believe that there is a considerable amount of settled order and inevitable development in the universe. But the materialist is not allowed to admit into his spotless machine the slightest speck of spiritualism or miracle... The Christian admits that the universe is manifold and even miscellaneous, just as a sane man knows that he is complex. The sane man knows that he has a touch of the beast, a touch of the devil, a touch of the saint, a touch of the citizen. Nay, the really sane man knows that he has a touch of the madman. But the materialist's world is quite simple and solid, just as the madman is quite sure he is sane. The materialist is sure that history has been simply and solely a chain of causation, just as [a madman] is quite sure that he is simply and solely a chicken. Materialists and madmen never have doubts."

—**G. K. Chesterton**, *Orthodoxy*

manmade climate change or the health hazards of processed foods) and ignore the latest findings that contradict them (for example, on the importance of being raised by both a mother and a father or the health hazards of artificial birth control). Worse, scientists who defy leftist pieties are quickly ostracized by their colleagues and defunded by big government or bootlicking universities.

But even if all scientific research were conducted, evaluated, and applied impartially, it would still be wrong to reduce truth to what is empirically verifiable. It is reasonable to embrace the conclusions of *science*, but it is not reasonable to embrace *scientism*, the belief (and note, it is nothing more than that) that the mind can gain knowledge *only* through the empirical scientific method. From Greek antiquity up to the late Middle Ages, Western man had an impressive faith in reason as something that is capable of canvasing the whole of reality, from the lowly bugs beneath his feet to the angels above his head. But thanks to modern developments such as the ironically named Age of Reason, reason's scope has gotten smaller and smaller: religion is out, metaphysics is out, ethics is out—all that is left is the world of matter, the world studied by modern empirical science. And if you subscribe to Nietzschean postmodernism, even that is out, leaving nothing but a yawning abyss.

It is scientism that leads to the breathtaking arrogance of a Richard Dawkins, a biologist who thinks that because he knows his way around a lab he can pontificate on theology. But our broader point here is that reducing reason to the empirical is not only bad for religion and ethics, it is bad for reason itself. And the retreat from reason has led to a crisis in Western civilization. Since science can only answer *how* things happen and never the deeper question of *why* we are here, the person drunk on scientism is left with no answers about the purpose of life. When enough citizens start thinking this way, you have a slow-burning crisis of the first order.

Third, scientism is closely linked to materialism, the view that the only thing that is real is empirical matter. And once again, this is bad not only for religion but bad for reason itself. Because if materialism is true, *reason* is out. Atoms can't know atoms, neurons can't know neurons, and gray matter can't know gray matter. Only the mind (which is different from the brain) can know matter. Again we find ourselves up against the issue of self-referential incoherence. If materialism is true, all rational thought is impossible; and if rational thought is impossible, so too is materialism.

The Second Deadly Sin of Modernity: Moral Relativism

With intellectual relativism comes moral relativism, the belief that man cannot know what is truly good or bad and that all convictions about good and evil are radically subjective. Whereas earlier generations acknowledged a fixed moral code greater than themselves, many Westerners currently subscribe to

A Book You're Not Supposed to Read

Who Am I to Judge? Responding to Relativism with Logic and Love by Edward Sri (San Francisco: Ignatius Press, 2016).

a loose sort of relativism of "values," insubstantial and fluid aspirations that *I* happen to value but that have no purchase on objective reality. Popular values such as "self-expression," "autonomy," and "tolerance" are representative of the loss of faith in an objective moral order.

In his bestselling 1987 book *The Closing of the American Mind*, Allan Bloom observed that the dogma of open-mindedness on which his college students had been fed paradoxically made them close-minded. Relativism, Bloom charged, makes its disciples conformist, apathetic, and flat-souled. After all, if I can't make any real moral judgments in light of an eternal standard of right and wrong, why spend any energy trying to figure out how I should live? The reliably discussion-killing question *Who am I to judge*? is more often than not code for *I'm too lazy or uninterested to think about it.* "Nobody really believes in anything anymore," Blooms concludes as he channels Nietzsche's critique of modern society, "and everyone spends his life in frenzied work and frenzied play so as not to face the fact, not to look into the abyss."

The Real Problem

"It is not the immorality of relativism that I find appalling. What is astounding and degrading is the dogmatism with which we accept such relativism, and our easygoing lack of concern about what that means for our lives."

—Allan Bloom, *The Closing of the American Mind*

Of course, to say that there is no such thing as absolute right and wrong is one thing; to mean it is another. Most people who call themselves relativists actually have a number of values that they treat as non-negotiable. Consider the growing list of taboos in society today. On the affirmative side, Thou Shalt Be in favor of recycling and sustainability, affirmative action (except for Asian students, according to some liberal colleges), safe and consensual sex, diversity (except in thought), toleration (except of conservatives), handicapped access, transgender bathrooms, universal health care, and borderless countries. On the negative side, Thou Shalt Not practice bullying, smoking (except for legalized marijuana), violence (especially against women and blacks—not so much against police officers), polluting the earth, microaggressions, and trigger words. If you look closely, you will notice that every item on this list falls into one of three categories: they are sins against bodily or planetary health, against radical equality, or against personal autonomy. These are the only gods left, and even though they sometimes come into conflict with each other, they are all worshiped with fervor. If you think I'm wrong, try parking in a handicapped spot in front of a Whole Foods Market without the designated tag dangling from your rearview mirror, or writing a coherent critique on how your employer Google makes an "ideological echo chamber" and calls it "diversity."

Acknowledging an Absolute

"If your moral ideas can be truer, and those of the Nazis less true, there must be something—some Real Morality—for them to be true about."

—**C. S. Lewis,** *Mere Christianity*

And so we are left with the worst of both worlds: moral zealotry which often borders on hysteria and sometimes spills over into violent riots, and no recognition that there is a transcendent moral standard by which this zealotry can be evaluated. And of course, there is that recurring issue of self-referential coherence: when you denounce others for judging, you are judging them; when you are intolerant of intolerance, you are an intolerant and intolerable hypocrite; and when you hate haters, you are a hater and therefore have become what you hate.

The Third Deadly Sin of Modernity: The Cult of the Ugly and the Cheap

Along with intellectual relativism and moral relativism comes aesthetic relativism, the denial of objective beauty. Instead of Keats's "beauty is truth,

truth beauty," today we are inundated with the cliché, "Beauty is in the eye of the beholder." Just as we are not supposed to judge moral behavior (unless it runs up against the idols of bodily and planetary health, radical equality, or personal autonomy), so too are we not allowed to make claims about beauty. As a result, we live in quite possibly the ugliest age in human history.

The contemporary war against beauty is waged on two different fronts. On the first front, the ugly is elevated as a metaphysical or moral statement or as an expression of personal freedom and autonomy. While beautiful works of the past are routinely denounced as products of "white privilege," grotesque modern art is applauded because it is "iconoclastic" and "transgressive" and "pushes the envelope." Such art is considered desirable because rejecting artistic norms is also rejecting any notion of a universe filled with meaning or charged with the grandeur of God. Ugly art, in other words, is seen as an honest mirror reflecting an ugly and meaningless universe. How can the world have meaning, so the argument goes, in a world that has experienced Auschwitz? (Thank goodness no one said that to Auschwitz survivor Victor Frankl or he might not have written the beautiful book *Man's Search for Meaning in the Universe*). As our philosophers have stopped believing in truth and our ethicists in goodness, so too have our artists stopped believing in beauty.

Ugly art is not entirely without its value when it serves as a window into the existential despair of modern life or the dark side of humanity. As Pope St. John Paul II is reputed to have said, "We owe secular artists appreciation for showing us what the world without God looks like." Yet what happens to our souls when this ugliness becomes the dominant art form?

Contemporary society is inclined to reject timeless notions of integrity, form, proportion, and meaning in favor of the mere assertion of self-expression and autonomy—and often simply for shock value. A talented student of mine dropped her music major after her teachers kept pressuring her to compose jarring and ugly atonal music instead of the classical progressions and chords that she found so appealing and beautiful. Another student expressed to me his dismay at how indifferent his classmates were to the masterpieces of art history such as the Sistine Chapel; instead they babbled on excitedly about Marcel Duchamp's 1917 *Fountain*, which was made out of a urinal, as the paragon of artistic expression.

On a second front, beauty today is commodified, reduced to serving our lusts for acquisition or domination. We see this instrumentalized beauty in its mild to moderate forms in marketing and advertising and the entertainment industry, and in its more extreme and even demonic forms in pornography and sex trafficking. The commercial cheapening and coarsening of beauty is something that all should lament, not because it is an offense against good taste (as if it were no more serious than using the wrong fork) but because it is an offense against the Good. As we have already seen in our section "The Rays of Beauty" in chapter six, beauty is significant because it calls us out of our selfish little selves and invites us to rise up to the heights and into a world of wonder. The false beauty of advertising, commercialism, and pornography, on the other hand, only locks us more deeply into ourselves. As Joseph Ratzinger explains, "Such beauty does not reawaken a longing for the Ineffable, readiness for sacrifice, the abandonment of self, but instead stirs up the desire, the will for power, possession and pleasure. It is that type of experience of beauty of which Genesis speaks in the account of the Original Sin. Eve saw that the fruit of the tree was 'beautiful' to eat and was 'delightful

The Limits of Creativity

"It is impossible to be an artist and not care for laws and limits. Art is limitation; the essence of every picture is the frame. If you draw a giraffe, you must draw him with a long neck. If, in your bold creative way, you hold yourself free to draw a giraffe with a short neck, you will really find that you are not free to draw a giraffe."

—**G. K. Chesterton,** *Orthodoxy*

to the eyes.' The beautiful, as she experienced it, aroused in her a desire for possession, making her, as it were, turn in upon herself."

Alas, virtually every segment of American society has been complicit in our loss of beauty. Both the Left and the Right have had a hand in making things ugly: ugly "urban renewal" projects, ugly strip malls, ugly music, ugly fashion, and ugly tattoos and piercings. Even God-fearing folk aren't immune from this trend. For at least the past half-century, Protestant and Catholic Christians alike have been producing kitsch art, sappy or libidinous music, vacuous and cloying worship services, and churches that on a good day look like a high school gymnasium or an airplane hangar. Adding to the tragedy of this deformation is the fact that whereas our penniless forebears skimped and saved to erect magnificent churches that exude a timeless beauty, we their flush descendants waste our money on tawdry architectural fads that are dated before the paint is dry. It's sad. In ignoring the power of beauty and succumbing to the cult of cheap beauty, we are throwing away a powerful tool of evangelization.

The Fourth Deadly Sin of Modernity: The Myth of Progress

Modern secularism does not want you to believe in objective truth, goodness, or beauty. What, then, does it want you to believe in? Progress—and God help you if you stand in its way. You will be accused of that most heinous of all crimes: "turning back the clock." This charge is highly effective in our day and age, as it conjures up images of African Americans enslaved and lynched, women forced to stay at home barefoot and pregnant, and heretics burned at the stake. But the accusation is a straw man. Among those accused of turning back the clock, I doubt there is one person in a thousand who is actually attempting the impossible task of restoring *everything* from a bygone era, like lynchings and leechings. Usually the dreaded clock-turner is simply trying to enrich the present with one or two elements from the past, which is what any reasonable and responsible person *should* want to do when he sees something out of whack in the present that could be remedied by something good from the past. "Would you think I was joking," C. S. Lewis asks, "if I said that you *can* put a clock back, and that if the clock is wrong it is often a very sensible thing to do?"

As Lewis's question implies, the clock-turning charge assumes that there is nothing wrong about the present and nothing right about the past. But does anyone, even among self-styled progressives, really believe this? No, the reason that the accusation of turning back the clock is rhetorically powerful today is not because it rests on a truth but because it safeguards a falsehood: secularism's sacred belief in the Myth of Progress, the conviction that History (with a capital "H") is on the march towards a perfect Utopian society. According to this view, mankind as a whole is getting better from age to age; each generation is less sexist and less racist and more tolerant and more diverse than the one that went before it and therefore more just, more humane, and more enlightened than its ancestors.

Real Progress

"We all want progress. But progress means getting nearer to the place where you want to be. And if you have taken a wrong turning, then to go forward does not get you any nearer. If you are on the wrong road, progress means doing an about turn and walking back to the right road; and in that case the man who turns back soonest is the most progressive man."

—C. S. Lewis, *Mere Christianity*

The Myth of Progress is secularism's way of compensating for the loss of truth and goodness. An expanding History replaces a shrinking Reason; man is no longer the "rational animal" capable of slipping the surly bonds of Earth and grasping truth, goodness, and beauty but the "historical animal," the mere product of an ever-evolving and impersonal historical process. Secularists love the Myth of Progress because it enables them to be moralistic while simultaneously denying morality. They can claim that although there is no eternal Moral Law there *is* a historical process that is making society more enlightened and more moral over time. In fact this argument implies an eternal, non-historical standard towards which History is moving, but never mind that now. All that matters is that you are "on the right side of history," with the "right side" usually being defined by the Left. How convenient.

The Myth also provides the Left with a justification for violence. Violence in self-defense or in defense of one's country is so-o-o bourgeois (only the déclassé Right still believes in such quaint things), but violence to advance the End of History is quite another matter, since History advances primarily through conflict and violence. One of the pioneers of the Myth of Progress, the German philosopher Hegel, famously described History as "the slaughter-bench on which the happiness of peoples, the wisdom of States, and the virtue of individuals are sacrificed." Oddly, the more one is convinced of the inevitability of a Utopian end to which History is moving, the more one is likely to use violence to usher in the inevitable. (I have no idea why the true believers in the Myth of Progress don't just kick back and let History do its violent thing on its own without getting their own hands dirty.) Hence, the bloodiest ideology in the twentieth century was communism, the brainchild of Hegel's disciple Karl Marx. Over an eighty-year period, communism was responsible for the deaths of ninety-four million people. To paraphrase Victor Laszlo in *Casablanca*, even Nazis couldn't kill that fast.

Not every leftist is a Marxist or as violent as one, but my point is that when you scratch the Left's Age-of-Aquarius pacifist rhetoric, you find a broad mandate for violence against any enemy perceived to be standing in the way of History. Hence the violent riots against Donald Trump, the "Bronze-Age warlord" and "Neanderthal" who is allegedly (gasp!) turning back the clock. Hence the leftist reliance on abortion, which ensures the "liberation" of women at the expense of their unborn children. And hence the Left's blindness about Islam, which gets a free pass because it has accorded Muslim extremists the coveted status of victim, a celebrated component of its Utopian vision.

Yet however handy it is for the Left, the Myth of Progress is only that—a myth for which there is no demonstrable proof. And the widespread belief in this myth comes at a high cost. For starters, it rules out everything from the past as benighted, outdated, and inferior, including the Good News about our salvation.

A Book You're Not Supposed to Read

The Black Book of Communism: Crimes, Terror, Repression by Stéphane Courtois et al. (Cambridge: Harvard University Press, 1997).

And there are other costs. Surprisingly, the man who saw them most clearly is the man who launched an attack of his own against Christianity. In a remarkable essay "On the Use and Abuse of History for Life," Friedrich Nietzsche (1844–1900) explained how the Myth of Progress harms human living and, ironically, impedes authentic progress:

- The Myth of Progress weakens human personality. By attacking our past, we attack and diminish ourselves, for the past is a part of us. And by believing in a blind historical process rather than eternal truths worth living and dying for, we no longer take the bull by the horns and produce a real culture. Instead, we pride ourselves on having a knowledge of cultures (think of our current self-congratulation about "multiculturalism"). Nietzsche impishly compares such feckless enthusiasts to eunuchs guarding a great historical world-harem.
- The Myth of Progress makes modern man presumptuous, as he assumes that he is wiser and more just than his predecessors, and presumption is a formula for self-delusion and stagnation. Just because I have gay or black friends, am I really a

better person than my ancestors? Is possessing the demanding virtue of justice really that easy? Modern man can be persuaded to learn *about* the past, as if he were perusing curios in a museum; but thanks to historicism, it is difficult to convince him to learn *from* the past, that is, from the past masters about the highest things in life. Consequently, Nietzsche opines, "sterling mediocrity becomes even more mediocre."

- The Myth of Progress renders modern man perpetually snarky and ironic, cynical and egotistical, but never heroic or great. Historicism destroys the horizon of meaning that inspires man to greatness; once it is gone, he has little choice but to retreat into his own ego. The result: we are better at producing characters from *South Park* than men like George Washington.

The Myth of Progress is ubiquitous today, affecting culture, politics, and even Christian self-understanding. As Nietzsche saw over a century ago, "recent theology appears quite innocently to have taken up History and even now is hardly aware that in doing so" it has entered the service of Voltaire's project to crush the Church. When you hear Christian leaders talk about needing to change the dogmas of their faith or lower their moral standards in order to "get with the times," you are hearing the howl of a historicist wolf in pious sheep's clothing.

The Problem with Historicism

"Scientific evolution... taught men to think that so long as they were passing from the ape they were going to the angel. But you can pass from the ape and go to the devil."

—**G. K. Chesterton,** *Orthodoxy*

The Fifth Deadly Sin of Modernity: The Idol of Equality

If History is on a dialectical march of progress, towards what is it marching? A classless and "diverse" society predicated on radical equality, of course. Progressives essentially take Euclid's axiom—"things which are equal to the same thing are equal to each other"—and then conveniently blanket over particular inequalities in order to insist on equal treatment for the individual or group in question. So, for instance, the push for "gay marriage" has been made on the grounds of equality, despite the fact that two persons of the same sex cannot naturally unite to beget offspring, an important component in the institution of marriage. Whereas the Right wants equality of opportunity (giving everyone a fair shot at the start of the race), the Left wants equality of result (giving everyone a blue ribbon at the end of the race no matter how poorly they did). The difference between these two notions of equality is the difference between egalitarianism and radical egalitarianism. Egalitarianism says that all men were created equal, but it does not say that all inequalities are bad. Radical egalitarianism does.

Radical egalitarianism was first championed by Jean-Jacques Rousseau (1712–1778), who taught that *all* inequality is a form of injustice. Before Rousseau, words like "master," "hegemony" (which used to mean the rule of one who *ought* to rule), and "hierarchy" were all considered good things; thanks to his influence, they are now dirty words. The transformation of "hierarchy" is particularly telling. The word, which in Greek literally means a holy order or ranking, was coined by the great fifth-century Christian mystic Pseudo-Dionysius to describe the differentiated panoply of celestial beings in Heaven and the pecking order of God's ordained ministers on Earth. Hierarchy was something positive, a great and sacred chain of being that links all of us together, lifting up the downtrodden and compelling the mighty to be responsive to them. When animated by love, a hierarchy unifies and elevates; it is a ladder to, rather than a ceiling obstructing, human solidarity and human flourishing. Yet when the word "hierarchy" is used today, it is often with pejorative or cynical connotations, suggesting an intrinsically oppressive order. Indeed, most of the politically incorrect

Vive la Différence

"Equity requires inequality. I don't treat an elderly person the same as I treat someone of my own age. I don't ask my wife to climb the roof to fix the shingles. You don't hold your 16-year-old boy to a calorie count equal to that consumed by his ten year old brother, or his twin sister."

—**Anthony Esolen,** "The Church of Intersectionality Offers Nothing for Sinful Man"

concepts on the ever-growing list of things that the secular Left denounces—things such as "patriarchy" and "heteronormativity"—are on that list because they allegedly involve some sort of hierarchy.

So Rousseau's radical egalitarianism has proved to be enormously influential, especially on the Left. But is it true that all forms of inequality are unjust? Christianity takes a much less extreme point of view. On the one hand, it affirms the spiritual equality and equal dignity of all human beings—man and woman, Jew and Gentile, and so forth. On the other hand, it recognizes the goodness of various kinds of *natural* inequalities or rankings, such as the nine orders of angels, the headship of the husband in the family, the rule of parent over child, and the taxonomic hierarchy of plants and animals. Indeed, if an inequality is truly natural (that is, a normal part of creation), then it is good. That is not to say that natural inequalities are incapable of being abused: on the contrary, sin can easily warp good things towards an evil end. Nor is it to deny that people can mistake their own (artificial) prejudices for natural inequalities, as in the ugly case of racism. And, of course, there are many immoral artificial inequalities, such as a caste system or a corporate structure that oppresses the worker.

Still, none of this renders *all* inequality evil. *Abus non tollit usum*, as the medieval used to say: the abuse of a thing does not negate its proper use. Even the Left relies on inequality: in order to advance the agenda of radical egalitarianism, a superior elite takes it upon itself to enlighten and guide the ignorant masses. In the Soviet Union, the *nomenklatura* filled this function; in Western society, it is tycoons like George Soros in confederacy with various privileged institutions and industries including the media, Hollywood, and progressive universities.

Christians gladly call Jesus Christ their "Lord" and "master" and recognize a glorious hierarchy instituted by Him. Are leftists equally honest about their own hierarchies of power as they preach the gospel of radical egalitarianism?

The Sixth Deadly Sin of Modernity: The Abolition of Man

The secular Left wants you to believe in radical egalitarianism. But the only way to convince you of their project is to run slipshod over nature. And this brings us to the dark side of the modern secular agenda. If man is not the rational but the historical animal, then he is nothing but an ever-changing product of an ever-evolving historical process; being in constant flux, he has no permanent essence. Both classical philosophy and the Christian faith see man as possessing a determinate nature that, even when damaged by sin, is essentially good. Thus happiness can be achieved by healing or completing our damaged nature; in the case of Christianity, our wounded natures can even participate in the Divine Nature with the help of sanctifying grace, which does not violate our original nature but elevates and transfigures it.

In modern secular thought, on the other hand, our nature (if it is even acknowledged that we have one) is seen either as raw material to be molded according to our own druthers or as an impediment to our happiness. Seeing human nature as neutral at best and as an enemy at worst is not very cheery, but leftist propaganda like Disney's *Zootopia* (2016) find clever and upbeat ways of selling the cynicism. "Anyone can be anything!" tout the lovable characters in the movie. Their acclamation of limitless possibility and hope almost makes one forget the deeper message—that your nature is merely a repressive stereotype to evolve out of. The utopia of *Zootopia* does not celebrate the natural diversity of the animal kingdom but obliterates it in the name of self-determination.

The "abolition of man," as C. S. Lewis famously called this project, has been going on for a while. It began at the dawn of modernity when thinkers such as Machiavelli, Hobbes, and Bacon declared war on nature through technological conquest and social engineering. As a result we have enjoyed the fruits of modern science and the wonderful advances of modern medicine, but we have also suffered the environmental devastation so much in the news today. Other factors compounded the problem. Modern economic systems reduced man to a mere consumer or producer, losing sight of the fact that humanity is so much more than that. Materialism masquerading as science reduced man to a living bipedal piece of meat and nothing more (see the First Deadly Sin). Social engineering sought to create the perfect society by controlling human beings as if they were rats in a lab.

Such was the plight of the West a century ago, and its ills were already evident to those who had eyes to see. But instead of returning to a classical Christian worldview, twentieth-century man doubled down, leaping out of the frying pan into the fire by moving even more explicitly from a war on nature to a war on human nature.

Transgenderism and transhumanism are both good examples of the latest escalation. According to transgender theory, your biological sex is irrelevant to who you are: your XX or XY chromosomes, your generative organs, your maleness or femaleness, offer no normative clues into how to live your life. What matters instead is your self-determined gender. Some LGBT activists claim that the gender with which you identify is your true "nature," but their claims ring hollow. For one thing, the growing list of gender options is not the product of nature but of fertile and recent imagination; for another, the very concept of gender rests on the conviction that nothing is objectively determinate and that all identification is culturally or personally fluid. What is really meant by gender is not nature but "self," an autonomous, independent, and self-willed identity.

And if this is true of transgenderism, it is all the more true of transhumanism, the belief that all of the limits of our humanity can and should be overcome by means of science and technology. Transhumanism is true to its name; its adherents really do wish to go beyond the human condition and leave it in the dust. Transhumanists dream of a day when we can achieve immortality by uploading our self-conscious minds onto some kind of hardware more durable than our vile bodies (I swear I am not making this up). The website "What is Transhumanism" makes no bones about transhumanists' disdain for human nature. "Isn't this tampering with nature?" the website asks. "Absolutely," is the reply, "and it is nothing to be ashamed of. It is often right to tamper with nature."

Runaway Technology

"A significant and perhaps irreversible process that, I believe, threatens to advance substantially in the 21st century is humanity's hazardous crossing from a natural existence into a 'technosphere.' Technical progress, which for centuries grew by devouring nature, now proceeds at the expense of culture and man himself."

— Aleksandr Solzhenitsyn

Well, not so fast. Intervening in nature is a good thing when it serves to restore nature to its proper function but bad when it serves to redefine nature or rob it of its integrity (This rule of thumb, incidentally, explains why some Christian churches have no objections to a wide array of medical and surgical procedures but oppose medical sterilization and artificial birth control, the goals of which are not to help nature do what it is designed to do but to stop nature from fulfilling its purpose). When a doctor gives a burn victim a skin graft, he is not rewriting nature but repairing it, not "tampering" with nature but helping it return to its normal operations. On the other hand, when a doctor does plastic surgery on a patient so that he looks like a genderless extra-terrestrial alien—as in the case of twenty-two year-old Vinny Ohh

Medical Experiments

"These professionals are using the myth that people are born transgender to justify engaging in massive, uncontrolled, and unconsented experimentation on children who have a psychological condition that would otherwise resolve after puberty in the vast majority of cases. Today's institutions that promote transition affirmation are pushing children to impersonate the opposite sex, sending many of them down the path of puberty blockers, sterilization, the removal of healthy body parts, and untold psychological damage. These harms constitute nothing less than institutionalized child abuse. Sound ethics demand an immediate end to the use of pubertal suppression, cross-sex hormones, and sex reassignment surgeries in children and adolescents, as well as an end to promoting gender ideology via school curricula and legislative policies."

—Michelle Cretella

from Los Angeles—he *is* tampering with nature. The poor fellow, who thinks of himself as a sexless E.T., did not need to spend $50,000 on science and technology to be "himself." He needs a good therapist to heal whatever psychological wounds caused this disconnect from reality.

The same goes for children experiencing confusion about their gender in what the *Diagnostic and Statistical Manual of Mental Disorders* (DSM-5) calls "gender dysphoria." The solution to this psychological condition is not the invasive artificial measures aggressively promoted by LGBT-backed "gender clinics" across the country, including hormone blockers, sterilization, and the removal of healthy body parts. These treatments do not liberate the patient's "true nature" but increase the likelihood of depression and suicide. Michelle Cretella, president of the American College of Pediatricians, is right: such experimentation on our children at such a tender stage of their sexual development is institutionalized child abuse.

We should be the masters of the things we make but the servants of our nature. Yet modern man has reversed this order: in trying to make ourselves masters of our nature, we have made ourselves servants of our technology. As Henry David Thoreau put it, "Men have become the tools of their tools." And if we really have made ourselves tools (in both

The Conquest of Nature and the Abolition of Man

"The final stage is come when Man by eugenics, by pre-natal conditioning, and by an education and propaganda based on a perfect applied psychology, has obtained full control over himself. Human nature will be the last part of Nature to surrender to Man... The man-moulders of the new age will be armed with the powers of an omnicompetent state and an irresistible scientific technique: we shall get at last a race of conditioners who really can cut out all posterity in what shape they please.

"It is not that they are bad men. They are not men at all. Stepping outside the *Tao* [moral law] they have stepped into the void. Nor are their subjects necessarily unhappy men. They are not men at all: they are artefacts. Man's final conquest has proved to be the abolition of Man."

—C. S. Lewis, *The Abolition of Man*

the strict and slang senses of the word), we have foolishly contributed to our own dehumanization. Technology is not intrinsically bad, nor is technological abuse the only way to dehumanize ourselves. The principal culprit is an attitude that treats God's gifts as machine-like things for us to manipulate and exploit. Transgenderism does this with the body and transhumanism does this with the mind. When all of human nature is mechanized or "electronicized," what is left is not nature but machine. And man is abolished.

The Seventh Deadly Sin of Modernity: Victimhood Culture

We saw with the Fifth Deadly Sin how the doctrine of radical egalitarianism is not internally consistent because it relies on a guiding elite that sees itself as superior. Similarly, the Left champions victimhood in the name of equal justice but it also elevates the victim to a privileged status while demoting and even demonizing the purported oppressor. This campaign to promote victimology has become so successful that it is helping to spawn what sociologists Bradley Campbell and Jason Manning call an entire culture of victimhood.

The best way to understand victimhood culture is to contrast it with honor culture, which prevailed around the time of the American Revolution and in the antebellum South. In honor cultures, men are highly sensitive to insult—hence the prevalence of duels. They like to call attention to themselves, especially to their prowess or exploits in areas involving conquest or risk, not only with respect to virtuous acts of bravery but also with respect to vicious acts such as gambling, drinking, and philandering. Honor seekers do not hesitate to exaggerate their successes or even lie about them, for by maintaining the appearance of being winners, they maintain their status and intimidate competitors. Honor cultures are tight-knit communities where word of mouth and age-old custom prevail and supervening legal authority is disdained. Men of honor love their family and their country but scorn the government and the court system, for there is more honor and glory in resolving conflict through one's own skill or bravery than in invoking the help of a third party.

A victimhood culture is an almost perfect photographic negative of an honor culture. Like honor culture, victimhood culture is highly sensitive to insult (hence the proliferating lists of "microaggressions" and "trigger words"), and it encourages its members to call attention to themselves. But whereas members of an honor culture like to mention their own exploits, people in a victimhood culture like to mention their own hardships, to dwell on their suffering at the hands of others on account of their race, class, or gender—and if they qualify as a victim in all three categories,

Not Living Up to Our Potential

"The victim mindset dilutes the human potential. By not accepting personal responsibility for our circumstances, we greatly reduce our power to change them."

—Steve Maraboli

they have hit the jackpot of what is now called "intersectionality." The status of victim is so coveted and the status of oppressor so loathed that there even emerges, to borrow another term from Campbell and Manning, a culture of "competitive victimhood." As with honor cultures, members in a competitive victimhood culture often exaggerate or lie in order to obtain the status they seek—only now it is about their victimization. Hence the rise of "hate crime hoaxes," with individuals fabricating stories of being attacked by members of an oppressor group. And hence the remarkable case of Rachel Dolezal, the woman who feigned being black and falsely claimed that she was the victim of nine hate crimes before it was discovered that she was a blue-eyed blonde from western Montana and forced to resign from her leadership position in the NAACP.

Victimhood culture thrives in highly egalitarian societies, where the only kind of "deviance" that is despised is not an act of cowardice or moral depravity but a sin against equality or diversity. It also thrives where there is a high degree of social atomization, that is, where individuals are no longer tightly bound to family or clan or any other stable group that would serve as intermediaries between them and the rest of society and the government. Unlike an honor culture, which disdains the interventions of a third party, victimhood culture requires a superior third party, such as a college administration or the federal government, which is pressured through protests or public shaming to side with the alleged victim group and condemn the ostensible oppressors.

Every cultural arrangement for doling out recognition has its strengths and weaknesses. The obvious strength of a victimhood culture is that it embraces and consoles victims. Victims of rape, for example, might be inclined to "hide their shame" in an honor culture, but in a victimhood culture they are rightly considered innocent of any wrongdoing and encouraged not to feel any self-recrimination for the terrible ordeal they have suffered.

But victimhood culture also has its fair share of weaknesses. As with an honor culture, it is all too easy in a victimhood culture to confuse genuine injustices with the desire for self-promotion. Moreover, defining oneself as a victim has several bad side effects:

1. It keeps you from self-knowledge, because you think that you already know who or what you are. But no matter how much you have been victimized, you are always more than a victim—you are an image of God.
2. It discourages a deeper quest for truth, because the painful, disorienting, and humiliating quest for the truth is replaced in a victimhood culture with the quest to protect victims from all "microaggressions," even the ones that may happen to be true. Hence on many college campuses today, the older model of education as a challenging tournament of ideas in which egos can get bruised has been replaced by a newer model in which education becomes a comforting therapy guaranteeing high self-esteem among the students.
3. It discourages the drive for excellence because persons in a victimhood culture can easily obtain an elevated status by claiming to be a victim and foregoing all the pain and sacrifice involved in excelling in any field. Victimhood becomes a shortcut to success but not to genuine achievement.
4. It encourages psychological frailty. In an article entitled "Colleges Are Promoting Psychological Frailty and We Should All Be Concerned," psychology professor Clay Routledge contends that "victim protection campaigns many colleges are engaged in not only underestimate human resilience, they may actually cause the problems they are designed to solve because they suggest to students who wouldn't otherwise feel like victims

that they are, in fact, victims." This identification as victims undermines their natural capacity to be "perfectly capable of remaining psychologically healthy in the face of offensive Halloween costumes, distasteful jokes or comments, and sensitive course material."

5. Social atomization, social media, and victimhood culture create conditions that easily lead to witch hunts and other forms of hysteria that ruin the careers or lives of innocent people. Just ask Justine Sacco, who (in)famously became the object of mass hatred during an eleven-hour flight because of one stupid tweet that went viral. Instead of protecting alleged victims, victimhood culture often creates real ones.
6. With its reliance on superior third parties, victimhood culture increases the power of those parties, further weakening both stable intermediary groups and individual rights. Hence today we see the increasing power of college administrations and the decreasing power of faculty, the increasing power of the federal government and the decreasing power of counterbalancing groups such as churches, businesses, clubs, and so forth. The danger of giving these third parties, which tend to be vast and impersonal bureaucratic organizations, so much power is expressed well by President Gerald Ford: "A government big enough to give you everything you want is a government big enough to take from you everything you have."
7. Finally, as the power of these third parties expands, a phenomenon that Campbell and Manning call "legal overdependency" may develop in which individuals become increasingly unwilling or unable to use other forms of conflict management. A generation or two ago, most Americans more or less knew how to settle their differences among themselves, either

> by talking directly to each other or through the intervention of neighbors or the local minister. Today, it is more common to take immediate recourse to social media, the police, and the courts. The combined increase of government power and the decrease of other forms of conflict resolution are particularly dangerous when a third element is added: an increasing intolerance of views deemed "microaggressive." According to a 2015 Pew poll, 40 percent of millennials, the generation most imbued with the culture of victimhood, think that it is proper for the government to prevent citizens from making statements that minority groups would find offensive. By contrast, only 12 percent of the so-called Silent Generation (Americans between the ages of seventy and eighty-seven) feel the same. To put it cynically and I hope with exaggeration, victimhood culture makes tempests out of teapots and then requires the expansion of tyrannical powers to quiet the storm.

Victimhood culture is especially congenial to the New Left and is now actively promoted by it, but the culture of competitive victimhood has become so intoxicating that it has even affected conservatives, such as the men who respond to feminist denunciations with charges of "reverse sexism" or the people who fabricate black-on-white hate crime hoaxes. Such responses are not effective. As Campbell and Manning note, victimhood culture is concerned "with offenses against minority or otherwise less powerful cultures, not offenses against historically dominant ethnic groups such as whites or historically dominant religious groups such as Christians"—even when those groups are currently being victimized. Muslims qualify as victims because they are seen as the innocent targets of Western hatred and intolerance stretching from the First Crusade to Fox News—this despite the fact that Islam has markedly illiberal attitudes towards other

Rejecting Victimhood

"In the late 1990s I was reading *Anatomy of the Spirit*, a then recent bestseller by Caroline Myss. Myss described having lunch with a woman named Mary. A man approached Mary and asked her if she were free to do a favor for him on June 8th. No, Mary replied, 'I absolutely cannot do anything on June 8th because June 8th is my incest survivors' meeting and we never let each other down! They have suffered so much already! I would never betray incest survivors!' Myss was flabbergasted. Mary could have simply said 'Yes' or 'No.'

"Reading this anecdote, I felt that I was confronting the signature essence of my social life among leftists. We rushed to cast everyone in one of three roles: victim, victimizer, or champion of the oppressed. We lived our lives in a constant state of outraged indignation. I did not want to live that way anymore. I wanted to cultivate a disposition of gratitude. I wanted to see others, not as victims or victimizers, but as potential friends, as loved creations of God. I wanted to understand the point of view of people with whom I disagreed without immediately demonizing them as enemy oppressors."

—**Danusha V. Goska**, "Top 10 Reasons I Am No Longer a Leftist"

"victim groups" such as women, homosexuals, and the transgendered, and despite the fact that Islam itself facilitates a virulent honor culture.

Christianity and Victimhood Culture

There is a supreme irony in disqualifying Christianity from victimhood status, for: 1) it is Christianity that gave the world concern for the victim in the first place, and 2) the Left is ruthlessly scapegoating Christianity by accusing it of being an oppressor.

Regarding the first point: Before Christianity, myths and the cultures that made them assumed that the victim was guilty and therefore never took the victim's side *even when*, weirdly enough, they later worshiped the victim as a god. First Judaism and then Christianity changed all this. Many of the Psalms record the voice of an innocent victim scapegoated by an angry mob, and the Gospels proclaim the innocence of Jesus Christ, a fact known both to His disciples and to His persecutors who sacrificed Him lest the whole nation perish (see John 11:50). Christianity exposes once and for all the Satanic nature of scapegoating an innocent person or minority group for the sake of political stability.

Scapegoating continued to exist after Christianity, of course, even among Christians themselves—we have already discussed how Christians sometimes scapegoated Jews in the Middle Ages. But because cultures influenced by Christianity now acknowledge that scapegoating is wrong, they must be more subtle and self-deceiving than they were before; they must convince themselves that they are not scapegoating when in fact they are. Enter the Left and its culture of victimhood (and our second point). On the one hand, the Left has taken over Christianity's concern for the victim; on the other, it turns this concern against Christianity, portraying it as oppressive in a breathtakingly intolerant and totalitarian manner. As Girard puts it, the Left's new totalitarianism reproaches Christianity "for not defending victims with enough ardor. In Christian history they see nothing but persecutions, acts of oppression, inquisitions." This new totalitarianism "presents itself as the liberator of humanity," but in fact it is trying to demonize the one religion that delivers humanity from the darkness. Girard goes so far as to call the Left's new victimology a kind of Antichrist, for it apes the teachings of Christ while ushering in something quite different: "The Antichrist boasts of bringing to human beings the peace and tolerance that Christianity promised but has failed to deliver. Actually, what the radicalization of contemporary victimology produces is a return to all sorts of pagan practices: abortion, euthanasia, sexual undifferentiation, Roman circus games galore but without real victims, etc."

Beneath the current Christ-like slogans of tolerance, diversity, equality, and, above all, concern for the victim, does there lurk the cry of "Crucify him"? It will be interesting, to say the least, to see what happens next.

Acknowledgments

I wish to express my gratitude to Alex Novak, Harry Crocker, and Tom Spence at Regnery Publishing for asking me to write this volume and for the amazing editorial skills of Elizabeth Kantor, who helped turn a sow's ear into a proper PIG.

Bibliography

Alinsky, Saul. *Rules for Radicals: A Practical Primer for Realistic Radicals*. Vintage, 1989.

Ambrose of Milan. *The Hexameron*. Trans. John J. Savage. *Fathers of the Church*, vol. 42. Catholic University of America Press, 1961.

Amorth, Gabriele. *An Exorcist Tells His Story*. Ignatius Press, 1999.

Anfenson, Dave. Online response to Roger Olson, "Be Careful What We Read into the Bible," *Waco Tribune-Herald*, July 14, 2017, http://www.wacotrib.com/opinion/columns/board_of_contributors/roger-olson-board-of-contributors-be-careful-what-we-read/article_ffe6f1a6-3893-5962-897a-7157762e11dc.html.

Anselm. *Cur Deus Homo: Why the God-Man?* Trans. Jasper Hopkins. CreateSpace Independent Publishing Platform, 2016.

Aquilina, Mike. *Why Me? When Bad Things Happen*. 30-Minute Read series. *Our Sunday Visitor*, 2009.

Aquinas, Thomas. *Summa contra Gentiles*. Trans. Anton C. Pegis and Vernon J. Bourke. Hanover House, 1955–57, http://dhspriory.org/thomas/ContraGentiles.htm.

———. *Summa Theologiae*. Trans. Fathers of the English Dominican Province. 2016, http://www.newadvent.org/summa/.

Athanasius. *On the Incarnation*. Trans. by a Religious of C.S.M.V. St. Vladimir Seminary Press, 1977.

Augustine. *Confessions*. Trans. F.J. Sheed, 2nd ed. Hackett, 2006.

———. *On the Catechising of the Uninstructed*. Trans. S.D.F. Salmond. http://www.newadvent.org/fathers/1303.htm.

———. *On Christian Doctrine*. Trans. James Shaw. http://www.newadvent.org/fathers/12022.htm.

———. *On the Good of Marriage*. Trans. C.L. Cornish. http://www.newadvent.org/fathers/1309.htm.

———.*On Order*. Trans. by the author.

Averill, Graham. "Republicans Drink Bourbon, Democrats Drink Vodka According to New Study," *Paste Magazine*, January 22, 2014, https://www.pastemagazine.com/articles/2014/01/republicans-drink-bourbon-democrats-drink-vodka-ac.html.

Bacci, Pietro Glacomo. *The Life of Saint Philip Neri*, vol. 1. Kegan Paul, Trench, Trübner & Company, Ltd., 1902.

Basil the Great. *Moralia*, quoted in *The Liturgy Documents*, vol. 4. Liturgy Training Publications, 2013.

Barna Group and Cornerstone Knowledge Network, "Designing Worship Spaces with Millennials in Mind," *Millennials* & *Generations*, November 5, 2014. https://www.barna.com/research/designing-worship-spaces-with-millennials-in-mind/.

Baskerville, Stephen. *The New Politics of Sex*: *The Sexual Revolution and Civil Liberty*. Angelico Press, 2017.

Baudelaire, Charles. "The Generous Gambler," in *The Prose Poems and La Fanfarlo*. Trans. Rosemary Lloyd. Oxford's World Classics. Oxford University Press, 1991.

Beard, Mary. *Woman as Force in History*. Macmillan, 1946.

Belloc, Hilaire. "The Catholic Sun." https://www.poemhunter.com/poem/the-catholic-sun-2/.

Berliner Morganpost. As quoted in Margherita Marchione, *Crusade of Charity: Pius XII and POWs (1939–1945)*.

Bloch, Ernst. See Kołakowski, Leszek (1981). *Main Currents of Marxism: Volume III, The Breakdown*. Oxford University Press, 436–40. Quoting *Dans Prinzip Hoffnung*, 1380–628.

Bloom, Allan. *The Closing of the American Mind: How Higher Education Has Failed Democracy and Impoverished the Souls of Today's Students*. Simon & Schuster, 1987.

Bogle, James. "The Real Story of Pius XII and the Jews," *Salisbury Review*, Spring 1996, https://www.catholicculture.org/culture/library/view.cfm?recnum=7086.

Bradley, Gerard. "One Cheer for Inquisitions," *Catholic Dossier* 2:6 (November–December 1996), http://archive.li/gRvbm.

Broussard, Karlo. *20 Answers: Miracles*. Catholic Answers Press, 2016.

Buck, Roger. *The Gentle Traditionalist: A Catholic Fairy-Tale from Ireland*. Angelico Press, 2015.

Byrne, Patrick. "Evolution, Randomness, and Divine Purpose: A Reply to Cardinal Schönborn," *Theological Studies* 67 (2006), 653–65.

Cabasilas, Nicholas. *The Life in Christ*. As quoted by Joseph Ratzinger, "The Feeling of Things, the Contemplation of Beauty." August 2002, http://www.vatican.va/roman_curia/congregations/cfaith/documents/rc_con_cfaith_doc_20020824_ratzinger-cl-rimini_en.html.

Calvin, John. *Institutes of the Christian Religion*. http://www.biblestudytools.com/history/calvin-institutes-christianity/.

Campbell, Bradley and Jason Manning. "Microaggression and Moral Cultures," *Comparative Sociology* 13:6 (January 2014), 692–726.

Camus, Albert. *The Myth of Sisyphus, and Other Essays*. Trans. Justin O'Brien. First Vintage International Edition, 1991.

Carter, Joe. "Why Evangelicals Love the Jews," *First Things*, May 27, 2010, https://www.firstthings.com/blogs/firstthoughts/2010/05/why-evangelicals-love-the-jews.

Catherine of Siena. As quoted in Matthew Knisely. *Framing Faith*. W. Publishing Group, 2014.

Chesterton, G. K. *Orthodoxy*. Ignatius Press, 1995.

———. "Social Reform versus Birth Control" and "Woman and the Philosophers" in *Brave New Family*: *G.K. Chesterton on Men & Women, Children, Sex, Divorce, Marriage & the Family*, ed. Alvara de Silva. Ignatius Press, 1990.

Church of England, "The Order of the Burial of the Dead," *The Book of Common Prayer*, 1662 edition, https://www.churchofengland.org/prayer-worship/worship/book-of-common-prayer/at-the-burial-of-the-dead.aspx.

Clark, Kevin. "A Memo to Google Employees on the Recent Outrage," *Crisis*, August 10, 2017, http://www.crisismagazine.com/2017/memo-google-employees-recent-outrage.

Commission for Religious Relations with the Jews, "Notes on the Correct Way to Present the Jews and Judaism in Preaching and Catechesis in the Roman Catholic Church," 1985, http://www.vatican.va/roman_curia/pontifical_councils/chrstuni/relations-jews-docs/rc_pc_chrstuni_doc_19820306_jews-judaism_en.html.

Compassion International. "The Heart of Compassion Beats Stronger Than Ever." https://www.compassion.com/history.htm.

Consolmagno, Guy. "The Virtuous Astronomer: How Studying the Stars is Shaped by Faith, Hope, and Love," presentation to Baylor University's Institute for Faith and Learning, March 2, 2010, unpublished.

Courcelle, Pierre. *Connais-toi toi-meme*; *de Socrate a Saint Bernard* [*Know Thyself*: *From Socrates to St. Bernard*]. Etudes Augustiniennes, 1974–75.

Crawford, Paul F. "Four Myths About the Crusades," *The Intercollegiate Review* (2011), 13–22.

Cretella, Michelle. "I'm a Pediatrician. How Transgender Ideology Has Infiltrated My Field and Produced Large-Scale Child Abuse," *The Daily Signal*, July 3, 2017, http://dailysignal.com/2017/07/03/im-pediatrician-transgender-ideology-infiltrated-field-produced-large-scale-child-abuse/.

Cruz, Eliel. "9 of the Biggest Lies Christianity Tells Us about Sex and Marriage," *Everyday Feminism Magazine*, May 14, 2015, http://everydayfeminism.com/2015/05/christianity-lies-sex-marriage/.

Dalin, David G. *The Myth of Hitler's Pope*. Regnery Publishing, 2005.

———. "Pius XII and the Jews: A Defense," *Weekly Standard*, February 26, 2001, http://www.weeklystandard.com/pius-xii-and-the-jews/article/1806.

Daniel, Lillian. "Spiritual but Not Religious? Please Stop Boring Me." *Huffington Post*. September 13, 2011, http://www.huffingtonpost.com/lillian-daniel/spiritual-but-not-religio_b_959216.html.

Daniels, Anthony. "The Worldview that Makes the Underclass," *Imprimis* 43:5/6 (June 2014), https://imprimis.hillsdale.edu/the-worldview-that-makes-the-underclass/.

Darwin, Charles. Letter to William Graham, July 3, 1881, https://www.darwinproject.ac.uk/letter/DCP-LETT-13230.xml.

———. *Origin of Species by Means of Natural Selection, or The Preservation of Favoured Races in the Struggle for Life*. Penguin Classics, 2009.

Dawkins, Richard and Robyn Blumer, "Atheists Aren't the Problem, Christian Intolerance Is the Problem," *Time*, September 30, 2015, http://time.com/3450525/atheists-arent-the-problem-christian-intolerance-is-the-problem/.

DeGuzman, Maria. *Spain's Long Shadow: The Black Legend, Off-Whiteness, and Anglo-American Empire*. University of Minnesota Press, 2005.

Dostoevsky, Fyodor. As quoted in Michael O'Brien, "Will Beauty Save the World?"

Downey, Patrick. *Desperately Wicked: Philosophy, Christianity, and the Human Heart*. IVP Academic, 2009.

Driscoll, Mike. *20 Answers: Angels and Demons*. Catholic Answers Press, 2016.

Eberstadt, Mary. "Eminem is Right," *Policy Review*, December 1, 2004, http://www.hoover.org/research/eminem-right.

———. *It's Dangerous to Believe*. Harper, 2016.

Esolen, Anthony. "The Church of Intersectionality Offers Nothing for Sinful Man," *Crisis Magazine*, August 3, 2017, http://www.crisismagazine.com/2017/church-intersectionality-offers-nothing-poor-sinful-man.

———. *The Politically Incorrect Guide® to Western Civilization*. Regnery Publishing, 2008.

Enûma Elish from Leonard William King, *The Seven Tablets of Creation*, 1902. http://www.sacred-texts.com/ane/enuma.htm.

"Epistle of Mathetes to Diognetus." Trans. Alexander Roberts and James Donaldson, in *Ante-Nicene Fathers*, vol. 1. Eds. Alexander Roberts, James Donaldson, and A. Cleveland Coxe. Christian Literature Publishing Company, 1885. http://www.newadvent.org/fathers/0101.htm.

Ferdman, Roberto A. "Americans Are Having Dogs instead of Babies," *Quartz*, April 10, 2014, https://qz.com/197416/americans-are-having-dogs-instead-of-babies/.

Foley, Michael P. "Does Nature Abhor a Vacuum of Patriarchy? Missing Fathers in the Films of Whit Stillman," *Logos: A Journal of Catholic Thought and Culture* 20:3 (Summer 2017), http://www.stthomas.edu/media/catholicstudies/center/logosjournal/archives/2017vol20/203/01-20.3Foleycopy.pdf.

———. "Male Subjection and the Case for an All-Male Liturgical Ministry," *Antiphon: A Journal for Liturgical Renewal* 15:3 (2011), 262–98.

———. "Showing the Tree to the Acorn: Feasts about the Resurrection of the Body." *The Latin Mass* 20:3 (Summer 2011), 38–42.

———. *Why Do Catholics Eat Fish on Friday? The Catholic Origin to Just About Everything.* Palgrave MacMillan Ltd., 2005.

Ford, Gerald. Address to a Joint Session of Congress. August 12, 1974.

Fortin, Ernest L. "The Bible Made Me Do It: Christianity, Science, and the Environment" in *Ernest L. Fortin: Collected Essays*, vol. 1. Ed. J. Brian Benestad. Lanham, MD: Rowman & Littlefield, 1996.

Frankl, Viktor E. *Man's Search for Meaning.* Rev., updated edition. Pocket Books, 1997.

Freud, Sigmund. *Future of an Illusion.* Ed. James Strachey. W. W. Norton & Company, 1989.

Garrigou-Lagrange, Reginald. *God, His Existence and Nature*, vol. 2. Herder, 1936.

Girard, René. "Are the Gospels Mythical?" *First Things* (April 1996), https://www.firstthings.com/article/1996/04/are-the-gospels-mythical.

———. *I See Satan Fall like Lightning.* Trans. James G. Williams. Ossining, NY: Orbis Books, 2001.

Girgis, Shirif, Ryan T. Anderson, and Robert P. George. *What Is Marriage? Man and Woman: A Defense.* Encounter Books, 2012.

Glendon, Mary Ann. "The Pope's New Feminism," *Crisis* 15, no. 3 (March 1997), http://www.crisismagazine.com/1997/the-popes-new-feminism.

"God Apologizes for Gendered Language in Bible," *Babylon Bee.* November 15, 2016, http://babylonbee.com/news/god-apologizes-gendered-language-bible/.

Graham, Anne. "The September 13th Interview of Anne Graham Lotz by Jane Clayson on CBS' *Early Show*," September 13, 2001, http://www.prayerfoundation.org/billy_grahams_daughter.htm.

Graves, Dan. *Scientists of Faith: Forty-Eight Biographies of Historic Scientists and Their Christian Faith.* Kregel Publications, 1996.

Greene, Graham. *The Power and the Glory.* Penguin Classics, 2003.

Gregory of Nazianzus. *On God and Christ* trans. Frederick Williams and Lionel Wickham. St. Vladimir's Seminary Press, 2002.

Grossman, Miriam. *You're Teaching My Child What? A Physician Exposes the Lies of Sex Ed and How They Harm Your Child.* Regnery Publishing, 2009.

Guruswamy, Lakshman. As quoted in University of Hawai´i at Mānoa, "International energy law expert to present public lecture on energy justice," November 18, 2014," https://manoa.hawaii.edu/news/article.php?aId=6865.

———. *International Environmental Law in a Nutshell – 5th Edition.* West Academic Publishing, 2017.

Hadiths. As translated and quoted in Meschini, "On Wars Thought Holy."

Hamilton, Bernard. *The Crusades.* Sutton Publishing, 1998.

Hegel, Georg W. H., *Reason in History, A General Introduction to the Philosophy of History.* Trans. Robert S. Hartman. Prentice-Hall, 1953.

Hitchcock, James. "The Crusades and Their Critics," *Catholic Dossier* 8:1 (January–February 2002), 27–28.

Hanby, Michael. *No God, No Science: Theology, Cosmology, Biology.* Wiley-Blackwell, 2013.

Hart, David Bentley. *Atheist Delusions: The Christian Revolution and Its Fashionable Enemies.* Yale University Press, 2009.

———. *The Doors of the Sea: Where Was God in the Tsunami?* Eerdmans, 2011.

Hertzog, Isaac. As quoted in David Dalin, "Pius XII and the Jews: A Defense."

History of the World, Part I. Brooksfilms, 1981.

Hitler, Adolf. *Mein Kampf: My Struggle.* Trans. James Murphy. Free Thought Library, 2015.

Hobbes, Thomas. *Leviathan.* Penguin Classics, 1982.

Hoffman, Sarah and Ian Hoffman. *Jacob's New Dress*. Albert Whitman & Company, 2015.

Holy Bible, King James Version. Zondervan, 2010.

Horn, Trent. *Hard Sayings: A Catholic Approach to Answering Bible Difficulties*. Catholic Answers Press, 2016.

———. *20 Answers: Death & Judgment*. Catholic Answers Press, 2016.

Horner, Christopher. *The Politically Incorrect Guide® to Global Warming (and Environmentalism)*. Regnery Publishing, 2007.

"Individuals and groups assisting Jews during the Holocaust," *Wikipedia*. https://en.wikipedia.org/wiki/Individuals_and_groups_assisting_Jews_during_the_Holocaust.

Ingersoll, Robert Green. "Individuality," 1873, https://infidels.org/library/historical/robert_ingersoll/individuality.html.

Innocent III. *Constitution for the Jews*. http://www.jewishvirtuallibrary.org/pope-innocent-iii#a.

International Theological Commission. "The Hope of Salvation for Infants who Die without Being Baptised," Congregation for the Doctrine of the Faith, April 19, 2007, http://www.vatican.va/roman_curia/congregations/cfaith/cti_documents/rc_con_cfaith_doc_20070419_un-baptised-infants_en.html.

"Is There a Santa Claus?" *New York Sun*, September 21, 1897, http://www.nysun.com/editorials/yes-virginia/68502/.

Jaki, Stanley L. *The Savior of Science*. Eerdmans, 2000.

———. *Science and Creation: From Eternal Cycles to an Oscillating Universe*. Scottish Academic Press, 1986.

Jenkins, Philip. *The New Anti-Catholicism: The Last Acceptable Prejudice*. Oxford University Press, 2003.

John Chrysostom. *On Marriage and Family Life*. Trans. Catherine P. Roth and David Anderson. St. Vladimir's Seminary Press, 1986.

———. *Homily 23 on St. Matthew.* As quoted in Horn, Trent. *20 Answers: Death & Judgment.* Catholic Answers Press, 2016.

Kamen, Henry. "The Secret of the Inquisition," *New York Review of Books*, February 1, 1996, http://www.nybooks.com/articles/1996/02/01/the-secret-of-the-inquisition/.

Kengor, Paul. *Takedown: From Communists to Progressives, How the Left Has Sabotaged Family and Marriage.* WND Books, 2015.

Kirsch, Jonathan. *The Grand Inquisitor's Manuel: A History of Terror in the Name of God.* HarperOne, 2008.

Knox, Ronald. *The Creed in Slow Motion.* Aeterna Press, 2015.

Krause, Edward. "Anti-Semitism and the Church," *Encyclopedia of Catholic Social Thoughts, Social Science, and Social Policy.* Eds. Michael Coulter, Stephen M. Krason, Richard S. Myers, Joseph A. Varacalli, Scarecrow Press, 2007, 45–46.

Kuby, Gabriele. *The Global Sexual Revolution: Destruction of Freedom in the Name of Freedom.* Angelico Press, 2015.

Kuhns, Elizabeth. "Sister Patriots: American Catholic Nuns– Heroines of History," *Faith & Family* (Summer 2003), 48–52.

Lapide, Pinchas. *Three Popes and the Jews.* Hawthorn, 1967.

Langford, Jerome L. *Galileo, Science and the Church.* University of Michigan Press, 1992.

Lefebvre, Gaspar. *Saint Andrew Daily Missal.* E. M. Lohmann Company, 1952.

Lewis, C. S. *The Abolition of Man.* HarperOne, 2015.

———. *God in the Dock.* Eerdmans, 2014.

———. *A Grief Observed.* HarperOne, 2009.

———. *Letters to Malcolm, Chiefly on Prayer.* Reissue ed. HarperOne, 2017.

———. *Mere Christianity.* Rev. ed. HarperSanFrancisco, 2009.

———. *The Problem of Pain.* Rev. ed. HarperOne, 2015.

———. *The Screwtape Letters.* Reprint ed. HarperOne, 2015.

Lichten, Joseph L. "The Vatican & the Holocaust: A Question of Judgment—Pius XII & the Jews," National Catholic Welfare Conference, 1963, available at the Jewish Virtual Library, http://www.jewishvirtuallibrary.org/a-question-of-judgment-pius-xii-and-the-jews.

Limbaugh, David. *Jesus on Trial: A Lawyer Affirms the Truth of the Gospel.* Regnery Publishing, 2014.

Lonergan, Bernard J.F. *Insight: An Inquiry into Human Understanding.* Harper & Row, 1978.

Luther, Martin. *On the Jews and Their Lies.* Trans. Martin Bertram. CreateSpace Independent Publishing Platform, 2017.

———. *Martin Luther's Large and Small Catechisms.* Trans. F. Bente and W. H. T. Dau. CreateSpace Independent Publishing Platform, 2014.

Madden, Thomas F. *A New Concise History of the Crusades.* Rowman & Littlefield Publishers, 2005.

———. "Clinton's Folly," *American Outlook* (Fall 2001), 16–17, http://www.americanoutlook.org/uploads/1/3/3/1/13311122/startled_giant.pdf.

———. "Crusade Myths," *Catholic Dossier* 8:1 (January–February 2002), 4–8.

———. "The Real Inquisition," *National Review*, June 18, 2004, http://www.nationalreview.com/article/211193/real-inquisition-thomas-f-madden.

Mansfield, Harvey. As quoted in Austin Ruse, "Reasoned Analysis vs. Blah, Blah, Sneer, and Blah," *Crisis Magazine*, August 26, 2016, http://www.crisismagazine.com/2016/reasoned-analysis-vs-blah-blah-sneer-blah.

Maraboli, Steve. As quoted in Joanna Barclay, *Conscious Culture.* Morgan James Publishing, 2015.

Marchione, Margherita. *Crusade of Charity: Pius XII and POWs (1939–1945).* Paulist Press, 2006.

Mansfield, Harvey. *Manliness.* Yale University Press, 2007.

MassResistance. *The Health Hazards of Homosexuality: What the Medical and Psychological Research Reveals.* CreateSpace Independent Publishing Platform, 2017.

Mattson, Daniel. *Why I Don't Call Myself Gay: How I Reclaimed My Sexual Reality and Found Peace.* Ignatius Press, 2017.

Mayer, Lawrence S. and Paul R. McHugh. "Sexuality and Gender Findings from the Biological, Psychological, and Social Sciences," *The New Atlantis* 50 (Fall 2016), http://www.thenewatlantis.com/docLib/20160819_TNA50SexualityandGender.pdf.

McGuire, Ashley. *Sex Scandal: The Drive to Abolish Male and Female.* Regnery Publishing, 2017.

Meschini, Marco. *Il Jihad e La Crociata* [*The Jihad and the Crusade*]. Edizioni Ares, 2007.

———."On Wars Thought Holy: Interview With Marco Meschini," ZENIT, June 5, 2007, https://zenit.org/articles/on-wars-thought-holy/.

Meyerhofer, Jane. *1000 Years of Catholic Scientists*, 6th ed. Ye Hedge School, 2016.

Morris, Henry M. *Men of Science Men of God.* Master Books, 1982.

Most, William G. "The Inquisition," EWTN, http://www.ewtn.com/library/ANSWERS/INQUIS.htm.

Muench, Aloisius. As quoted in Dorothy M. Brown and Elizabeth McKeown, *The Poor Belong to Us: Catholic Charities and American Welfare.* Harvard University Press, 2000.

My Fair Lady. Warner Bros., 1964.

The Myth of the Spanish Inquisition. Documentary by BBC and A&E, 1994.

National Center for Fathering, "The Consequences of Fatherlessness," http://www.fathers.com/statistics-and-research/the-consequences-of-fatherlessness/.

Newman, John Henry. Letter to J. Walker of Scarborough, May 22, 1868, http://inters.org/Newman-Scarborough-Darwin-Evolution.

Nietzsche, Friedrich. *On the Advantage and Disadvantage of History for Life*. Trans. Peter Preuss. Hackett, 1980.

Nussbaum, Martha. October 21, 1993 affidavit in the 1993 Colorado district court case *Evans v. Romer*, eventually decided by the Supreme Court, 517 U.S. 620 (1996).

O'Brien, Michael. "Will Beauty Save the World?" *Dappled Things*, SS. Peter and Paul 2007, http://dappledthings.org/4266/will-beauty-save-the-world/.

O'Connell, Marvin. "The Spanish Inquisition: Fact Versus Fiction," *Catholic Dossier* 2:6 (November–December 1996), http://archive.li/gRvbm.

O'Connor, Flannery. As quoted in Mary Ann Glendon, "The Pope's New Feminism."

"On Wars Thought Holy: Interview With Marco Meschini," ZENIT, June 5, 2007. https://zenit.org/articles/on-wars-thought-holy/.

Pacepa, Ion Mihai. *Disinformation*: *Former Spy Chief Reveals Secret Strategies for Undermining Freedom, Attacking Religion, and Promoting Terrorism*. WND Books, 2013.

Pascal, Blaise. *Penseés*. Trans. A. J. Krailsheimer. Penguin Classics, 1995.

Pius XI. *La Documentation Catholique*, 29 (1938), col. 1460.

Pius XII. *Summi Pontificatus*. October 20, 1939, http://w2.vatican.va/content/pius-xii/en/encyclicals/documents/hf_p-xii_enc_20101939_summi-pontificatus.html.

Pieper, Josef. *Happiness and Contemplation*. St. Augustine's Press, 1998.

Planned Parenthood v. Casey, 505 U.S. 833 (1992).

Plantinga, Alvin. *God, Freedom, and Evil*. Eerdmans, 1989.

Pope, Charles. "The Bible is Not Just a Book, It Is a Library. And This is Key to Interpreting Scripture," Community in Mission, April 7, 2011, http://blog.adw.org/2011/04/the-bible-is-not-a-book-it-is-a-library-and-this-is-key-to-interpreting-scripture/.

Poushter, Jacob. "40% of Millennials OK with Limiting Speech Offensive to Minorities," Pew Research Center, November 20, 2015, http://www.pewresearch.org/fact-tank/2015/11/20/40-of-millennials-ok-with-limiting-speech-offensive-to-minorities/.

"The Pope's Message," *New York Times*, December 25, 1941, available at the Catholic League, http://www.catholicleague.org/the-new-york-times-editorials-praising-pope-pius-xii/.

Pruss, Alexander R. *One Body: An Essay in Christian Sexual Ethics*. University of Notre Dame Press, 2012.

Pseudo-Dionysius. *Pseudo-Dionysius: The Complete Works*. Trans. Colm Luibheid. Paulist Press, 1987.

Qu'ran. As translated and quoted in Meschini, "On Wars Thought Holy."

Ratzinger, Joseph. "The Feeling of Things, the Contemplation of Beauty," Congregation for the Doctrine of the Faith, August 2002, http://www.vatican.va/roman_curia/congregations/cfaith/documents/rc_con_cfaith_doc_20020824_ratzinger-cl-rimini_en.html.

Regnerus, Mark. *The Transformation of Men, Marriage, and Monogamy*. Oxford University Press, 2017.

Reilly, Robert R. *Making Gay Okay: How Rationalizing Homosexual Behavior Is Changing Everything*. Ignatius Press, 2014.

Riley-Smith, Jonathan. *The Crusades, Christianity, and Islam*. Columbia University Press, 2008.

Robinson, Jonathan. *The Mass and Modernity: Walking to Heaven Backward*. Ignatius Press, 2005.

Roosevelt, Theodore. *Fear God and Take Your Own Part*. CreateSpace, 2017.

Rousseau, Jean Jacques. "Discourse on Inequality," in *The Essential Rousseau*. Trans. Lowell Bair. Mentor Books, 1974.

Routledge, Clay. "Colleges Are Promoting Psychological Frailty and We Should All Be Concerned," James G. Martin Center for Academic Renewal, November 9. 2016, https://www.jamesgmartin.center/2016/11/colleges-promoting-psychological-frailty-concerned/.

Russell, Burton. *Inventing the Flat Earth*: *Columbus and Modern Historians*. Praeger, 1991.

Rychlak, Ronald. *Hitler, the War, and the Pope*, revised and expanded.

Salvation Army. "About Us," Salvation Army International, http://www.salvationarmy.org/ihq/about.

Sarah, Robert. *The Power of Silence*: *Against the Dictatorship of Noise*. Ignatius Press, 2017.

Schlanger, Zoë. "We Need to Talk about 'Ecoanxiety': Climate Change Is Causing PTSD, Anxiety, and Depression on a Mass Scale," *Quartz*, April 3, 2017, https://qz.com/948909/ecoanxiety-the-american-psychological-association-says-climate-change-is-causing-ptsd-anxiety-and-depression-on-a-mass-scale/.

Schmidt, Mike. "Being 'Spiritual but Not Religious' Carries Consequences," Bulldog Catholic, June 9, 2016, http://bulldogcatholic.org/being-spiritual-but-not-religious-carries-consequences/.

Schweizer, Peter. *Makers and Takers*: *Why Conservatives Work Harder, Feel Happier, Have Closer Families, Take Fewer Drugs, Give More Generously, Value Honesty More, Are Less Materialistic and Envious, Whine Les.... and Even Hug Their Children More Than Liberals*. Doubleday, 2008.

Sheed, Frank J. *Theology for Beginners*. 3rd ed. Servant Books, 1981.

Sheen, Fulton J. *The World's First Love*: *Mary, Mother of God*, 2nd ed. Ignatius Press, 2010.

———. As quoted in Joseph Morse, *Now and at the Hour of Our Death*. New Classic Books, 2013.

Silverman, David. As quoted in Trent Horn, *Hard Sayings*.

Soskis, Benjamin. "Both More and No More: The Historical Split between Charity and Philanthropy," *Hudson Institute*, October 15th, 2014, https://www.hudson.org/research/10723-both-more-and-no-more-the-historical-split-between-charity-and-philanthropy.

"The Spanish Inquisition," *Monty Python's Flying Circus*. British Broadcasting Corporation and Python Pictures, 1970.

Spencer, Robert. *The Politically Incorrect Guide® to Islam (and the Crusades)*. Regnery Publishing, 2005.

Spitzer, Robert J. *New Proofs for the Existence of God: Contributions of Contemporary Physics and Philosophy*. Eerdmans, 2010.

Stark, Rodney. *The Triumph of Christianity: How the Jesus Movement Became the World's Largest Religion*. HarperOne, 2011.

Swinburne, Richard. *Is There a God?* Oxford University Press, 2010.

De Thaon, Philippe. *The Bestiary of Philippe de Thaon*. Trans. Thomas Wright. The Royal Society of Northern Antiquaries of Copenhagen, 1841, http://bestiary.ca/etexts/wright1841/bestiary%20of%20philippe%20de%20thaon%20-%20wright.pdf.

Tischner, Józef. As quoted in Filip Mazurczak, "Judging Religion by the Actions of its Adherents," *Crisis Magazine*, March 7, 2017, http://www.crisismagazine.com/2017/judging-religion-actions-adherents.

De Tocqueville, Alexis. *Democracy in America*. Trans. Harvey Mansfield. University of Chicago Press, 2002.

Tucker, William. "Monogamy and Its Discontents," in *Wing to Wing, Oar to Oar: Readings on Courting and Marrying*. Eds. Amy and Leon Kass. University of Notre Dame Press, 2000.

The Usual Suspects. Polygram Filmed Entertainment and Spelling Films International, 1995.

Vitz, Paul C. *Faith of the Fatherless: The Psychology of Atheism*. Spence Publishing, 1999.

von Hildebrand, Alice. *Man & Woman: A Divine Invention*. Sapientia Press, 2002.

———. *The Privilege of Being a Woman*. Sapientia Press, 2005.

Wallace-Wells, David. "The Uninhabitable Earth," *New York*, July 9, 2017, http://nymag.com/daily/intelligencer/2017/07/climate-change-earth-too-hot-for-humans.html.

Walls, Jerry L. *Heaven, Hell, and Purgatory: Rethinking the Things That Matter Most*. Brazos Press, 2015.

———. *Purgatory: The Logic of Total Transformation*. Oxford University Press, 2011.

Walsh, William T. *Characters of the Inquisition*, TAN Books, 2005.

Ward, Keith. *Pascal's Fire: Scientific Faith and Religious Understanding*. Oneworld Publications, 2006.

Wiker, Benjamin. *The Darwin Myth: The Life and Lies of Charles Darwin*. Regnery Publishing, 2009.

Woodward, Chris, and Fred Jackson. "Planned Parenthood: Record Year for Abortions, Taxpayer Funding," One News Now, January 8, 2013, https://onenewsnow.com/pro-life/2013/01/08/planned-parenthood-record-year-for-abortions-taxpayer-funding#.UkSep7wmbMk.

Yad Vashem, "The Righteous Among the Nations" database, http://www.yadvashem.org/righteous?WT.mc_id=ggcamp&WT.srch=1.

Zinmeister, Karl. "Charitable Giving and the Fabric of America," *Imprimis* 45:1 (January 2016), https://imprimis.hillsdale.edu/charitable-giving-and-the-fabric-of-america/.

———. "Some People Love to Call Names," The Philanthropy Roundtable, 2017, http://www.philanthropyroundtable.org/topic/excellence_in_philanthropy/some_people_love_to_call_names.

Index

J

K

L

M

N

O

P

Q

R

S

T

U

V

W

Z